Christian Origins and the New Testament in the Greco-Roman Context

Essays in Honor of
Dennis R. MacDonald

Christian Origins and the New Testament in the Greco-Roman Context

Essays in Honor of Dennis R. MacDonald

Margaret Froelich,

Michael Kochenash,

Thomas E. Phillips

&

Ilseo Park, editors

CLAREMONT STUDIES IN
NEW TESTAMENT &
CHRISTIAN ORIGINS

Christian Origins and the New Testament in the Greco-Roman Context
Essays in Honor of Dennis R. MacDonald
©2016 Claremont Press
1325 N. College Ave
Claremont, CA 91711

ISBN 978-1946230003

Library of Congress Cataloging-in-Publication Data

Table of Contents

Abbreviations

AB	Anchor Bible
ABD	*Anchor Bible Dictionary*. Edited by David Noel Freedman. 6 volumes. New York: Doubleday, 1992.
AnBib	Analecta Biblica
ANEP	*The Ancient Near East in Pictures Relating to the Old Testament*. Second Edition. Edited by James B. Pritchard. Princeton: Princeton University Press, 1994.
ASP	*American Studies in Papyrology*
AUSDDS	Andrews University Seminary Doctoral Dissertation Series
BECNT	Baker Exegetical Commentary on the New Testament
BETL	Bibliotheca Ephemeridum Theologicarum Lovaniensium
Bib	*Biblica*
BibInt	*Biblical Interpretation*
CBET	Contributions to Biblical Exegesis and Theology
CBQ	*Catholic Biblical Quarterly*
CC	Continental Commentaries
CCSL	Corpus Christianorum Series Latina
CGLC	Cambridge Greek and Latin Classics
CP	*Classical Philology*
ECL	Society of Biblical Literature Early Christianity and Its Literature
ESEC	Emory Studies in Early Christianity
FAT	Forschungen zum Alten Testament

GCS	Die greichischen christlichen Schriftsteller der ersten [drei] Jahrhunderte
HALOT	*Hebrew and Aramaic Lexicon of the Old Testament.* Ludwig Koehler and Walter Baumgartner. 5 volumes. Leiden: Brill, 1996.
HSCP	*Havard Studies in Classical Philology*
ICC	International Critical Commentary
JBL	*Journal of Biblical Literature*
JHS	*Journal of Hellenic Studies*
JR	*Journal of Religion*
JSNTSup	Journal for the Study of the New Testament Supplement Series
LCL	Loeb Classical Library
LEC	Library of Early Christianity
LSJ	*A Greek-English Lexicon.* H. G. Liddell, R. Scott, H. S. Jones, and R. McKenzie, eds. New edition. Oxford: Clarendon Press, 1940.
LNTS	Library of New Testament Studies
MnemosSup	Mnemosyne Supplements
MP	*Modern Philology*
NovT	*Novum Testamentum*
NovTSup	Novum Testamentum Supplement Series
NIGTC	New International Greek Testament Commentary
NTGL	New Testament and Greek Literature
NTS	*New Testament Studies*
PRS	*Perspectives in Religious Studies*
REA	*Revue des études anciennes*
SBLSP	*Society of Biblical Literature Seminar Papers*
SBLSym	Society of Biblical Literature Symposium Series
SCJ	Studies in Christianity and Judaism
Sem	*Semeia*

SNTSMS	Society for New Testament Studies Monograph Series
SUNT	Studia zur Umwelt des Neuen Testaments
SP	Sacra Pagina
TSAJ	Testi e ricerche di scienze religiose
WUNT	Wissenschaftliche Untersuchungen zum Neuen Testament
ZPE	*Zietschrift für Papyrologie und Epigraphik*

Bibliography of
Dennis MacDonald's Writings

Books

The Dionysian Gospel: The Fourth Gospel and Euripides. Minneapolis: Fortress Press, 2017.

The Gospels and Homer: Imitations of Greek Epic in Mark and Luke-Acts. NTGL 1. Lanham, MD: Rowman & Littlefield, 2015.

Luke and Vergil: Imitations of Classical Greek Literature. NTGL 2. Lanham, MD: Rowman & Littlefield, 2015.

Mythologizing Jesus: From Jewish Teacher to Epic Hero. Lanham, MD: Rowman & Littlefield, 2015.

Two Shipwrecked Gospels: The Logoi of Jesus and Papias's Exposition of Logia about the Lord. ECL 8. Atlanta: Society of Biblical Literature, 2012.

My Turn: A Critique of Critics of "Mimesis Criticism." Occasional Papers of the Institute for Antiquity and Christianity 53. Claremont: Institute for Antiquity and Christianity, 2009.

The Intertextuality of the Epistles: Explorations of Theory and Practice (edited with Thomas L. Brodie and Stanley E. Porter). New Testament Mono-graphs 16. Sheffield: Sheffield Phoenix Press, 2006.

Acts of Andrew (translated with introduction). Early Christian Apocrypha 1. Santa Rosa: Polebridge, 2005.

Does the New Testament Imitate Homer? Four Cases from the Acts of the Apostles. New Haven: Yale University Press, 2003.

Mimesis and Intertextuality in Antiquity and Christianity
(editor). Studies in Antiquity and Christianity.
Harrisburg: Trinity Press International, 2001.

The Homeric Epics and the Gospel of Mark. New Haven: Yale
University Press, 2000. Greek Translation: *Τα*
Ομηρικά Έπη και το κατά Μάρκον Ευαγγέλιο. Tr. Kostas
Tsapogas. Athens: Cactus, 2004.

Christianizing Homer: The Odyssey, Plato, and The Acts of
Andrew. Oxford: Oxford University Press, 1994.

The Acts of Andrew and the Acts of Andrew and Matthias in the
City of the Cannibals (translated with introduction
and commentary). Texts and Translations 33.
Christian Apocrypha 1. Atlanta: Scholars, 1990.

There Is No Male and Female: The Fate of a Dominical Saying in
Paul and Gnosticism. Harvard Dissertations in
Religion 20. Philadelphia: Fortress, 1987.

The Apocryphal Acts of the Apostles (editor). Semeia 38.
Atlanta: Scholars, 1986.

The Legend and the Apostle: The Battle for Paul in Story and
Canon. Philadelphia: Westminster, 1983.

Articles and Chapters

"Luke's Antetextuality in Light of Ancient Rhetorical
Education." *Ancient Education and Early Christianity*,
155–63. Edited by Matthew Ryan Hauge and
Andrew W. Pitts. London: Bloomsbury T&T Clark,
2016.

"Mimesis." *Exploring Intertextuality: Diverse Strategies for*
New Testament Interpretation of Texts, 93–105. Edited
by B. J. Oropeza and Steve Moyise. Eugene, OR:
Cascade, 2016.

"Jesus and Dionysian Polymorphism in the *Acts of John*."
Early Christian and Jewish Narrative: The Role of Religion in Shaping Narrative Forms, 97–104. Edited by Ilaria Ramelli and Judith Perkins. WUNT 348. Tübingen: Mohr Siebeck, 2015.

"John's Radical Rewriting of Luke-Acts." *Forum*, third series 4.2 (2015): 111–24.

"Toward an Intertextual Commentary on Luke 7." *The Elijah-Elisha Narrative in the Composition of Luke*, 130–52. Edited by John S. Kloppenborg and Joseph Verheyden. London: Bloomsbury, 2014.

"Pseudo-Luke's Imitation of the 'We-Voyages' in Homer's *Odyssey*." *Forum*, third series 2.2 (2013): 231–51.

"Classical Greek Poetry and the Acts of the Apostles: Imitations of Euripides' *Bacchae*." *Christian Origins and Greco-Roman Culture: Social and Literary Contexts for the New Testament*, 463–96. Edited by Stanley E. Porter and Andrew W. Pitts. Texts and Editions for New Testament Study 9. Early Christianity in Its Hellenistic Context 1. Leiden: Brill, 2013.

"Gospel Fictions and Historical Jesus, Again." *Alive and Well and Talking Jesus: Doing Theology at Pilgrim Place*, vol. 8, 61–76. Edited by Paul Kittlaus, Pat Patterson, and Connie Kimos. Shelbyville, KY: Wasteland, 2013.

"Luke's Use of Papias for Narrating the Death of Judas." *Reading Acts Today: Essays in Honour of Loveday C. A. Alexander*, 43–62. Edited by Steve Walton, Thomas E. Phillips, Lloyd Keith Petersen, and F. Scott Spencer. Library of New Testament Studies 427. London: T&T Clark, 2011.

"An Alternative Q and the Quest for the Earthly Jesus." *Sources of the Jesus Tradition: Separating History from Myth*, 17–44. Edited by R. Joseph Hoffmann. Amherst, NY: Prometheus, 2010.

"The Synoptic Problem and Literary Mimesis: The Case of the Frothing Demoniac." *New Studies in the Synoptic Problem: Oxford Conference, April 2008: Essays in Honour of Christopher M. Tuckett*, 509–21. Edited by Paul Foster, Andrew F. Gregory, John. S. Kloppenborg, and Joseph Verheyden. BETL 239. Leuven: Peeters, 2011.

"The Pastoral Epistles against 'Old Wives' Tales.'" *The Writings of St. Paul*, 303–18. Second edition. Edited by Wayne A. Meeks and John T. Fitzgerald. New York: W. W. Norton, 2007.

"A Categorization of Antetextuality in the Gospels and Acts: A Case for Luke's Imitation of Plato and Xenophon to Depict Paul as a Christian Socrates." *The Intertextuality of the Epistles: Explorations of Theory and Practice*, 211–25. Edited by Thomas L. Brodie, Stanley E. Porter, and Dennis R. MacDonald. New Testament Monographs 16. Sheffield: Sheffield Phoenix Press, 2006.

"Imitations of Greek Epic in the Gospels." *The Historical Jesus in Context*, 372–84. Edited by Amy-Jill Levine, Dale C. Allison, and John Dominic Crossan. Princeton Readings in Religions. Princeton: Princeton University Press, 2006.

"Who Was That Chaste Prostitute? A Socratic Answer to an Enigma in the *Acts of John*." *A Feminist Companion to the New Testament Apocrypha*, 88–97. Edited by Amy-Jill Levine with Maria Mayo Robbins. Feminist Companion to the New Testament and Early Christian Writings 11. London: T&T Clark International, 2006.

"The Breasts of Hecuba and Those of the Daughters of Jerusalem: Luke's Transvaluation of a Famous Iliadic Scene." *Ancient Fiction: The Matrix of Early Christian and Jewish Narrative*, 239–54. Edited by Jo-Ann A. Brant, Charles W. Hedrick, and Chris Shea. SBLSym 32. Atlanta: Society of Biblical Literature, 2005.

"Υπήρχε η Μαρία Μαγδαληνή πριν την επινοήσει ο Μάρκος?" ("Did Mary Magdalene Exist before Mark Invented her?") *Delition Biblikon Meleton* 23 (2005): 97–113.

"Lydia and Her Sisters as Lukan Fictions." *A Feminist Companion to the Acts of the Apostles*, 105–10. Edited by Amy-Jill Levine with Marianne Blickenstaff. Feminist Companion to the New Testament and Early Christian Writings 9. London: T&T Clark, 2004.

"Paul's Farewell to the Ephesian Elders and Hector's Farewell to Andromache: A Strategic Imitation of Homer's *Iliad*." *Contextualizing Acts: Lukan Narrative and Greco-Roman Discourse*, 189–203. Edited by Todd Penner and Caroline Vander Stichele. SBLSym 20. Atlanta: Society of Biblical Literature, 2003.

"The Spirit as a Dove and Homeric Bird Similes." *Early Christian Voices: In Texts, Traditions, and Symbols: Essays in Honor of François Bovon*, 333–39. Edited by David H. Warren, Ann Graham Brock, and David W. Pao. Biblical Interpretation Series 66. Boston: Brill, 2003.

"Renowned Far and Wide: The Women Who Anointed Odysseus and Jesus." *A Feminist Companion to Mark*, 128–35. Edited by Amy-Jill Levine with Marianne Blickenstaff. Sheffield: Sheffield Academic Press, 2001.

"Tobit and the *Odyssey*." *Mimesis and Intertextuality in Antiquity and Christianity*, 11–40. Edited by Dennis R. MacDonald. Studies in Antiquity and Christianity. Harrisburg: Trinity Press International, 2001.

"The Ending of Luke and the Ending of the *Odyssey*." *For a Later Generation: The Transformation of Tradition in Israel, Early Judaism and Early Christianity*, 161–68. Edited by Randal A. Argall, Beverly Bow, and Rod Werline. Harrisburg: Trinity Press International, 2000.

"Luke's Emulation of Homer: Acts 12:1–17 and *Iliad* 24." *Forum*, new series 3.1 (2000): 197–205.

"The Shipwrecks of Odysseus and Paul." *NTS* 45 (1999): 88–107.

"Secrecy and Recognitions in the *Odyssey* and Mark: Where Wrede Went Wrong." *Ancient Fiction and Early Christian Narrative*, 139–53. Edited by Ronald F. Hock, J. Bradley Chance, and Judith Perkins. SBLSym 6. Atlanta: Scholars, 1998.

"Which Came First? Intertextual Relationships among the Apocryphal Acts of the Apostles." *The Apocryphal Acts of the Apostles in Intertextual Perspective. Semeia* 80 (1997): 11–41.

"From Faith to Faith." *Leaving the Fold: Testimonies of Former Fundamentalists*, 109–16. Edited by Edward T. Babinski. Amherst, NY: Prometheus Books, 1995.

"Is There a Privileged Reader? A Case from the Apocryphal Acts." *Semeia* 71 (1995): 29–43.

"Luke's Eutychus and Homer's Elpenor: Acts 20:7–12 and *Odyssey* 10–12." *Journal of Higher Criticism* 1 (1994): 5–24.

"Legends of the Apostles." *Eusebius, Christianity, and Judaism*, 166–79. Edited by Harold W. Attridge and Gohei Hata. Detroit: Wayne State University Press, 1992.

"*The Acts of Paul* and *The Acts of John*: Which Came First?"
Society of Biblical Literature 1992 Seminar Papers, 506–
10. Edited by Eugene H. Lovering. Atlanta: Scholars,
1992.

"*The Acts of Paul* and *The Acts of Peter*: Which Came First?"
Society of Biblical Literature 1992 Seminar Papers, 214–
24. Edited by Eugene H. Lovering. Atlanta: Scholars,
1992.

"*The Acts of Peter* and *The Acts of John*: Which Came First?"
Society of Biblical Literature 1992 Seminar Papers, 623–
26. Edited by Eugene H. Lovering. Atlanta: Scholars,
1992.

"A Response to R. Goldenberg and D. J. Harrington, S.
J." The Sabbath in Jewish and Christian Traditions, 57–
61. Edited by Tamara C. Eskenazi, Daniel J.
Harrington, S. J., and William H. Shea. New York:
Crossroad, 1991

"Apocryphal and Canonical Narratives about Paul." Paul
and the Legacies of Paul, 55–70. Edited by William S.
Babcock. Dallas: Southern Methodist University
Press, 1990.

"Intertextuality in Simon's 'Redemption' of Helen the
Whore: Homer, Heresiologists, and The Acts of
Andrew." Society of Biblical Literature 1990 Seminar
Papers, 336–43. Edited by David J. Lull. Atlanta:
Scholars, 1990.

"Corinthian Veils and Gnostic Androgynes." Images of the
Feminine in Gnosticism, 276–92. Edited by Karen L.
King. Studies in Antiquity and Christianity.
Philadelphia: Fortress, 1988.

"The Acts of Andrew and Matthias and the Acts of Andrew."
The Apocryphal Acts of the Apostles, 9–26. Edited by
Dennis R. MacDonald. Semeia 38. Atlanta: Scholars,
1986.

"From Audita to Legenda: Oral and Written Miracle
       Stories." *Forum* 2 (1986): 15–26.
"Odysseus's Oar and Andrew's Cross: The Transformation
       of a Homeric Theme in the Acts of Andrew." *Society
       of Biblical Literature 1986 Seminar Papers*, 309–13.
       Edited by Kent Harold Richards. Atlanta: Scholars,
       1986.
"Pseudo-Chrysostom's Panegyric to Thecla: The Heroine of
       The Acts of Paul in Homily and Art." Coauthored
       with Andrew D. Scrimgeour. *The Apocryphal Acts of
       the Apostles*, 151–59. Edited by Dennis R.
       MacDonald. Semeia 38. Atlanta: Scholars, 1986.
"In Memoriam et Imitationem." A sermon remembering
       the life of George W. MacRae. *HTR* 78 (1985): 237–
       242.
"A Conjectural Emendation of 1 Cor. 15:31–32; Or the Case
       of the Misplaced Lion Fight." *HTR* 73 (1980): 265–76.

Other Selected Publications

The Oxford Encyclopedia of the Bible and Ethics (2014): *s.v.*
       "Imitation" and "Mimesis Criticism."
Acts and Christian Beginnings: The Acts Seminar Report (2013):
       s.v. "Prison Breaks in Luke's Literary World" (72–
       74), "Shipwrecks in Luke's Literary World," (313–
       15) and "We-Passages in the Acts of the Apostles"
       (191–93).
Jesus in History, Thought, and Culture: An Encyclopedia (2003):
       s.v. "Homer."
The Anchor Bible Dictionary (1992): *s.v.* "Thecla," "Andrew,
       Traditions of," and "Acts of Andrew and Matthias."
*The Oxford Study Bible: Revised English Bible with the
       Apocrypha* (1992): *s.v.* "Early Christian Literature."
"Andrew and the Ant People." *The Second Century* 8 (1991):
       43–49.
"Areté." *The Iliff Review* 44 (1987): 39–43.

"The Forgotten Novels of the Early Church." *Harvard Divinity Bulletin* 16.4 (1986): 4–6.

"Response," to Jean-Marc Prieur. *The Apocryphal Acts of the Apostles*, 35–39. Edited by Dennis R. MacDonald. *Semeia* 38. Atlanta: Scholars, 1986.

The New Harper's Bible Dictionary (1985): *s.v.* "Apocryphal New Testament," "Bithynia," "Galatia," "Nicolaitans," "Phrygia," "Pontus," and "Thrace."

"The Role of Women in the Production of the Apocryphal Acts of Apostles." *The Iliff Review* 41 (1984): 21–38.

Preface

New Testament scholars are a peculiar lot. They examine a very small corpus of material that has been intensively studied for nearly two thousand years. It is no hyperbole to say that absolutely every single word in the New Testament has been the subject of thousands of independent analyses and commentaries. As a result, it's tough to be a truly original New Testament scholar. Few fields are as self-derivative as is New Testament studies.

The work of Dennis MacDonald is a refreshing exception to the generally repetitive and ceaselessly redundant nature of most New Testament scholarship. *No living scholar of the New Testament and Christian origins has presented as clear and compelling challenges to the status quo of New Testament scholarship as has Dennis MacDonald.* In the early years of his distinguished career, MacDonald was a driving force in the scholarly trend to incorporate the study of early Christian fiction, most importantly the apocryphal Acts of the Apostles, into the study of Christian Origins. In his mid-career, MacDonald almost single-handedly established the discipline of memesis criticism, the scholarly endeavor to identify when early Christian writers — including the canonical writers — imitated other ancient texts, most notably the Homeric epics. In his most recent work, MacDonald has challenged the most sacred of New Testament scholarship's sacred cows. He has sought to revise widely held theories about Q and the classic two source theory of the synoptic traditions.

For most scholars, it would be a monumental achievement to play even a supporting role in any one of these three scholarly innovations — helping to establish the study of fiction narratives within the field of Christian Origins, developing the entirely field of memesis criticism, and presenting a bold new conception of gospel formation. Yet, MacDonald has led in all three innovations!

It is with great admiration and sincere appreciation that we present these honorific essays to our colleague, mentor and friend, Dr. Dennis R. MacDonald.

Thomas E. Phillips
Editor, CST Press

Introduction

What has Troy to do with Jerusalem? How can the venerable Greek traditions of epic poetry, drama, and mythology help us understand early Christians and their literary products? Dennis MacDonald has helped put this question to the forefront of New Testament scholarship. While the study of ancient Near- and Middle-Eastern epic and mythologies is a staple of Hebrew Bible scholarship, it is only in recent decades that any modern researcher in New Testament has given serious attention to the Greek equivalents. We have no Pritchard-esque storehouse of relevant mythological, historical, and legal texts, not to mention the pictures.[1] Nonetheless, an expanding and intergenerational body of scholars, many of whom were taught by MacDonald, are recognizing the disservice to knowledge that comes of limiting the New Testament and other early Christian narratives to only their Judean contexts. As the twenty-first century comes into its own, the growing field of Greco-Roman backgrounds to early Christianity owes, if not its existence, certainly its increasing prominence in large part to MacDonald.

---

[1] See James B. Pritchard, *Ancient near Eastern Texts Relating to the Old Testament* (2nd corr. and enl. ed.; Princeton: Princeton University Press, 1955).

Most importantly, I believe MacDonald's work embodies a kind of playful "what-if" approach to study. What happens if we read Euripides' *Bacchae* immediately before reading the Gospel of John? What if we take seriously the idea that nearly every literate person in the ancient Mediterranean — even the Christian ones — cut their teeth on Homer? Not every investigation pans out, and it can be fascinating to discuss which of MacDonald's proposals resonate with a given reader and which do not (to my memory I have not encountered a student of his who rejects mimesis criticism outright). But the payoff, and for MacDonald the obvious joy, seems to come of simply asking the question and seeing where it leads.

Therefore, in the following chapters, students, former students, friends, and colleagues of MacDonald demonstrate the range of questions his work has inspired.

First, Michael Kochenash adopts conceptual metaphor theory to advance a sophisticated understanding of the relationship between Luke-Acts and Virgil's *Aeneid* in his essay, "Reconsidering Luke-Acts and Virgil's *Aeneid*: Negotiating Ethnic Legacies." Jumping off from recent work comparing the two narratives, including that of MacDonald, Kochenash argues that Luke-Acts shares the *Aeneid*'s concerns with the blending of ethnic identities as well as divine legitimization of a new dynasty. He shows that Luke-Acts adapts the logic and of Virgil's epic at several crucial narrative points in order to position the kingdom of God as the preeminent power over and against the Roman Empire.

Gregory Riley, a pioneer of the Greco-Roman origins school, in this volume interrogates the ethnic roots of

Christianity itself. In his essay, "What Has Galilee to Do with Jerusalem?", he ventures into the Hellenistic and early Roman history of that tiny region, including reference to the New Testament, 1 Maccabees, and the Hebrew Bible. This contribution demonstrates that although Jesus and his closest followers are all understood to be Jews, their home ground had long been politically and culturally separate from Judea, a fact reflected in its majority-Gentile population. This has profound implications for our understanding of Jesus's message and the earliest stages of his movement. Riley goes on to position Jesus's most important teachings within the cultural and philosophical traditions of the Hellenized world.

Marvin A. Sweeney provides a compelling reminder of the importance and continued relevance of literary approaches to biblical texts. In his essay "Shabbat: An Epistemological Principle for Holiness, Sustainability, and Justice in The Pentateuch," he calls into question a *creatio ex nihilo* understanding of Genesis 1:1–2:3 in favor of a process of creation that requires a more integrated than domineering role for humanity. Through exegesis of a number of the Pentateuch's legal codes, Sweeney characterizes Shabbat as a fundamental basis not only of Torah but of humanity's relationship to itself and the rest of creation, grounded in restoration, relief, and justice. By beginning his analysis with the looming and increasingly realized dangers of climate change and drought, Sweeney cautions us to consider the consequences of our interpretations of biblical texts.

In "Can Homer Be Read with Profit? A Delightful Response—and Then Some," Richard I. Pervo regales us with the philosophical conundrum of poetry's usefulness. In the tug-of-war between moral instruction and entertainment, thinkers like Plato, Plutarch, and Strabo attempt to discern which texts are worthy not only of imitation, but of reading at all (and why), and in the process invent critical exegesis. Pervo turns the attention of this argument to fictive/historiographical texts such as the Acts of the Apostles and 2 Maccabees to show that pleasure can act in the service of instruction, as a lure and a hook.

John S. Kloppenborg's essay, "James 3:7–8, Gen 1:26, and the Linguistic Register of the Letter of James," examines the vocabulary of the epistle of James as a window into the social location and rhetorical purposes of the text and its audience. Acknowledging some previous scholars' doubts, on the basis of syntax, concerning James's literary level, Kloppenborg instead highlights word choice to demonstrate the author's familiarity with the Greek philosophical, epic, and poetic traditions. He concludes that James paraphrases both the LXX and a number of sayings from the Jesus tradition using *aemulatio* in a manner consistent with other philosophical and psychogogic rhetoric in both the Jewish and non-Jewish Greek traditions.

A distinctive feature of MacDonald's work on the New Testament and ancient epic is its sparse interaction with more traditional scholarship. His task is to establish the connections; it falls to those of us continuing his work to investigate whether and how his proposals integrate with earlier ones, and to judge between the two when necessary. My own contribution, "Irony and Interpretability in Mark's Passion Narrative," is an attempt at this step. I analyze various proposals for the textual ancestry of Mark's Passion narrative and conclude that the death of Hector in the *Iliad* as a literary model for the Markan narrative more fully explains the story's intense irony than Psalm 22 (LXX 21).

On a more theoretical note, Matthew Ryan Hauge's "The Forgotten Playground" contextualizes MacDonald's work within modern literary approaches. Hauge begins with a description of Hellenistic and early-imperial period educational practices to show how Homeric epic and themes were tightly woven into the literary tradition of the ancient world, as well as the importance and sophistication of imitation in ancient composition. He identifies three modern schools for the recognition of literary dependence — the "philological fundamentalist," the "literary universalist," and, occupying the middle range of the spectrum, MacDonald and others who perceive the variety of mimetic strategies and the complex work of identifying them.

Besides his focus on the literature of Greco-Roman culture, an important part of MacDonald's legacy will be his willingness to challenge the common knowledge of the field. Thomas E. Phillips likewise bucks the scholarly trend in his piece, "When Did Paul Become a Christian? Rereading Paul's Autobiography in Galatians and Biography in Acts." In this study, Phillips resists what he calls the "crossbreeding" of the Lukan image of Paul with the one that he presents of himself in the letters. In order to form a more accurate picture of the life of the historical Paul, Phillips reads Galatians 1 and 2 with reference only to the other Pauline letters, particularly 1 Corinthians, endeavoring to remove the spectre of Acts from his consideration. The paper challenges the assumption that Paul only persecuted the church *before* his conversion, and instead proposes that Galatians 2 describes Paul's early opposition to the inclusion of Gentiles in the Jesus movement.

We hope that our offerings in this book will demonstrate the wide relevancy of MacDonald's work and spirit, and advance the scholarly understandings of the literary, cultural, and philosophical forebears of early Christian texts. To the implicit question of MacDonald's work, "What has Troy to do with Jerusalem?" we have answered, and we hope that others will likewise, "Let's find out!"

Margaret Froelich

Reconsidering Luke-Acts
and Virgil's Aeneid
Negotiating Ethnic Legacies

Michael Kochenash

Foundation stories allow communities to wrestle with their identities. Whether a community is defined by cultural traits (which can be acquired) or ethnicity (which cannot), "foundation stories help to define who is in, who is out, and whether membership is open or closed."[1] Foundation stories are sometimes situated in the mythic past, like Virgil's *Aeneid*, and at other times they are situated in the more recent past, as with Luke-Acts. Whatever else we may think about the relationship between Luke's and Virgil's narratives, they both negotiate the inclusion of different ethnic groups within a superordinate identity, whether Roman or Christian. In this way, both narratives function as foundation stories. Although most biblical scholars reject an intertextual relationship between Luke-Acts and the *Aeneid*, a few have seen value in comparing them. In this essay, I will review three recent comparisons — by Marianne Palmer Bonz, Dennis R. MacDonald, and Aaron Kuecker — after which I will propose a different

---

[1] Gary B. Miles, "The *Aeneid* as Foundation Story," *Reading Vergil's* Aeneid: *An Interpretive Guide* (ed. C. Perkell; Norman: University of Oklahoma Press, 1999), 232.

framework for reading the two narratives together that advances the insights of these scholars: reading Luke's story of the kingdom of God as appropriating the language of Rome, understood through the framework of conceptual metaphor theory.

Reasoning is often metaphorical. People often use the language, images, and/or logic from well-known domains in order to communicate meaningfully about others. In the New Testament, metaphors and analogies abound in an effort to express the significance of Jesus and the kingdom of God. Sometimes, metaphors and analogies are used in a straightforward fashion. Clear examples can be found in Jesus's teachings: the kingdom of God is "like a mustard seed" and "yeast" (Luke 13:19, 21). Other times, New Testament texts explain the kingdom of God through conceptual metaphors and/or conceptual blending.[2] In these cases, the New Testament texts can be read as appropriating the language, images, and/or logic from well-

---

[2] For conceptual metaphor theory, see George Lakoff and Mark Johnson, *Metaphors We Live By* (Chicago: University of Chicago Press, 1980); George Lakoff, *Women, Fire, and Dangerous Things: What Categories Reveal about the Mind* (Chicago: University of Chicago Press, 1987); Mark Johnson, *The Body in the Mind: The Bodily Basis of Meaning, Imagination, and Reason* (Chicago: University of Chicago Press, 1987). For an application of this theory to New Testament texts, see Jennifer Houston McNeel, *Paul as Infant and Nursing Mother: Metaphor, Rhetoric, and Identity in 1 Thessalonians 2:5–8* (ECL 12; Atlanta: Society of Biblical Literature, 2014). For conceptual blending theory, see Gilles Fauconnier and Mark Turner, *The Way We Think: Conceptual Blending and the Mind's Hidden Complexities* (New York: Basic Books, 2002); Seana Coulson, *Semantic Leaps: Frame-Shifting and Conceptual Blending in Meaning Construction* (New York: Cambridge University Press, 2001). For an application of this theory to New Testament studies, see Robert H. von Thaden, Jr., *Sex, Christ, and Embodied Cognition: Paul's Wisdom for Corinth* (ESEC 16; Blanford Forum, UK: Deo, 2012).

known domains. Of particular significance for this essay is the existence of Roman language, images, and logic in New Testament descriptions of the kingdom of God. Although these texts never explicitly describe the relationship metaphorically or analogically — e.g., "The kingdom of God is (like) the Roman Empire" — they depend on the audience's first-hand experiences with Roman self-representation to recognize the source domain of the language and to draw appropriate conclusions regarding God's kingdom. In this essay, I argue that the relationship of Luke-Acts to Virgil's *Aeneid* can be read in this way: elements within Luke's narrative evoke Virgil's epic — in terms of macrostructure, literary strategies, and allusive language and images — and readers who recognize the parallels are able to draw meaningful conclusions about the kingdom of God via contrast with Rome and its foundation story. Of particular interest are the ways in which Luke and Virgil portray deities intervening in order to unify different ethnic groups.

Recent Work on Luke and Virgil

Recent comparisons of Luke-Acts and the *Aeneid* have primarily operated within one of two frameworks: compositional practices in the Roman Mediterranean world or social identity theory. Two scholars, Marianne Palmer Bonz and Dennis R. MacDonald, have compared Luke-Acts with Virgil's *Aeneid* within the former framework. This approach foregrounds both the practice of imitation in composing literature in the agonistic Roman Mediterranean world and the importance of intertextual references in the creation of meaning. The difference between Bonz and

MacDonald is of degree: Bonz proposes that Luke is directly imitating Virgil—much like late first-century Latin poets did—whereas MacDonald claims that Luke's rivalry with the *Aeneid* is mediated through the imitation of Greek classics, primarily Homer's *Iliad* and *Odyssey*. A third scholar, Aaron Kuecker, compares Luke's and Virgil's works within the framework of social identity theory, applying the theoretical insights about superordinate subgroup identities to Virgil's treatment of Roman identity in the *Aeneid* and Luke's treatment of Christian identity in Luke-Acts. He observes a significant contrast among the similarities: Roman identity entails acting with violence toward outsiders, whereas Christian identity is characterized by "neighborly love."[3]

The most extensive recent treatment of the relationship between Luke-Acts and the *Aeneid* is Bonz's *The Past as Legacy: Luke-Acts and Ancient Epic*.[4] Whereas scholars generally locate Luke-Acts under the umbrella of historiography, Bonz identifies it as "a Christian prose adaptation of heroic epic."[5] Unlike the comparanda appealed to by advocates of Luke-Acts as historiography, Luke's narrative foregrounds a divinely ordained mission with a universal scope: "to proclaim the kingdom of God

---

[3] Aaron Kuecker, "Filial Piety and Violence in Luke-Acts and the *Aeneid*: A Comparative Analysis of Two Trans-Ethnic Identities," *T&T Clark Handbook to Social Identity in the New Testament* (ed. J. B. Tucker and C. A. Baker; London: Bloomsbury, 2014), 222–23, 226–32.

[4] Marianne Palmer Bonz, *The Past as Legacy: Luke-Acts and Ancient Epic* (Minneapolis: Fortress Press, 2000).

[5] Bonz, *Past as Legacy*, 190.

and to establish the composition of its chosen people."[6] Luke's narrative is replete with prophecies (especially in the form of Septuagintal citations), visions, and other forms of divine intervention that ensure the mission's success. These features are more characteristic of the epics of Homer and Virgil than the Greek histories commonly cited.

Previous intertextual interpretations of Luke-Acts, Bonz contends, focus too myopically on allusions to and citations of the Septuagint. Although Lukan scholars do need to address this Septuagintal intertextuality, they ought to adopt a wider purview. She writes:

> For just as traditional Virgilian scholarship at one time had focused almost exclusively on Homeric influence, neglecting the importance of the Alexandrian themes and perspectives that many interpreters now consider to be substantive, so, too, has traditional Lukan scholarship tended to focus too narrowly on scriptural typologies and motifs, ignoring the more immediate influence of Greco-Roman religious, political, and literary paradigms.[7]

Indeed, especially with the publication of Georg Knauer's *Die Aeneis und Homer*, for a time attention to Virgil's intertextual relationship with Homer's *Iliad* and *Odyssey* dominated scholarship on the *Aeneid*.[8] More

---

[6] Bonz, *Past as Legacy*, 190. For discussions of the genre of and comparanda for Luke-Acts, see Thomas E. Phillips, *Acts within Diverse Frames of Reference* (Macon: Macon University Press, 2009), 46–77; Bonz, *Past as Legacy*, 1–14, 22.

[7] Bonz, *Past as Legacy*, 91–92. She singles out MacDonald's work as an exception (92 n. 2).

[8] Georg N. Knauer, *Die* Aeneis *und Homer. Studien zur poetischen Technik Vergils mit Listen der Homerzitate in der* Aeneis (Hypomnemata 7; Göttingen: Vandenhoeck & Ruprecht, 1964). Cf. Alessandro Barchiesi,

recently, Damien Nelis's *Vergil's* Aeneid *and the* Argonautica *of Apollonius Rhodius*, for instance, demonstrates Virgil's debt to Apollonius's *Argonautica* and exemplifies the current disposition of today's classicists: reading Virgil as influenced both by Homeric *and* Alexandrian texts.[9] Bonz envisions a future when scholars will interpret Luke-Acts within frameworks that encompass both the Septuagint *and* the Greek and Latin texts that pervaded the Roman Mediterranean. Such a purview, she observes, led Thomas Brodie to observe that Septuagintal allusions in Luke-Acts appear to function in ways that are strikingly similar to Homeric allusions in the *Aeneid*.[10]

Bonz situates her reading of Luke-Acts as a "Christian prose adaptation of heroic epic" among first-century "adaptations" of Virgil's *Aeneid* that sought "to refute the equation of Augustan imperial rule with the will of heaven, an equation made famous by Virgil's epic."[11] The Julio-Claudian dynasty, supposedly fulfilling the prophecy of Aeneas's "empire without end" (*Aen.* 1.278–79; cf. 6.792–95), began to crumble during Nero's reign. Disillusioned by

---

Homeric Effects in Vergil's Narrative (Princeton: Princeton University Press, 2015), originally published in Italian in 1984.

[9] Damien Nelis, *Vergil's* Aeneid *and the* Argonautica *of Apollonius Rhodius* (Leeds: Francis Cairns, 2001). Other studies explore the possible influence of other poets, such as Ennius, Callimachus, Catullus, and Lucretius.

[10] Thomas L. Brodie, "Greco-Roman Imitation of Texts as a Partial Guide to Luke's Use of Sources," *Luke-Acts: New Perspectives from the Society of Biblical Literature Seminar* (ed. Charles H. Talbert; New York: Crossroads, 1984), 17–46. Cf. Bonz, *Past as Legacy*, 191: "Virgil incorporates Homeric allusions with the same ubiquity and for essentially the same reasons that Luke employs allusions to the Septuagint."

[11] Bonz, *Past as Legacy*, 65.

Nero's despotism, Lucan anticipated the end of the Julio-Claudian dynasty in his dysphoric *De bello civili*, in which he counters much of the *Aeneid*'s nationalistic optimism. After Nero's suicide—ending the Julio-Claudian dynasty—poets associated with the Flavian dynasty similarly challenged aspects of the *Aeneid* in their own poetry. One such poet, Statius, identified Domitian as the true heir to Aeneas's eternal empire in the *Silvae*, explicitly contrasting him with Augustus.[12] His epic, the *Thebaid*, similarly echoes Lucan's "anti-Virgilian" ethos.[13] Valerius Flaccus's *Argonautica* and Silius Italicus's *Punica* both likewise contest Virgil's Augustan themes. These poets rival Augustan claims to salvation, peace, succession from Aeneas, and realized eschatology.[14] Situating Luke-Acts among such agonistic literature, Bonz claims that Luke "presents a rival vision of empire, with a rival deity issuing an alternative plan for universal human salvation."[15]

Whereas Bonz argues that Luke knew the text of the *Aeneid*—possibly a Greek prose translation similar to the one referred to by Seneca—Dennis MacDonald challenges the idea that access to a physical copy of Virgil's epic is necessary to explain the similarities it shares with Luke-Acts.[16] The relationship between Luke and Virgil,

---

[12] Statius, *Silvae*, 4.1.5–8; 4.2.1–2; 4.3.114–17; 4.3.128–44. Cf. Bonz, *Past as Legacy*, 72–74.

[13] Bonz, *Past as Legacy*, 77.

[14] For Bonz's discussion of these epic rivals of Virgil, see *Past as Legacy*, 61–86.

[15] Bonz, *Past as Legacy*, 182.

[16] Bonz, *Past as Legacy*, 24–25; Dennis R. MacDonald, *Luke and Vergil: Imitations of Classical Greek Literature* (NTGL 2; Lanham, MD:

MacDonald claims, is not mimetic; at the very least, it is not the same as Luke's relationship to his Greek literary models. Instead, Luke "was aware of the *Aeneid* and shaped his book to rival it. The affinities between Luke and Vergil thus pertain... to narrative structure and development, not to imitations of particular episodes or characterizations."[17] Knowledge of the structure and content of the *Aeneid* — including its own imitations of Homer — was made available through a number of nontextual media for the general public in the Roman Mediterranean. Such knowledge was not the exclusive possession of the literate elite.[18]

In *Luke and Vergil: Imitations of Classical Greek Literature*, MacDonald explores the remarkable affinities shared between Luke-Acts and the *Aeneid*, primarily in terms of "narrative structure and analogous imitations of Homer."[19] Structurally, Virgil's *Aeneid* can be read as a Roman "Odyssey-Iliad": *Aeneid* 1–6 follows Aeneas's sea voyages from Troy to Carthage to Italy and includes a shipwreck; *Aeneid* 7–12 details the conflict between the Trojans and the Latins, culminating in Aeneas's slaying of Turnus.[20] The structure of Luke-Acts reverts to the Homeric

---

Rowman & Littlefield, 2015), 3–4. MacDonald does allow that Luke may have been able to read Latin himself or known someone who could.

[17] MacDonald, *Luke and Vergil*, 1.

[18] Cf. MacDonald, *Luke and Vergil*, 3–4; Chris Shea, "Imitating Imitation: Vergil, Homer, and Acts 10:1–11:18," *Ancient Fiction: The Matrix of Early Christian and Jewish Narrative* (ed. J. A. Brant, C. W. Hedrick, and C. Shea; Atlanta: Society of Biblical Literature, 2005), 44–46.

[19] MacDonald, *Luke and Vergil*, 4 (cf. 125–204).

[20] Barchiesi observes that Apollonius (*Argonautica*) and Naevius (*Bellum Punicum*) precede Virgil with similar strategies (*Homeric Effects*, 71). For more nuanced analyses of Virgil's Homeric structure, see Francis Cairns, *Virgil's Augustan Epic* (Cambridge: Cambridge University Press,

order, a Christian "Iliad-Odyssey": the Gospel of Luke climaxes with the death of Jesus;[21] the Acts of the Apostles features a number of first-person sea-voyages and includes a shipwreck. Moreover, Luke's and Virgil's narratives both conclude in Rome and feature the progression of divinely ordained, kingdom-oriented missions. Within this framework, MacDonald observes that a number of the Homeric imitations he identifies in Luke-Acts are analogously imitated in Virgil's *Aeneid*. One example is Hector's farewell to Andromache (*Il.* 6) in *Aeneid* 2.647–794 and 3.294–380, Luke 24:37–40, and Acts 20:18–38.[22] A second example — the double portent of Agamemnon's lying dream and the sign of the serpent (*Il.* 2) — will be discussed at length below.

MacDonald situates his reading of Luke-Acts and Luke's construction of Christian identity among the constructions of Greek identity within the Roman Empire. According to Tim Whitmarsh, "In literary terms, 'becoming Greek' meant constructing one's own self-representation through and against the canonical past."[23] Luke certainly constructs the kingdom of God that Jesus inaugurates "through and against" narratives and prophecies of the Septuagint; MacDonald has argued that foundational Greek narratives — those by Homer, Euripides, Plato, and

---

1989); Edan Dekel, *Virgil's Homeric Lens* (New York: Routledge, 2012); and Barchiesi, *Homeric Effects*, 69–93.

[21] In this respect, it may be worth noting that Luke corrects Mark's designation of the "Sea" of Galilee by identifying it as a "lake." Luke reserves sea adventures for Paul and the Mediterranean.

[22] MacDonald, *Luke and Vergil*, 151–56.

[23] Tim Whitmarsh, *Greek Literature and the Roman Empire: The Politics of Imitation* (Oxford: Oxford University Press, 2001), 27.

Xenophon—also serve as mimetic points of reference.[24] Like Bonz, MacDonald also wants to bring the most famous Roman narrative within Lukan scholars' purview. Luke's rivalry with Homer and Virgil communicates to the reader that Luke's heroes, "Jesus and Paul, are more powerful than and morally superior to their Homeric and Vergilian counterparts, just as Vergil's Aeneas generally is morally superior to the likes of Achilles and Odysseus."[25] MacDonald argues that Luke-Acts can be read as contesting "Vergil's Roman appropriation of Greek epic by depicting the superiority of his heroes—especially Jesus and Paul—to Aeneas and Augustus."[26] According to MacDonald, Luke constructs Christian identity and the significance of Jesus by comparison and contrast with both the canonical past—Jewish and Greek—and the ubiquitous present of Roman self-representation, not least of all in Virgil's *Aeneid*.

From a different perspective, Aaron Kuecker, in a recent essay, draws a compelling comparison between the negotiations of superordinate social identities in Virgil's *Aeneid* and in Luke-Acts.[27] In both works of literature, superordinate identities are constructed by appeal to filial piety; the major contrast lies in how these identities are manifest.[28] Whereas the filial piety of Roman identity inevitably precipitates violence in the *Aeneid*, the filial piety

---

[24] Cf. MacDonald, *The Gospels and Homer: Imitations of Greek Epic in Mark and Luke-Acts* (NTGL 1; Lanham, Md.: Rowman & Littlefield, 2015); MacDonald, *Luke and Vergil*, 11–123.

[25] MacDonald, *Luke and Vergil*, 3.

[26] MacDonald, *Luke and Vergil*, 4.

[27] Kuecker, "Filial Piety and Violence," 211–33.

[28] Kuecker, "Filial Piety and Violence," 216–17.

of Christian identity in Luke-Acts is grounded in "neighborly love." Within both Virgil's and Luke's narratives, the presence of a superordinate identity allows for the maintenance of subgroup identities: Trojans, Latins, and other conquered subgroups within Roman identity; Judeans, Greeks, Cretans, and others within Christian identity.[29]

Kuecker begins "with the rather straightforward observation that in the first century CE Roman citizenship and Christian identity stood as unique parallels with regard to their interest in reconciling still salient ethnic subgroup identities within a larger, trans-ethnic social group."[30] Perhaps unlike in Luke-Acts, such reconciliation cannot be credibly identified as one of the intended functions of the *Aeneid*. In terms of identity, Virgil's epic is primarily about the union of Trojan and Latin peoples; however, there were no "Trojans" to speak of in Virgil's time. He is concerned, rather, with the appropriation of an ancient identity, a heritage, by a contemporary people who were ethnically distinct from those ancient people.

When Luke-Acts and Virgil's *Aeneid* are compared within Kuecker's identity theory framework, a contrast comes into focus: Roman violence toward outsiders and the neighborly love of the kingdom of God. As opposed to the violence toward outsiders characterizing Roman identity — think of the war of the Trojans against the Latins and Aeneas's slaying of Turnus — Christian identity fosters

---

[29] Of course, in the *Aeneid*, Trojan identity does not endure beyond the merger of Latins and Trojans. See the discussion below on *Aeneid* 12.

[30] Kuecker, "Filial Piety and Violence," 212.

neighborly love. Kuecker identifies Luke 9:51-56 — a passage that alludes to the Elijah narrative — as exemplifying the Christian option for neighborly love over violence. He writes, "When the Samaritans refuse to join the family, so to speak, the logical implication for James and John is violent destruction of the village. This sounds eerily similar to the way filial piety functions in Vergil's description of the relationship between *Romanitas* and those outside the Roman ingroup."[31] Similarly, Kuecker observes how the filial piety of the fictional Samaritan (Luke 10:25-37) and the post-Damascus Road Paul lead them away from violent opposition.

The hinge of filial piety swings toward violence, for instance, in the reaction of a subset of Judeans — including the pre-Damascus Road Paul — at the idea of God's benefactions being extended to those beyond their own in-group. This violent tendency among opponents of Jesus's message of inclusion recurs throughout Luke and Acts, including Luke 4:16-30 and Acts 17:1-14. Luke calls followers of Jesus to bestow God's benefactions upon outsiders, rather than to be hostile toward them. For instance, in the Good Samaritan episode, "The question of the lawyer, 'And who is my neighbor?', invites Jesus to engage in the sort of social categorization *that could limit social obligation or access to benefits* of the lawyer's own Israelite ingroup."[32] Jesus rejects such limitations. In contrast to Roman violence toward outsiders — Rome's instrument for inclusion — Christian identity is characterized by filial

---

[31] Kuecker, "Filial Piety and Violence," 227. Cf. 2 Kings 1:10-12.
[32] Kuecker, "Filial Piety and Violence," 228, emphasis added.

piety, precipitating the peaceful inclusion of those on the margins of Judean society and beyond.

Negotiating Ethnic Identities and Legacies

As I have already suggested, the theme of negotiating Trojan identity among Italians recurs throughout the *Aeneid*. Why this theme? The Roman arrogation of the legacy of Troy had begun centuries before Virgil composed his epic; moreover, any significant remnant of Trojan ethnicity among the Romans—if there ever was one—had long since dissipated. One explanation for this theme is that it makes sense of Italian people in the first century BCE, who are not ethnically Trojan, claiming the legacy of Troy. Virgil situates his Roman foundation epic at the imagined point in the ancient past when two people groups—Trojans and Latins—merged, all the while providing divine justification for his first-century-BCE situation. Luke-Acts exhibits a similar theme: the kingdom of God inaugurated by Jesus expands to include not only marginalized Jews/Judeans, but also Gentiles, who also become heirs to the legacy of Israel. Bonz writes, "The promise of ancient Troy reaches its fulfillment in the creation of the Roman people, just as, in Luke's narrative, the promise of ancient Israel reaches its fulfillment in the establishment and growth of the new community of believers."[33] Luke's narrative appeals to Israelite prophecies and highlights the supernatural intervention involved in bringing about this inclusion. At the time Luke-Acts was composed—whether in the late first century or early second century—many

---

[33] Bonz, *Past as Legacy*, 192–93; cf. 87–128 (especially 124–28).

Christian communities faced a quandary similar to Rome's: how to reconcile the ethnic composition of the churches (predominantly Gentile) with the church's claim to Israel's legacy. Luke and Virgil negotiate this issue in remarkably similar ways.

Luke's use of prophecies and divine intervention constitutes a major part of Bonz's comparison of Luke-Acts with the *Aeneid*. Moreover, most comparisons of Luke's and Virgil's narratives similarly observe the common goal of establishing a unified identity comprising distinct ethnic groups.[34] The comparison that follows in this essay explores the role of deities in orchestrating these negotiations in the *Aeneid* and Luke-Acts. The similarities are so striking, I argue, that it is credible to read Luke's language in a dialectic relationship with that of the *Aeneid*, playing with it as a conceptual metaphor.

The Ghost of Hector and the Resurrected Jesus

Before exploring the issue of divine intervention to merge ethnic groups in the *Aeneid* and Luke-Acts, I ask: Are there any distinctive parallels between the narratives of Luke-Acts and Virgil's *Aeneid* that lend credibility to a

---

[34] Cf. John Taylor, *Classics and the Bible: Hospitality and Recognition* (London: Duckworth, 2007), 133; Kuecker, "Filial Piety and Violence;" and MacDonald, *Luke and Vergil*, 2. Others recognize the Roman quality of this theme, without discussing the *Aeneid*. Cf. Vernon K. Robbins, "Luke-Acts: A Mixed Population Seeks a Home in the Roman Empire," *Images of Empire* (ed. L. Alexander; Sheffield: JSOT Press, 1991), 202–21; David L. Balch, "The Cultural Origin of 'Receiving All Nations' in Luke-Acts: Alexander the Great or Roman Social Policy?" *Early Christianity and Classical Culture: Comparative Studies in Honor of Abraham J. Malherbe* (ed. J. T. Fitzgerald, T. H. Olbricht, and L. M. White; NovTSup 110; Leiden: Brill, 2003), 483–500.

comparison of the two? Peter's healing of a man who bears the name of Virgil's protagonist (Acts 9:32–35) may be intriguing in this respect, but the name Aeneas was famous well before the publication of the *Aeneid*, as Loveday Alexander has previously observed, and does not necessitate Luke's knowledge of Virgil.[35] Instead, I will briefly consider a confluence of distinctively Virgilian features surrounding the appearance of Jesus to Paul in Acts 23. The distinctiveness of these similarities adds credibility to the subsequent comparison of how each narrative negotiates ethnic legacies.

In Acts 22, Paul delivers an apologia to a Jerusalem mob that had been roused at the idea of Paul introducing "Greeks" beyond the Court of the Gentiles in the Jerusalem Temple (cf. 21:27–29). His defense closes with his commission to minister to Gentiles (22:21), at which the crowd erupts in demonstrative disapproval. Claudius Lysias, the Roman tribune, extracts Paul from the tumult. In an effort to understand the excitement, Lysias brings Paul before the Sanhedrin. Several details from this account (Acts 23:1–8) echo Jesus's time in Jerusalem in Luke's Gospel, perhaps none more than Paul's appeal to the resurrection of the dead, creating dissension between Pharisees and Sadducees.[36] The dissention becomes violent, so the

---

[35] Loveday Alexander, *Acts in its Ancient Literary Context: A Classicist Looks at the Acts of the Apostles* (LNTS 298; London: T&T Clark, 2005), 170–71. Cf. Michael Kochenash, "You Can't Hear 'Aeneas' without Thinking of Rome," *JBL* (forthcoming).

[36] Cf. Richard I. Pervo, *Acts: A Commentary* (Hermeneia; Minneapolis: Fortress Press, 2009), 533–34. For the topic of Sadducees opposing resurrection during Jesus's time in Jerusalem, see Luke 20:27–39.

tribune's soldiers once again extract Paul and return him to the barracks (23:10).

Those who read Luke-Acts within a Virgilian framework may be struck by what Luke narrates in the following verse. Still in Jerusalem, within the Roman barracks: "That night the Lord stood near [Paul] and said, 'Keep up your courage! For just as you have testified for me in Jerusalem, so you must bear witness also in Rome'" (23:11). This encouragement confirms the Roman direction of the narrative previously made explicit in Acts 19:21.[37] Commentators typically classify this as a "vision" or a "dream."[38] The text of Acts 23:11 makes neither classification self-evident, however. Although the episode in Acts 23 takes place at night, there is no indication that the Lord (i.e., Jesus) is appearing in a dream or vision.[39] Instead, Luke straightforwardly presents Jesus standing near Paul and instructing him that he must bear witness to him in Rome.[40]

---

[37] It also anticipates the reassurance brought by an angel during Paul's perilous voyage to Rome in Acts 27:24. MacDonald compares Acts 23:11 with Circe's prophetic directions in *Odyssey* 12, which may have served as a model for Helenus's prophecies for Aeneas in *Aen.* 3.374–462. Paul and Aeneas are both directed to Italy. Cf. MacDonald, *Luke and Vergil*, 156.

[38] E.g., Joseph A. Fitzmyer, *The Acts of the Apostles: A New Translation with Introduction and Commentary* (AB 31; New York: Doubleday, 1998), 720; C. K. Barrett, *A Critical and Exegetical Commentary on the Acts of the Apostles* (2 vols.; ICC 34; Edinburgh: T&T Clark, 1994–1998), 2: 1068; Pervo, *Acts*, 576; and Craig S. Keener, *Acts: An Exegetical Commentary* (4 vols.; Grand Rapids: Baker Academic, 2012–2015), 3:3299. Richard Pervo notes a parallel between Acts 23:11 and an episode in Josephus's autobiography (*Life* 208–9) in a footnote (*Acts*, 576 n. 51).

[39] Circumstances of dreams, visions, and trances are elsewhere made explicit: Acts 9:10; 10:3, 10; 16:9; 18:9; 22:17.

[40] If the interpretation of these commentators is correct, however, the parallel with the *Aeneid* may be strengthened.

The narrative of the Acts of the Apostles is situated, of course, after the events of the Gospel of Luke, which climaxes with the death of Jesus, the protagonist, and ends with his resurrection and ascension. In Acts 23:11, the protagonist of the earlier narrative appears to the current protagonist in the middle of the night and commissions him with a task that involves going to Rome. The confluence of these circumstances corresponds to remarkably similar features of Virgil's narrative, a matrix of distinctive features that, to my knowledge, is not replicated elsewhere in ancient literature.

In book 2 of the *Aeneid*, like Odysseus in Phaeacia, Aeneas entertains his Carthaginian hosts with stories of the Trojan War and of his own sea voyages. Among his recollections, Aeneas narrates how, while he was sleeping and the Greeks were overtaking Troy, he was met by the ghost of Hector (*Aen.* 2.270–71).[41] The narrative of Virgil's *Aeneid*, just like Homer's *Odyssey*, is situated in the aftermath of the *Iliad*. The *Iliad*, of course, reaches its climax when Achilles slays Hector, arguably the hero of the epic, in book 22. In *Aeneid* 2, Hector's ghost returns to the realm of the living and charges Aeneas with leading a remnant of Trojans out from the burning city in order to establish them "over the seas" (*Aen.* 2.289–95). The reader knows Hector is

---

[41] Curiously, Latin scholars have translated this episode ambiguously, leaving it unclear as to whether Hector "seems" to appear to Aeneas in a dream (as the translations suggest) or whether Hector's ghost is actually present with him (as the Latin text would suggest, like a Homeric dream). Cf. Raymond J. Clark, "The Reality of Hector's Ghost in Aeneas' Dream," *Latomus* 57 (1998): 832–41.

referring to Italy, specifically the area that will become Rome, and the narrative later confirms it.

Reading Acts 23:11 through a Virgilian lens thus reveals a striking similarity: both Luke and Virgil narrate a nighttime scene wherein the fallen hero of a related antecedent narrative appears to the present protagonist and tasks him with a mission that involves going to Rome (or the region that will later become Rome).[42] Obvious differences exist between the *Aeneid* and Luke-Acts, ranging from language to style to content. Nevertheless, there are remarkable similarities in terms of scope: Virgil composed a foundation epic for the Roman Empire, detailing how a group of Trojan refugees merged with the Latin people and established the roots of both the Romans and the Julio-Claudian dynasty itself. Luke-Acts can be read as functioning similarly, comprising a foundation narrative for the kingdom of God that details how the kingdom inaugurated by Jesus expanded to include not only Judeans but also Gentiles.

---

[42] Interestingly, before leaving Troy, Aeneas encounters another ghost, that of his wife, Creusa, who makes Aeneas's destination explicit: Italy (*Aen.* 2.776–89; cf. 3.163–68, 374–462); Paul likewise encounters a second divine figure, this time an angel, who affirms that Paul is "to stand before the emperor" (Acts 27:23–24). Aeneas, however, encounters a third ghost, that of his late father, in *Aeneid* 5.529–31, who similarly sends him to Italy.

Virgil's Aeneid

Karl Galinsky affirms that the fusion of Trojans and Latins is "a significant theme" of the *Aeneid*.[43] By the first century BCE, the Roman connection to the ancient Trojan people was well established. During the time of Augustus, "Rome's noblest families laid claim to Trojan descent and their scions participated in the elaborate equestrian Troy game (*lusus Troiae*)."[44] Not only were Romans identifying as descendants of Aeneas's Trojans corporately, Julius Caesar introduced an innovation: he, personally, was a direct descendant of Aeneas and heir to his legacy. Augustus inherited these claims and advertised them even further. Within this cultural environment, Virgil narrates the movement of a remnant of the Trojan people to Italy after the fall of Troy. The bard is explicit, early in his epic, about the task of the Trojans: "to found the Roman people" (*Aen.* 1.33).[45] Most of the relevant passages, incidentally, are concentrated in books 1, 6, 7, and 12, the first and final books in both halves of the *Aeneid*. In this brief discussion of the *Aeneid*, I highlight both the explicitly divine origin of the Trojans' mission and the ways in which the Olympians negotiated its accomplishment: subsuming the Trojans among the Latins.

In book 1 of the *Aeneid*, after observing Aeneas and his crew shipwreck at Carthage, Venus inquires about the

---

[43] Karl Galinsky, "Vergil's *Aeneid* and Ovid's *Metamorphoses* as World Literature," *The Cambridge Companion to the Age of Augustus* (ed. K. Galinsky; Cambridge: Cambridge University Press, 2005), 346.

[44] Galinsky, "Vergil's *Aeneid* and Ovid's *Metamorphoses*," 347.

[45] The translation of the *Aeneid* used here was made by Dennis MacDonald.

fate of the Trojans. She states, "Surely from these [Trojans] Romans— / from these, from the renewed bloodline of Teucer—will come rulers, / who will hold with authority the sea and all lands / because you promised it" (1.234–37). Jupiter affirms that "still unmoved / are the fates of your children" (1.257–58). He continues, "From this wonderful heritage a Trojan Caesar will be born who will limit his / empire with Oceanus and his fame with the stars; / Iulius, a name derived from the great Iulus [Aeneas's son]" (1.286–88). The emergence of Romans from the merger of Trojans and Latins is not only the will of the Olympians, it is destiny.

In the final book of the first half of the *Aeneid*, book 6, Aeneas travels to the underworld. Here he encounters his recently deceased father, Anchises, who explains to Aeneas the fate of the souls occupying the underworld.[46] In this context, Anchises reveals Aeneas's "destiny," the souls of his descendants "of Italian parents" and "of the Trojan race" (6.757, 759, 767). Aeneas's preview climaxes with Caesar Augustus, "son of a god, who will found a golden / age again in Latium" (6.792–93). Virgil here legitimizes the propaganda of Julius Caesar and Augustus, that they are direct descendants of Aeneas through the mixing of Latins and Trojans, and heirs to the eternal kingdom prophesied for him. This circumstance is not merely an accident of history, as Anchises explains; rather it has been predetermined.

Virgil's "Iliad," the conflict between Trojans and Latins, begins in book 7. Virgil declares that it is "by fate" that King Latinus had no male descendant, and "heavenly

---

[46] Virgil's account appears to imitate Plato's Myth of Er (*Resp.* 10.614–21).

portents" prevented the marriage of his daughter, Lavinia, to Turnus (7.50–51, 58). Both of these divine interventions facilitated Aeneas's marriage to Lavinia, making Latinus the "founder of the bloodline" (7.48–49) culminating in Augustus. Faunus, Latinus's father, instructed the king in an oracle:

> Do not seek to unite your daughter to a Latin / … Foreign peoples are coming, whose bloodline / will carry your name to the stars (7.96–99).

After Latinus welcomed the Trojans into his palace, the Trojan Ilioneus reveals that they (too) have been guided by oracles (7.241–42); Latinus then recalls Faunus's oracle and identifies Aeneas as the one appointed by fate (7.254–58).[47]

Prior to the epic's conclusion, Jupiter and Juno negotiate the fates of Latin identity and Trojan legacy. As Nicholas Horsfall indicates, Virgil's "resolution of the negotiations is to a large extent predetermined by the known facts of history and ethnography," but it is nevertheless remarkable that the poet credits the resolution to divine decree.[48] Juno requests that the Latin people be able to retain their name, language, and clothing, that they never change their name, and that the Trojan identity "be fallen" along with Troy (*Aen.* 12.819–28). Jupiter responds by granting her wish: the Latins will keep their language, identity, and their way of life; the Trojans will "merge" and "fade away," incorporated as Latins (12.833–37).[49] Thus, the only group

---

[47] Not all deities worked toward the union of Latins and Trojans. Juno explicitly opposes it (*Aen.* 7.286–322).

[48] Nicholas Horsfall, "Aeneas the Colonist," *Vergilius* 35 (1989): 22.

[49] Cf. Horsfall, "Aeneas the Colonist," 22–24. Clifford Ando observes the contradiction: the conquerors were subsumed within the

with a claim to the legacy of the Trojans is the Latin people. Kuecker identifies this section of the *Aeneid* as a "virtually technical [description] of the formation of a superordinate identity with ongoing subgroup salience."[50]

Luke-Acts

A major theme of Luke-Acts is the inclusion of the marginalized.[51] The narrative of Luke's Gospel exhibits a particular interest in Jesus's ministry to Samaritans, tax collectors, women, and poor people.[52] The kingdom of God that Jesus inaugurates, however, will also include Gentiles. Simeon encounters the baby Jesus and declares that he will be "a light for revelation to the Gentiles," though also "destined for the falling and the rising of many in Israel" (Luke 2:32, 34). John the Baptist, preparing the way for Jesus's ministry, recites Isaiah's prophecy that "all flesh shall see the salvation of God" (Luke 3:6; Isa 40:5). When Jesus inaugurates his ministry in Galilee, he similarly quotes from Isaiah—"The Spirit of the Lord is upon me, because he has

---

identity of the vanquished (*Imperial Ideology and Provincial Loyalty in the Roman Empire* [Berkeley: University of California Press, 2000], 53–54).

[50] Kuecker, "Filial Piety and Violence," 211–12. E.g., *Aen.* 12.834–37, 1055–1065.

[51] The inclusion of outsiders into the kingdom of God is by no means unique to Luke-Acts; the idea is found in Mark, Matthew, and Paul's letters, as well as much antecedent Jewish literature: e.g. Isaiah 2:1–4; 42:6; 49:6; 56:1–8; Tobit 13:11; 14:7; *1 Enoch* 10:21; 90:37–38; *Sibylline Oracles* 3:657–808. On the theme of divine intervention within Luke's narrative, see also Bonz, *Past as Legacy*, 158–64.

[52] On Samaritans, see Luke 9:51–56; 10:29–37; 17:11–19. On tax collectors, see Luke 5:27–32; 7:34; 15:1–12; 18:9–14; 19:1–10. On women, see Luke 7:11–17, 36–50; 8:1–3, 42–48; 10:38–42; 21:1–4; 23:27; 23:55–24:11. On the poor, see Luke 4:18; 6:20–21; 7:22; 12:16–21; 14:13, 21; 16:19–31; 18:22.

anointed me to bring good news to the poor" (Luke 4:18; Isa 61:1) — and then explains his fulfillment of this scripture by referring to the activity of Elijah and Elisha, how they ministered to those outside Israel (Luke 4:25-27). Although Jesus proceeds to have only limited contact with Gentiles throughout his ministry in Luke's Gospel (cf. Luke 7:1-10), he commissions his followers to continue his work among Gentiles (Luke 24:47; Acts 1:8); and so it is in the Acts of the Apostles that Gentiles gain inclusion into God's kingdom.[53]

The first Gentile in Luke-Acts to gain inclusion within the kingdom of God is Cornelius in Acts 10:1-11:18, a narrative replete with supernatural orchestration. An angel appears to Cornelius, "a centurion of the Italian cohort" (Acts 10:1), and gives him instructions to send for Peter; meanwhile, Peter witnesses a portent involving "all kinds of four-footed creatures and reptiles and birds" along with an interactive voice from heaven while in a trance (Acts 10:9-16).[54] These two incidents work together to bring about Cornelius's inclusion within the kingdom of God.

---

[53] A number of passages in the Acts of the Apostles attest to the idea that Jewish rejection of the gospel message precipitates the extension of that message to Gentiles. These passages, however, are primarily found within the schematized Pauline missionary work (though not exclusively; cf. possibly Luke 13:25-30), and they stand in tension with passages suggesting that Gentile inclusion was a foundational aspect of the kingdom of God inaugurated by Jesus, as foretold by the prophets, without first requiring Jewish rejection. For passages suggesting the latter, see Luke 2:32; 3:6; and (especially) Acts 10:1-11:18, where the first Gentile is included without a hint of Jewish rejection.

[54] John B. F. Miller notes, "Peter's dream-vision in Acts 10 is the only interpreted symbolic dream-vision in the New Testament outside of Revelation" ("Exploring the Function of Symbolic Dream-Visions in the Literature of Antiquity, with Another Look at 1QapGen 19 and Acts 10," *PRS* 37 [2010]: 449). He calls the others "message dream-visions" (453). Cf.

The details of Cornelius's vision are repeated four times in Acts 10:1–11:18, with many of the key details withheld until the final iteration (11:12–14).[55] Prior to the first vision, the narrator establishes Cornelius's ethos (10:1–2) and emphasizes his keen perception at the time of the vision: it is three o'clock in the afternoon, and he sees the vision "clearly" (10:3).[56] The angel of God "came in" to him, though Cornelius's location is unstated, and tells him that the vision is in response to his prayers and alms and that he needs to send for Peter, who is in Joppa (10:4–7).

The next day, Peter receives a dream-vision. While praying on a rooftop, he becomes hungry and falls into a trance (10:9–11; 11:5). He then sees "the heaven opened and something like a large sheet coming down" within which are "all kinds of four-footed creatures and reptiles and birds" (10:11–12; 11:5–6). Three times a voice from heaven orders Peter to kill and eat these animals; each time, Peter declines on account of their unclean status (10:13–16; 11:7–10). Peter is still puzzling over the meaning of the vision when Cornelius's men arrive.

The second iteration of Cornelius's vision is reported to Peter by the three men sent by Cornelius (10:22). This report establishes Cornelius's character for Peter by adding a note about his reputation among the whole Jewish

---

Edith M. Humphrey, "Collision of Modes? — Vision and Determining Argument in Acts 10:1–11:18," *Sem* 71 (1995): 65–84; Dennis R. MacDonald, *Does the New Testament Imitate Homer? Four Cases from the Acts of the Apostles* (New Haven: Yale University Press, 2003), 19–65.

[55] Humphrey, "Collision of Modes," 76.

[56] The pious character of Cornelius contrasts with Homer's depiction of Agamemnon. Cf. MacDonald, *Imitate Homer*, 44–45.

nation. Moreover, it provides a rationale not previously stated: the angel told Cornelius to send for Peter *in order to hear what he has to say*. Peter also learns that the three men will be taking him to the house of a Roman centurion. The third iteration of Cornelius's vision (10:30–32), attributed to Cornelius himself, is "more vivid" and adds two key details: the vision occurred while he was praying, and it took place inside his house.[57] His description of the angel as "standing" before him is also significant.[58]

Luke attributes the fourth iteration of the vision to Peter (11:12–14). According to Peter, the angel explained to Cornelius that Peter "will give you a message by which you and your entire household will be saved" (11:14). Edith Humphrey writes, "It is this picture of the angel entering the house of Cornelius for the ultimate purpose of the salvation of that household that would appear to be the masterstroke of the argument."[59] In Peter's rooftop vision, God declares all foods clean. If Peter objected to associating too closely with Gentiles because their diets made them ritually impure, God thus nullified the premise of his objection. The implications of this vision become clear to Peter when Cornelius's men invite him to stay at the house of a Gentile. (God's spirit had told Peter to go without hesitation.) The audience learns later that the angel of God had set a precedent for Peter's entrance within a Gentile's house (10:30). The narrative thus circumvents the objection of the circumcised men from Jerusalem—"Why did you go to

---

[57] Humphrey, "Collision of Modes," 76.

[58] MacDonald, *Imitate Homer*, 46. See below.

[59] Humphrey, "Collision of Modes," 77.

uncircumcised men and eat with them?" (11:3)—and presents an argument for including Gentiles within God's kingdom.[60] In the end, the "circumcised" express the conclusion of Luke's argumentation: "Then God has given even to the Gentiles the repentance that leads to life" (11:18). Jesus's followers in Jerusalem recognize the inclusion of this individual Gentile (and his household) as opening the door for all Gentiles. Gentiles are able to join the kingdom of God and become joint heirs to Israel's legacy, just as the prophets foretold.

MacDonald has compellingly argued that Acts 10:1–11:18 can be read as an imitation of episodes in book 2 of Homer's *Iliad*.[61] In *Iliad* 2, at the request of Thetis, the mother of Achilles, Zeus sends Oneiros ("Dream") with a duplicitous message for Agamemnon, one of the military commanders of the Greeks, to punish him for taking Achilles's concubine, Briseis. Standing over his head, Oneiros deceives Agamemnon, telling him that it is "now" the right time to attack Troy; victory is assured by Zeus (*Il.* 2.1–41). Energized by Oneiros, Agamemnon convokes his council and relays the message from his dream. Within the council is Odysseus, who recalls a portent from nine years prior: before the Greek armies embarked on their voyage to Troy, as they were offering sacrifices, a serpent emerged from under the altar, darted to the top of a nearby tree, and devoured eight baby sparrows and then also the mother (2.301–20). The prophet Calchas interpreted each of the birds

---

[60] Humphrey, "Collision of Modes," 78.

[61] MacDonald, *Imitate Homer*, 19–65 and MacDonald, *Gospels and Homer*, 33–46.

as a year of war against Troy; in the tenth year, the Greeks would overtake the city (2.321–29). Odysseus and the Greeks understand the earlier portent as confirming the validity of Agamemnon's vision. "Only after losing many heroes does Agamemnon recognize that [Zeus] had deceived them."[62] Although the Greeks do eventually overthrow the city of Troy, the Olympians—particularly Zeus—capitalize on the duplicitous dream's correspondence to a portent in order to sow destruction among the Greeks.

The correspondences between Acts 10:1–11:18 and *Iliad* 2 are dense, distinct, and relatively sequential, and Luke's use of Homer here is certainly interpretable.[63] Particularly notable is the way in which Cornelius's angelic visit and Peter's dream-vision interact to enact God's will for the inclusion of Gentiles.[64] The similarities between Acts 10:1–11:18 and *Iliad* 2 become all the more striking, however, for those familiar with Virgil's *Aeneid*. Virgil imitates both the lying dream sent to Agamemnon and the portent of the serpent and sparrows recalled by Odysseus, but he does so in two unrelated episodes in the *Aeneid*. Notably, both episodes retain the element of duplicity and result in many deaths. As Virgil tells it, the establishment of the Trojans in Italy—the foundation of the Roman Empire—came about amid violence driven by ethically questionable divine manipulation.

---

[62] MacDonald, *Imitate Homer*, 26.

[63] Cf. MacDonald, *Imitate Homer*, 56–65.

[64] For other ancient writings that imitate both the dream and portent from *Iliad* 2, see MacDonald, *Imitate Homer*, 37–43.

The portent of twin serpents in *Aeneid* 2.199–227 imitates the *Iliad*'s portent of the serpent and the sparrows.[65] In *Aeneid* 2, Aeneas describes the fall of Troy to the Carthaginians and focuses on the fateful act of accepting the wooden horse from the Greeks. The Trojan priest Laocoön suspected ill intentions on the part of the Greeks and so advised against receiving the gift. He suggested destroying the wooden horse (*Aen.* 2.40–49, 54–56). To the misfortune of the Trojans, while Laocoön was performing a sacrifice to Poseidon, twin serpents darted out from the sea and attacked Laocoön's two sons. When Laocoön tried to save them, the serpents caught him in their coils and squeezed the life out of him along with his sons (2.199–227). The witnesses quite reasonably interpreted this portent as a divine judgment against the priest and his advice regarding the wooden horse, which he had also assaulted with a spear (cf. 2.50–53, 229–31). Thus the fate of the Trojans was sealed. A divinely ordained portent ensured the destruction of the city of Troy and many of its inhabitants.

In *Aeneid* 7.406–34, Allecto's deception of Turnus imitates Oneiros's encounter with Agamemnon in *Iliad* 2.[66] Juno comes to the realization that her efforts to prevent the

---

[65] Cf. Knauer, *Aeneis und Homer*, 379; Adele J. Haft, "Odysseus' Wrath and Grief in the *Iliad*: Agamemnon, the Ithacan King, and the Sack of Troy in Books 2, 4, and 14," *Classical Journal* 85 (1990): 107–9; Hermann Kleinknecht, "Laokoon," *Hermes* 79 (1944): 66–111; MacDonald, *Imitate Homer*, 36; and MacDonald, *Luke and Vergil*, 148–51.

[66] Cf. Knauer, *Aeneis und Homer*, 236–37; Hans Rudolf Steiner, *Der Traum in der* Aeneis (Noctes Romanae 5; Bern: Paul Haupt, 1952), 62–66; Clyde Murley, "The Use of Messenger Gods by Vergil and Homer," *Vergilius* 3 (1939): 3–11; MacDonald, *Imitate Homer*, 32–33; and MacDonald, *Luke and Vergil*, 175–77.

union of the Latins and Trojans are futile, and so she resolves to delay the union by sowing the seeds of war (7.293–322). Juno summons Allecto and sends her with a deception for Turnus, the Rutulian king and former suitor of Lavinia (who was betrothed to Aeneas upon the arrival of the Trojans). While the king is sleeping, Allecto appears to him as an elderly priestess of Juno's temple. She rouses Turnus by reminding him of Latinus's betrayal and Aeneas's preemption. After explaining that she had been sent by Juno — a half-truth — she urges him to take up arms against the Trojans (7.406–34). When Turnus awakes, he gathers the "captains of his troops" and readies them for battle against the Trojans (7.467–70). Not only does the Trojan army defeat the Latins, the entire epic concludes with Aeneas taking Turnus's life. The intervention of Juno and Allecto thus resulted in many needless deaths.

Metaphors not only facilitate the explanation of something abstract by reference to something concrete; they also influence the logical framework within which the concept being explained is understood.[67] They do so by allowing auditors "to borrow patterns of inference from the source domain to use in reasoning about some target domain."[68] The narrative logic of Virgil's *Aeneid* can be found in Luke's reasoning about the kingdom of God, in this case regarding the union of different ethnic groups. Such a discovery should not be surprising; it simply suggests that

---

[67] Cf. Coulson, *Semantic Leaps*, 162–202; George Lakoff and Mark Turner, *More than Cool Reason: A Field Guide to Poetic Metaphor* (Chicago: University of Chicago Press, 1989), 57–139.

[68] Lakoff and Turner, *More than Cool Reason*, 65.

Luke's narrative utilizes culturally significant patterns of inference. As suggested above, however, Luke's narrative also breaks from the Roman schema in meaningful ways.

In Rome's foundation narrative, some deities actively opposed the union of the Trojans and Latins, going so far as to incite war between the two groups to delay it. Juno and Allecto's intervention — in the form of a duplicitous dream-vision — resulted in the deaths of many on both sides, with the Latins absorbing more casualties (including the life of Turnus himself). Moreover, the Trojans themselves had previously been the victims of divine meddling: a portent convinced them to accept the wooden horse full of Greek warriors, precipitating the fall of Troy. Nevertheless, the union of Trojans and Latins was inevitable, having been promised by Olympians and decreed by fate. Luke's narrative can be read as operating within this logical framework, where immortal beings intervene in order to fulfill divine mandates. When Luke narrates the first inclusion of Gentiles among the Jewish followers of Jesus, the union is divinely orchestrated by a dream-vision and a portent involving animals. Israelite prophets foretold this inclusion; Jesus's ministry in Luke's Gospel anticipates it. Luke breaks the pattern established by Homer and followed by Virgil, however. God's intervention does not bring death with it; instead it brings salvation. The God of the Israelites is morally superior to the Olympians.[69] Such a conclusion

---

[69] On the appropriateness of transvaluation when imitating literary models, see Dennis R. MacDonald, *My Turn: A Critique of Critics of "Mimesis Criticism"* (Occasional Papers of the Institute for Antiquity and Christianity 53; Claremont, CA: Institute for Antiquity and Christianity, 2009), 6–7. MacDonald here responds to objections raised by Margaret M.

may strike modern ears as underwhelming or perhaps trite. I would suggest, however, that Luke's comparison was powerful within the Roman Mediterranean, a culture that highly valued both Homer's *Iliad* and Virgil's *Aeneid*. In this way, Luke's narrative can be read as both appropriating and challenging a dominant cultural paradigm.

Conclusions

The foregoing discussion interprets Luke's negotiation of Israel's legacy among Jewish and Gentile Christians within the framework of Virgil's *Aeneid*. Due to the ubiquity of Virgil's story of Aeneas throughout the Roman Mediterranean, it is possible to read the ethnic negotiation in Luke's narrative as a reconfiguration of Roman self-representation. The similarities between Virgil's and Luke's narratives make sense within the framework of conceptual metaphor and conceptual blending theories, with Luke importing the language and logic of one domain (the Roman Empire) into another (God's kingdom). Once the schema (divine orchestration) is recognized, Luke's subversion of it stands out (salvation, not death).

The kingdom of God in Luke-Acts is similar to the Roman Empire in certain ways, but it also differs in significant ways. Both narratives are driven by prophecies, visions, and divine orchestration. Both narratives detail the merger of two ethnic groups and sort through issues of identity and ethnic heritage. Although the ethnic

---

Mitchell ("Homer in the New Testament?" *JR* 83 [2003]: 252) and Karl Olav Sandnes ("*Imitatio Homeri*? An Appraisal of Dennis R. MacDonald's 'Mimesis Criticism,'" *JBL* 124 [2005]: 715–32).

negotiations of Luke and Virgil are worked out in similar ways, even a superficial comparison reveals a striking contrast: the ethical behavior of the deity or deities. In the primary examples discussed above, a supernatural portent—the two-headed serpent consuming Laocoön—convinces the Trojans to accept the Greeks' wooden horse, filled with Troy's destruction; Juno sends Allecto to cajole Turnus into battle against the Trojans, who subsequently slaughter many Latins. In Homer's *Iliad*, Zeus sends a duplicitous dream to Agamemnon, which, when interpreted alongside Odysseus's recall of the serpent and sparrows portent, results in the death of many Greeks. The God of the Jews, however, sends truthful visions and portents, resulting in the salvation of ethnic outsiders and their inclusion into God's kingdom.

What has Galilee to do with Jerusalem?[1]

Gregory Riley

Sometime in the early third century of the common era, just after the year 200, Tertullian, a lawyer and major Christian apologist in Carthage in North Africa, wrote his treatise entitled, *Concerning the Proscription of Heresies.* In chapter seven he exclaims, "What has Athens to do with Jerusalem?"[2] He is contrasting the philosophers of Athens with the divinely inspired Scriptures, which he assigns to Jerusalem. The heresies that he was opposing stood on the philosophy of the Greeks, and not on God's word in the Scriptures. The title of this paper is a version of Tertullian's famous statement. The opposition here might perhaps be seen as Galilean ways to be Jewish over and against the ways to be Jewish in Judea and Jerusalem. So, one of the questions I would like to explore is: "How did being from Galilee and not from Judea influence Jesus the Jew?"

Judaism is, to state the obvious, a Jewish phenomenon. Christianity is a largely Gentile phenomenon, and has been for all of its history except for its first few years. However, early Christianity has often been described as a

---

[1] Originally presented on March 11, 2013, in Claremont, CA, as part of the *Voices of Wisdom* lecture series jointly sponsored by the Academy for Jewish Religion, CA; Bayan Claremont; Claremont Lincoln University; and the Claremont School of Theology.

[2] Tertullian, *Praescr.* 7.9: "Quid ergo Athenis et Hierosolymis? Quid academiae et ecclesiae? Quid haereticis et christianis?"

Jewish sect. It was founded by Jesus, a Jew, and according to our sources, all or nearly all of his early followers were Jews. Judaism certainly had its share of sects of one sort or another during the lifetime of Jesus. The most prominent sects that existed in the first century, those cited by Josephus, were Pharisees, Sadducees, Essenes, and a "fourth philosophy" with revolutionary political aspirations.[3] We might add Hellenized Jews such as Philo of Alexandria and his friends. Yet these sects, no matter how strong their differences with one another, remained Jewish. Christianity did not. It became a Gentile religion. Why was that? Why did a Jewish sect, founded by a Jew whose early followers were likely all Jews, become a Gentile religion?

A bit of explanation here on the word "Gentile": It is a Latin adjective of the noun *gens*, meaning "of the nations, the peoples of the world." The Romans used it to mean all the nations of the world who were not Romans, so it meant the "the other guys." It is used to translate the Greek word *ethnoi*, which had the same meaning and usage for the Greeks, to designate the non-Greeks, "the barbarians." So it passes over into Jewish and Christian usage as a designation for those who are not Jewish, or neither Jewish nor Christian. I thought it worth mentioning that the Romans, Greeks, Jews, and Christians were all using the same term, "Gentiles," to mean anyone other than themselves.

The fact that Christianity became a Gentile religion raises another major question here: "Who was responsible for this?" Or perhaps, depending on one's viewpoint, we should ask, "Whose fault was it? Who left the back door

---

[3] Josephus, *AJ* 18.1.2; 18.1.6.

open and let all these Gentiles in?" Different answers have been offered to this question. Jesus, according to some, limited his ministry to Jews only and so could not have been responsible for the Gentile mission. For example, Jesus in the Gospel of Matthew tells his disciples, when he is about to send them out on their first missionary journey, "Go nowhere among the Gentiles, and enter no town of the Samaritans, but go rather to the lost sheep of the house of Israel" (Matt 10:5–6). So perhaps it was the apostle Paul who opened the door, or some others of the later disciples who didn't get the original instructions or the follow-up email about Jews only.

Galilee and Jerusalem

The sect of Jesus began in Galilee. Recall our title, "What does Galilee have to do with Jerusalem?" The point of the question is to ask how close or distant were ties of Galilee to Jerusalem, with its Temple, priests, and culture of Jerusalem Judaism? The very phrase "Jerusalem Judaism" points to the fact that the varieties of Judaism found in Jerusalem and Judea were not shared by everyone who was Jewish in Israel. In fact, from the point of view of geography, if not numbers of people, two-thirds of the land of Israel were in some respects at odds with Judea and Jerusalem. If we divide the land of Israel into three parts, the south would be Judea, the central part Samaria, and the north Galilee. The view from the south looking north illustrates the kinds of differences that existed among these areas. As Jesus's parable of the Good Samaritan (Luke 10:30–37) reminds us, there was no such thing as a good Samaritan in the minds of Judean Jews. As for Galilee, in the Gospel of John, when Philip announces that they had found the Messiah, Jesus of

Nazareth (a small town in Galilee), Nathaniel answers, "Can anything good come out of Nazareth?" (John 1:46). In a later scene, when Nicodemus suggests to his fellow Jewish authorities in Jerusalem that they should at least give Jesus a hearing, they retort, "Surely you are not also from Galilee, are you? Search and you will see that no prophet arises from Galilee" (John 7:49–52).

And what is the problem with Galilee? It is a hundred miles north of Jerusalem, more or less, and in the days of no cars that was three or four days of walking. It was rural and rustic. The Temple, with its strict rituals, and Jerusalem, with its educated and observant upper classes, were a hundred miles away. Several of the noteworthy cites in Galilee were Gentile cities. A number were named after the Gentile rulers of the empire in Rome: we have the cities Tiberias, Caesarea Philippi, Ptolemais, and Livia. And that points to one important aspect of Galilee in the minds of Judeans: Galilee was largely Gentile in population. The prophet Isaiah had called it "Galilee of the Gentiles" (Isa 8:23 and 9:1).

That phrase, "Galilee of the Gentiles," appears again many years later in a very curious passage in 1 Maccabees. 1 Maccabees is an account of the successful rebellion of the Jews led by Judas Maccabeus of Judea and his brothers against the Greek overlords of Israel, which occurred between 167 and 164 BCE. According to this heroic story, Judas and his followers defeated the Greek armies, and purified the previously abused Temple in Jerusalem and restored it to proper Jewish function. In approximately 164 BCE, as the rebellion reached its successful conclusion and

42

Judea won its independence, the non-Jewish populations of Galilee in the north and across the Jordan river to the east reacted by threatening and preparing attacks on the Jews who lived among them. A report comes to Judas in Jerusalem from Jews in Galilee that "the people of Ptolemais and Tyre and Sidon, and all Galilee of the Gentiles had gathered together against them" (1 Macc 5:15). Note the use of Isaiah's phrase "Galilee of the Gentiles." Judas, the leader of the Jews in Judea, sends his brother Simon with a large force of soldiers to rescue the Jews in Galilee. The text reads: "So Simon went to Galilee and fought many battles against the Gentiles, and the Gentiles were crushed before him.... Then he took the Jews of Galilee... with their wives and children and all they possessed, and led them to Judea with great rejoicing" (1 Macc 5:21–23). Simon brought the Jews of Galilee to Judea. A literal reading of the text would mean that there were no Jews left in Galilee.

How should we understand this text? There certainly were Jews left in Galilee, as we are able to see from the archaeological record and from other written sources. The Jews were, however, in the minority. So how do we understand 1 Maccabees? One possible answer is that Simon brought all the people that *he* considered to be Jews to Judea, all who wanted to leave Gentile Galilee and relocate to Judea. In other words, the Jews who agreed with Judea and Jerusalem left with Simon, leaving behind the Jews who did not, who felt more at home in Galilee. These "left behind" Jews were perhaps not even considered real Jews by Simon, as the story seems to imply. And eventually, Galilee was the homeland of Jesus the Jew, but a Jew of Galilee and not of Jerusalem.

The Gentile Mission: Who Opened the Door?

We asked earlier, "How did the Jewish sect of Jesus become a Gentile religion?" and "Who was responsible?" To take second question first, I would like to use some unusual evidence to try to get at that question. Who opened the door to the Gentiles? One hears that Jesus limited his ministry to Jews, and that perhaps the apostle Paul was the one who opened the door of the promise to Abraham for the Gentiles. After all, he describes himself as the apostle to the Gentiles in his letter to the churches in Galatia in what is today central Turkey (Gal 2:7). But Paul was not always Paul the Christian Apostle. Formerly he was Saul the Pharisee, "far more zealous for the traditions of my ancestors," he says, than his other Jewish contemporaries (Gal 1:14). He was a Jew, committed to upholding Jewish traditional ways. He tells us in his letters that, before his conversion, before his encounter with the risen Jesus, he was a persecutor of Jesus' followers. Consider that fact. Paul was persecuting followers of Jesus before he himself became a follower. He could not have been persecuting Gentiles, Gentile Christians. He can only have been persecuting Jews who had become followers of Jesus.

And why was he persecuting? What was he persecuting them for? This is a question without an easy answer. But if we distill the information available to us, he was persecuting Jewish followers of Jesus because they had relaxed the markers that differentiated Jew from Gentile in daily life. They were hanging out with Gentiles, eating meals with Gentiles, eating Gentile food, not requiring the keeping

44

of the Sabbath or the other holy days, and not requiring Gentile males to be circumcised. This list may be not entirely accurate, but it is close. Saul the Pharisee was persecuting Jewish followers of Jesus for loosening the requirements for traditional Jewish observances and for accepting Gentiles with their Gentile ways into the people of God. These were Gentiles, just as they were, not converted into Jews, accepted into their communities as members of the people of God. It could not have been Saul the Pharisee who opened the door to the Gentiles. He was doing the persecuting. The one who opened the door was Jesus.

So our final question: "How was it possible that a Jewish sect, founded by a Jew whose early followers were likely all Jews, became a Gentile religion?" This is not an easy question either, and so far as I know, it has not been adequately answered. Let us note here that Gentiles had been associated with Jews and Judaism for a very long time. There was a Court of the Gentiles on the Temple precincts in Jerusalem that allowed a limited participation of Gentiles as observers and fellow worshippers in the Temple cult. In addition, we read of the "God-fearers" associated with the synagogues, Gentiles who attended the synagogues but were not converts. Yet Jesus takes this association and participation of Gentiles a major step further.

Jesus certainly believed, as did most of his fellow Jews, in the one God of Israel who was in fact the one God of the entire universe, and therefore the one God of every human being. He also believed, in a view shared by very few at the time, that every human being had been given by God an eternal soul. Many of our ancient texts talk about our eternal souls, but we forget that these educated writers were a small minority in their viewpoint. We learn from tombstone inscriptions, on the contrary, that nearly ninety-five percent of people, both inside of Israel and in the Greco-Roman world in general, thought that when one died, that was it; one was gone forever. One common sentiment is expressed by the tombstone inscription: "O Tettius, my brother. Farewell. No one is immortal." And one of the most common tombstone inscriptions, so common that it was abbreviated, much like our RIP for "rest in peace," was: "I was not; I was; I am not; I don't care."[4] In addition, for Jesus, one's soul was of immeasurable value. "What does it profit," he declared, "if you gain the world and lose your soul? And what can you give in exchange for your soul?" (Mark 8:36–37). The vision of the spiritual life and mission of Jesus is built on this premise, body/soul dualism, that we all have eternal souls in perishable and temporary bodies. To use a later poetic phrase, "We have this treasure in earthen vessels" (2 Cor 4:7). So when Jesus and his followers began to preach a message of the promise of eternal life, that was news to the majority of those around him; that was welcome, good news.

Jesus believed another thing that was again rare in his day and culture: that true religion was religion of a pure heart toward God. In this he is certainly in agreement with Biblical admonition. To quote just one of many examples, Psalm 24:4: "Those who have clean hands and pure hearts… will receive blessing from the Lord." This sounds much like the beatitude of Jesus: "Blessed are the pure in heart, for they

---

[4] Non fui; fui; non sum; non curo.

46

shall see God" (Matt 5:8). The prophets and Biblical writers certainly saw the importance of worship from the heart, as did, one may add, the philosophers of the Greco-Roman tradition. But they, like Jesus, were in a small minority. That this was a rare view is surprising to us today, since it seems obvious that real religion must come from a sincere and clean heart, and most of today's religions would readily agree. But it was not so in antiquity. What was required were the outer forms of religion, the rituals, even among those who understood the importance of religion in the inner soul.

Plato, for example, in the fourth century BCE, did not, so far as I can tell, believe in the traditional pagan gods at all. But in one of his last major books, the *Laws*, he still requires the traditional observances and rituals of the state cults. Cicero, in the first century BCE, who agreed with Plato's theology, thought that augury, the ritually necessary observations of the flights of birds to foretell the future, was foolish, scientifically wrong, and mostly mere trickery.[5]

Yet he held the office of Augur for much of his adult life. He watched birds fly and endorsed predictions because that was what tradition required. In a poignant example from the middle of the third century CE, Cyprian, bishop of the city of Carthage in North Africa, is arrested and put on trial for his Christian faith. After Cyprian explains his faith in the true God and denies the value of the pagan cults, the judge asks him, despite his beliefs about the state cults, "Will you nevertheless perform the rituals?" In other words, I don't care what you think; do the required rituals! Cyprian

---

[5] E.g., Cic. *Div* 2.

refuses and is executed.[6] For the vast majority of people, the rituals could not be dispensed with. They were far more important than one's beliefs. In fact, no one seemed to care much about what one believed, as long as the rituals were performed according to the traditional customs.

For Jesus, however, religion from a pure heart, from a sincere and clean soul, was the foundation and very substance of the human relationship with God. No ritual observance was important at all in comparison. To illustrate this, consider how he deals with the covenants between God and Israel. In one example from the Gospel of Matthew, Jesus refers to a commandment in the Law as follows: "You have heard that it was said, 'You shall not commit adultery.' But I say to you that everyone who looks at a woman with lust has already committed adultery with her in his heart" (Matt 5:27–28).

He specifies that the place of true obedience is within one's heart. He does the same with several others of the commandments, such as "Do not murder," and "Do not swear falsely." In a particularly stark example, when asked, "Why do your disciples not live according to the tradition of the elders, but eat with defiled hands?" (Mark 7:5), Jesus calls the crowd together and says, "There is nothing outside a person that by going in can defile, but the things that come out are what defile" (Mark 7:15). When later questioned by his disciples about what he meant, he explains: "whatever goes into a person from outside cannot defile, since it enters not the heart but the stomach and is eliminated in the

---

[6] Herbert Mursurillo, *The Acts of the Christian Mar-tyrs* (Oxford: Clarendon Press, 1972), 2: 168–175.

sewer.... It is what comes out of a person that defiles. For it is from within, from the human heart, that evil intentions come" (Mark 7:18–23).

One may see a similar viewpoint in Jesus's understanding of the Kingdom of God. The career and ministry of Jesus sparked among many of his followers' expectations that the kingdom promised to David and his descendants was imminent. "Lord," his disciples ask at one point, "is it at this time that you are restoring the kingdom to Israel?" (Acts 1:6). There is much controversy among scholars about how eschatologically oriented Jesus was, whether he carried around a sign saying, "The end is near!" There is disagreement within the New Testament itself about that issue, with different authors expressing different viewpoints. The core of Jesus's teachings, most scholars would agree, may be found in the organic growth parables, those wonderful farming stories about the sower sowing the seed in human hearts that grows slowly over time until it fully matures and bears fruit. Those stories do not foresee that the end is near at all, but the contrary. They require a lifetime to come to fruition. How long would it take, for example, for the smallest mustard seed to grow into the largest tree?

These stories cohere well with one of Jesus's most famous sayings. When asked whether the kingdom of God was coming, Jesus answered, "The kingdom of God is not coming with things that can be observed; nor will they say, 'Look, here it is!' or 'There it is!' For, in fact, the kingdom of God is within you" (Luke 17:20–21). So, the Kingdom is a spiritual entity found within the human soul. That is also

Paul's understanding. In a discussion of clean and unclean foods similar to the one Jesus had, mentioned earlier, Paul writes: "the kingdom of God is not food and drink but righteousness and peace and joy in the Holy Spirit" (Rom 14:17).

For Jesus then, the covenant that best summed up his understanding of God's relationship with Israel and in fact the whole world was the one predicted by Jeremiah: "Behold, the days are coming, says the Lord, that I will make a new covenant with the house of Israel, and with the house of Judah:... I will put my law within them, and write it in their hearts" (Jer 31:31–33). It was the New Covenant that Jesus saw coming; in the phrasing of the King James Bible, it was the "New Testament."

Conclusion

In the book of Genesis, God asks Abraham to leave his homeland and move to the land of Canaan, and he promises that in Abraham, all the nations of the world will be blessed. Isaiah (56:7) reiterates that promise and applies it to the Temple in Jerusalem, that it would become a "house of prayer for all the nations."

Jesus, during the final week of his life, goes to Jerusalem from Galilee. As the Gospel of Mark (11:15–16) tells it,

> he entered the Temple and began to drive out those who were selling and those who were buying in the Temple, and he overturned the tables of the money changers and the seats of those who sold doves; and he would not allow anyone to carry anything through the Temple.

This turns out to be a remarkably bad idea from the point of view of longevity, for the issue of the Temple comes up as one of the main accusations against Jesus at his arrest and trial. His explanation for his actions in the Temple underscores his understanding of the covenant with Abraham as used by Isaiah. He puts together two sayings, the one mentioned by Isaiah (56:7), and another by Jeremiah (7:13), "Is it not written, 'My house shall be called a house of prayer for all the nations'? But you have made it a den of robbers."

Jesus lived in Galilee among both Jews and Gentiles. Gentiles, in his view, were children of the same God as he and his fellow Jews were. Gentiles had the same eternal souls, and could relate to God as could all people, whatever their customs and rituals, if they would repent and approach God with clean hearts. Abraham had believed God and obtained the promise that in him all the nations of the world would be blessed. Jeremiah had promised that one day God would make a New Covenant wherein the Law would be written on people's hearts. Jesus saw that day arriving, and he opened to the Gentiles the door of the blessing of Abraham for the nations and the New Covenant of religion from a pure heart. The good things that God gave to Israel, we may be reminded, were blessings for the whole world.

Shabbat

*An Epistemological Principle for Holiness,
Sustainability, and
Justice in the Pentateuch*

Marvin A. Sweeney

In August 2014, my wife and I drove north through the San Joaquin Valley of Central California, once a fertile breadbasket that supplied some forty percent of the agricultural produce grown in the United States. Although we were well aware of the drought that has plagued California and other parts of the Western United States for several years now, we were shocked and dismayed at the devastation we witnessed all along Interstate 5. Coming from a declining agricultural area in Central Illinois, I shudder at the consequences that such drought and devastation portend for our food supply, particularly since the world human population has expanded from some two and a half billion when I was born to some seven billion today. I fear for the future of our children as they enter a world facing chronic shortages of food and the potential outbreak of violence as human beings begin to compete for resources in an increasingly overtaxed world.

Those of us who identify in one form or another with the Jewish and Christian traditions rooted in the foundational instruction of the Pentateuch and beyond must recognize that we human beings bear at least some degree of responsibility for ensuring the viability of the world in which we live. Genesis1:26–28 posits that G-d created human beings on the penultimate day of creation and charged us with responsibility for "mastering" the earth and "ruling" over the fish of the sea, the birds of the sky, and all the living things that creep about on earth as we become fruitful and multiply and fill the earth.

And yet in our own arrogance and conceit, we so frequently forget that we are a part of creation itself as we focus on ourselves as the ultimate masters of creation to the exclusion of the context of creation as a whole in which we were created. We forget that our roles as masters and rulers call for responsible action to recognize and ensure the holiness, justice, and sustainability of creation. Our own irresponsibility begins with the ways in which we read Genesis diachronically, by positing that the seven-day process of creation is Priestly and therefore not as worthy of consideration as the purportedly earlier J tradition, which focuses more on human beings in the world of creation rather than upon creation itself. Although some very useful work has been done on J in this regard, contemporary scholarship now questions the early date and even the existence of J.[1] In any case, a focus on J alone gives only a small part of the picture.

---

[1] E.g., Theodore Hiebert, *The Y-hwist's Landscape: Nature and Religion in Early Israel* (Oxford and New York: Oxford University Press, 1996); cf. James Barr, *The Garden of Eden and the Hope of Immortality* (Minneapolis: Fortress Press, 1992); Gary A. Anderson, *The Genesis of*

To that end, I propose reading the Pentateuch from a synchronic perspective, which recognizes that the seven-day process of creation points to the holy Shabbat as an epistemological principle that informs creation and the role of human beings within it. I do not intend that a synchronic reading would replace diachronic readings; rather, I see synchronic and diachronic readings as complementary.[2] I will attempt to demonstrate this contention by examining two fundamental issues. The first issue is the holy nature of creation itself and human responsibility in it as expressed in Genesis 1:1–2:3. The second issue is the laws of the Pentateuch that employ the seven-day Shabbat principle as the basis for governing the agricultural calendar and treatment of the land, and for ensuring social justice among the people of the land. Treatment of the legal materials will include the Covenant Code of Exodus 20–24 and its supplement in Exodus 34; the laws of the Tabernacle; Offerings, Holiness, and other matters in Exodus 25–30, 31, 35–40, Leviticus, and the supplements in Numbers; and the Book of Deuteronomy.

Perfection: Adam and Eve in Jewish and Christian Imagination (Louisville: Westminster/John Knox, 2001). For current discussion of the J stratum of the Pentateuch, see esp. Thomas B. Dozeman and Konrad Schmid, eds., *A Farewell to the Y-hwist? The Composition of the Pentateuch in Recent European Interpretation* (SBLSym 34; Atlanta: Society of Biblical Literature, 2006).

[2] For a methodological overview, see Marvin A. Sweeney, "Form Criticism," *To Each Its Own Meaning: Biblical Criticisms and their Application* (ed. S. L. McKenzie and S. R. Haynes; Louisville: Westminster John Knox, 1999), 58–89.

II

Genesis 1:1–2:3 presents an account of G-d's seven-day creation of the world that serves as the foundation for the entire Pentateuchal narrative when read synchronically.[3] Indeed, it serves as the foundation for the entire Bible, whether the Bible is understood as the Tanak, the Jewish form of the Bible, or the Old Testament, the first major portion of the Christian form of the Bible. Insofar as the process of creation presented in Genesis 1:1–2:3 culminates in the holy Shabbat, the Shabbat both completes and sanctifies that creation and thereby provides the epistemological basis which defines the character of creation and the means by which life, including human life, functions ideally within it.

In order to understand the Shabbat as the epistemological foundation of creation, we must consider several dimensions.

First is the initial statement of creation in Genesis 1:1–2. Until relatively recent times, non-Jewish interpreters have understood these verses to describe a process of creation out of nothing or *Creatio ex Nihilo*.[4] Such an understanding holds that G-d is the supreme creative power in the universe and the beginning point or Alpha of creation, which of course entails an Omega, or a point at which creation will come to an end. Such an understanding is based

---

[3] For full discussion of the synchronic literary structure of the Pentateuch, see Marvin A. Sweeney, *Tanak: A Theological and Critical Introduction to the Jewish Bible* (Minneapolis: Fortress Press, 2012), 45–167.

[4] For discussion of this point, see esp. Jon D. Levenson, *Creation and the Persistence of Evil: The Jewish Drama of Divine Omnipotence* (San Francisco: Harper and Row, 1988).

in Christian theological understanding of a creation that will ultimately reach its culmination with the second coming of Christ and thereafter cease to exist as we know it, ushering in a new age of eternal salvation. But such a conception is not supported by the text of Genesis 1:1–2. It presupposes a finite understanding of Genesis 1:1, "in the beginning, G-d created the heavens and the earth," followed by a second set of finite statements in Genesis 1:2, "and the earth was formless and void, and darkness was over the deep and the spirit of G-d was hovering over the face of the waters." Thus we have a sequence of statements in which the earth is first created out of nothing in v. 1, and then in v. 2 we have a description of the state of the earth following its initial creation.

But such a reading is grammatically impossible based on the traditional form of the Hebrew Masoretic Text (MT).[5] As the medieval Jewish Bible exegete, R. Solomon ben Isaac (Rashi, 1040–1105 CE), demonstrated nearly a millennium ago, the Hebrew term, *bereishit*, often translated, "in the beginning," cannot stand as an independent clause. The Hebrew term, *reishit*, is a construct form that must be read in relation to the following term in the sentence so that *bereishit* can only read, "in the beginning of..." Thus the sentence, *bereishit bara' Eloqim et ha-shamayim ve'et ha'aretz* must read in awkward English, "in the beginning of the creating of (by) G-d of the heavens and the earth." In better English, "when G-d began to create the heavens and the earth..." In such a reading, Genesis 1:1 can only be read as a

---

[5] See esp. Harry M. Orlinsky, *Notes on the New Translation of the Torah* (Philadelphia: Jewish Publication Society, 1969), 49–52.

subordinate clause that requires a following clause to serve as the primary assertion of the sentence, viz., "When G-d began to create the heavens and the earth, the earth was formless and void and darkness was upon the face of the deep and the wind of G-d was hovering over the waters." In such a statement, the earth is an unformed, preexisting entity at the outset of G-d's creation, i.e., the earth already existed in an undefined form prior to G-d's creation. G-d's act of creation is not *Creatio ex Nihilo* or Creation out of Nothing; rather, it is the shaping and definition of the unformed earth that existed before G-d's creation commenced.

Indeed, the traditional reading that presents the notion of *Creatio ex Nihilo* is derived from the Greek Septuagint (LXX) reading of the text, *En arche epoiesin ho Theos ton ouranon kai ten gen*, "in the beginning, G-d created the heavens and the earth," an interpretative reading of the Hebrew influenced by Hellenistic notions of creation circulating in the Egyptian Jewish community during the third–second centuries BCE.

Such a difference in interpretative perspective is not simply an exercise in semantics. Instead, it points to a divine model for human action in the world. Whereas the LXX reading of the text presents a model of divine action that humans are unable to emulate, the MT reading of the text presents a model of divine action that humans are indeed able — and perhaps expected — to emulate. Just as G-d takes a situation of unformed chaos and creates order and definition out of the chaos, so human beings, who are given "dominion" in creation, are expected to create order out of chaos in the world of creation in which we live. The MT statement becomes a basis for calling for human action based on the model provided by G-d.

But we must also recognize that the seven-day process of creation in Genesis 1:1–2:3 entails a dimension of sanctity that is inherent in creation. Creation in Genesis 1:1–2:3 proceeds on the basis of six days of divine action and one day of divine rest. As we well know, the six days of creation are highly ordered to provide the basic structure of creation in two parallel three-day sequences.[6] The first sequence, in days one through three, calls for the creation of the basic structures of creation, beginning with the differentiation between light and darkness on day one; the differentiation between the waters of the earth and the waters of the heavens on day two; and the differentiation between the dry land, which produces plant life, and the waters of the sea on day three. The second sequence, on days four through six, fills in some of the details for the basic structures created on the first three days. The second sequence therefore includes the lights of the heavens, which function to reckon time, and the sun and the moon, which function to distinguish day and night, on the fourth day; the creation of sea creatures and the birds of the heavens on day five; and the creation of living creatures, culminating in human beings, on day six. The subsequent Pentateuchal narrative will signal other creation, such as features associated with the Exodus from Egypt and the Wilderness narratives in Exodus–Numbers, but the basic foundations of creation are treated in Genesis 1:1–2:3.

---

[6] Michael Fishbane, "Genesis 1:1–2:4a: The Creation," *Text and Texture: Selected Readings of Biblical Texts* (New York: Schocken, 1979), 1–16.

Although Genesis 1:1–2:3 maintains that G-d completed the divine work of creation after six days, creation remains incomplete without the sanctification of the seventh day of Shabbat. Genesis 2:2 makes it clear that G-d completed the work on the seventh day, not on the sixth, i.e., "and G-d completed His work which He had done on the seventh day, and G-d ceased on the seventh day from all the work which He had done." In sum, the full creative process of creation requires both the six days of divine labor and the seventh holy day of cessation of labor and rest by G-d.

But this brings us to the role of the human being who was created on the sixth day within creation. The human, created as male and female in the image of G-d, is endowed with the responsibility to master the earth and to rule it. We must understand what such mastery or dominion entails. The usual interpretations of the Hebrew words used for mastery, Hebrew, *vekivshuha*, "and master it," and dominion, Hebrew, *uredu*, "and rule it," generally envision something akin to total domination. In the case of the Hebrew root, *kbš*, *HALOT* defines it as "to subjugate" in reference to nations and slaves and as "to violate" in reference to women.[7] In the case of the Hebrew root, *rdh*, *HALOT* defines it as "to tread" in reference to a wine press and as "to rule (with the associated meaning of oppression)" in reference to the earth, nations, peoples, etc.[8] Such understandings have suggested to interpreters that human beings are given virtually unlimited dominion over the earth

---

[7] *HALOT*, 460.
[8] *HALOT*, 1190.

and its creatures that would constitute unrestrained autocratic and oppressive rule.

But a basic principle of power politics holds that such autocratic rule is impossible without the consent of those governed. Such consent might be gained through use of force, but in the long run, such models of rule prove to be unviable. Rather, effective dominion is best gained by demonstrating to those ruled that they have something to gain from the leadership of those in power. In short, effective rule entails a sense of responsibility on the part of those in power to demonstrate to those ruled that they will benefit from the actions of their rulers. Such a model applies to the statements in Genesis 1:26–28 that humans are given dominion and rule over the earth and its creatures. The dominion and rule granted by G-d to humans in Genesis entails that they will exercise appropriate responsibility in exercising their power. Insofar as G-d creates the world according to a seven-day pattern that culminates in the holy Shabbat, human dominion entails responsibility for ensuring the holiness of creation as the foundation for its viability or sustainability.

But what does this mean? For one, Shabbat calls for a day of rest for all creation so that creation might rejuvenate itself and thereby better ensure its viability or sustainability. Such a principle of rejuvenation applies to land, animals, and human beings in the world of creation. But it is not limited to simple rest and rejuvenation. As the so-called Holiness Code in Leviticus 17–26 indicates, holiness also entails a combination of moral and ritual principles, such as the proper treatment of blood, appropriate marriage and sexual relations, appropriate ownership and care for land, proper observance of sacred times and offerings, proper actions by the priesthood, proper treatment of the elderly, and much more. In short, the use of Shabbat as an epistemological principle in creation signals an entire code of conduct that is incumbent upon human beings to ensure their proper, holy, just, and sustainable life in the land that G-d grants to them.

Finally, we must also consider the placement of the P account of creation in Genesis 1:1–2:3 immediately prior to the J account of creation in Genesis 2:4–4:26. Under the influence of source criticism and the self-contained character of each narrative, we have been accustomed to read these narratives diachronically and independently of each other. But the more recent recognition of intertextual reading strategies demands that we consider the synchronic literary context in which a narrative appears. In this case, Genesis 1:1–2:3 sets the terms by which Genesis 2:4–4:26 is read, and Genesis 2:4–4:26 draws out the meaning and implications of Genesis 1:1–2:3. To be brief, Genesis 1:1–2:3 sets the basic holy structure of creation and the place, role, and responsibility of human beings within it. Genesis 2:4–4:26 then examines the character of human beings within that creation, and it points to problems, e.g., human companionship, knowledge, the capacity for wrongdoing, and human mortality, that must be addressed.

III

The Covenant Code in Exodus 20–24 and its supplement in Exodus 34 are parts of the larger narrative concerning the revelation at Mt. Sinai in Exodus 19–

Numbers 10. Some recent studies have argued that the Covenant Code must date to the Babylonian period due to its well demonstrated dependence on both the casuistic formulations and the legal substance of Hammurabi's Law Code,[9] but such studies overlook Israel's relationship with the Neo-Assyrian Empire from the late ninth century BCE and Assyrian dependence on Hammurabi's Law Code for its own legal texts.[10] The Covenant Code includes apodictic legal forms that are dependent on analogous forms that appear throughout Neo-Assyrian suzerain-vassal treaty texts.[11] Furthermore, the mid-eighth-century BCE Judean prophet, Amos, cites the Covenant Code throughout his indictment of the northern kingdom of Israel in Amos 2:6–16.[12] The Covenant Code appears to be the earliest of Israel's law codes, written in the northern kingdom of Israel during the late ninth or early eighth century BCE. Its dependence on Neo-Assyrian suzerain-vassal treaty forms indicates an

---

[9] John Van Seters, *A Law Book for the Diaspora: Revision in the Study of the Covenant Code* (Oxford and New York: Oxford University Press, 2003) and David P. Wright, *Inventing G-d's Law: How the Covenant Code of the Bible Used and Revised the Laws of Hammurabi* (Oxford and New York: Oxford University Press, 2009).

[10] See the Black Obelisk of Shalmaneser III (ANEP, 355), which depicts the submission of King Jehu of Israel to King Shalmaneser III of Assyria in the late ninth century BCE, and the vassal list of the Assyrian monarch, Adad Nirari III (S. Page, "A Stela of Adad Nirari III and Negal-ereš from Tell al Rimlah," *Iraq* 30 (1968): 139–153), which lists King Joash of Israel as one of his vassals in the early eighth century BCE.

[11] See D. J. Wiseman, "The Vassal Treaties of Esarhaddon," *Iraq* 20 (1958): 1–99 and Pritchard, ANET 534–541.

[12] See my commentary on Amos 2:6–16, *The Twelve Prophets* (Berit Olam; Collegeville, MN: Liturgical, 2000), 1: 214–218.

interest in portraying YHWH as the great suzerain monarch who defines the terms of the relation to the vassal, Israel.[13]

The Covenant Code begins in Exodus 20:2–14 with a version of the Ten Commandments. Although some consider the Ten Commandments to be a form of ancient Israelite law, the commandments cannot function as such insofar as they do not include any form of legal adjudication or resolution for the various problems they address. Insofar as they include a combination of commands and prohibitions, the Ten Commandments function as a statement of moral and religious principles that inform the laws found within the following law collection.

We may note, however, that the Shabbat appears in Exodus 20:8–11, which commands Israel to "remember the Shabbat Day to sanctify it," and specifies this command by calling for the people of Israel, their children, their servants, their cattle, and resident aliens in their midst to rest on the seventh day. The text justifies this command by noting that YHWH created the heavens, earth, sea, and everything in them in six days of labor and then blessed and sanctified the seventh day as a day of rest. Although some posit that this is a P text, Hosea cites the Ten Commandments in Hosea 4; Jeremiah cites them in Jeremiah 7; and Isaiah notes the Shabbat in Isa 1:10–17. As part of the Ten Commandments, the command to remember the Shabbat Day and the basic

---

[13] See also Dennis J. McCarthy, *Treaty and Covenant: A Study in Form in the Ancient Oriental Documents and in the Old Testament* (AnBib 21A; Rome: Biblical Institute Press, 1978) and Dennis J. McCarthy, *Old Testament Covenant: A Survey of Current Opinions* (Atlanta: John Knox, 1972).

instructions concerning its observance and justification constitute a basic principle of the Israelite legal system.

The first instance of the application of the Shabbat principle to a case in Israelite law is the slave law in Exodus 21:2–11. This law stipulates that a man who becomes a slave may serve for a maximum of six years, but must be freed in the seventh year, unless he goes through a formal procedure to declare himself a slave for life. When he goes free, he receives no payment from his master. If his master provided him with a wife and he had children, they remain with the master. If a woman becomes a slave, she is not released like a man after six years of service because it is presumed that the master may marry her himself or give her as a bride to one of the men in his household. She may only go free if her husband does not provide her with food, clothing, and sexual relations, which ensure that she will have children who will care for her in her old age. Examples of the application of this law appear in the Jacob narratives of Genesis 29–31, in which Jacob serves his father-in-law, Laban, for six years each in return for the bride price to marry his daughters, Leah and Rachel, and another six years to acquire a share of the flocks which Jacob helped to produce so that he might support his family.

The slave law is clearly an application of the Shabbat principle to the practice of debt slavery, i.e., a man may assign himself to work as a slave for another because he is no longer able to support himself or his family. He works for six years, and then he goes free or rests in the seventh. Although it constitutes an early attempt to provide a just solution to the problem of poverty or indebtedness, there are clear problems with the formulation of this law. The failure to provide support for the newly released slave plays a role in ensuring the likelihood that he will return to debt slavery; the problems he faced when he first became a slave have not been resolved, and the chances of his return to slavery are high—and indeed supported by the current formulation of the law, which allows him to declare himself a slave for life. Furthermore, the refusal to release a wife given to him in slavery or children born to him in slavery provides a very powerful incentive to remain a slave in perpetuity. The refusal to release a woman sold into slavery may provide even greater incentive to avoid slavery, but nevertheless it does nothing to resolve the problem of poverty that motivates consideration of slavery in the first place. Even if the woman is released from slavery due to the negligence of her husband, she faces a life of poverty, lack of support, and little likelihood that she will find another husband apart from slavery.

The second instance of the application of the Shabbat principle to a case of Israelite law appears in Exodus 22:28–29, which calls upon the people to give the first produce of the grain and fruit harvest to YHWH, as well as the first-born sons and the first-born of the cattle and the flocks. The application of the Shabbat principle appears in the command to allow the first-born to remain with its mother for seven days prior to presentation as an offering to YHWH. First-born sons apparently served originally as priests for YHWH prior to the institutionalization and sanctification of the tribe of Levi (Num 3; 8; 17–18). The seven-day delay in offering the first-born son evolves into the practice of circumcision for Israelite/Judean men following the seventh day after birth (see Gen 17). As a result, Israelite/Judean men are consecrated for divine service.

The third and final instance of the application of the Shabbat principle in the Covenant Code appears in Exodus 23:10–12, which calls for the people to farm their land for six years and then let it lie fallow in the seventh. The principle here points to an underlying concern with allowing the land to renew itself without being depleted of its fertility to produce food. Such a practice continues in contemporary farming to avoid depletion of land. The principle is also applied to the replenishment and care of the poor in the land and the wild animals. Israelites should let the fallow land lie during the seventh year so that the poor may take whatever food grows up on the land during that seventh year. Animals are likewise allowed to feed from the plot without interference. The principle is also applied to vineyards and olive groves. A restatement of the command to observe the Shabbat concludes the paragraph by reiterating that the people should work for six days and then rest on the seventh, including draft animals, servants, and resident aliens in the land.

Overall, the Covenant Code applies the Shabbat principle to ensure the replenishment and viability of both human beings and land. The Shabbat principle thereby functions as an application of sustainability in creation and social justice in the human realm.

Similar perspectives appear in the supplement to the Covenant Code in Exodus 34, which presents a revised form of many of the laws of the Covenant Code following Moses's breaking of the tablets of the original covenant during the Golden Calf incident. In the narrative, Exodus 34 functions as a statement of the laws of the covenant written on the second set of tablets that were meant to replace the first set. In diachronic terms, they likely represent a J revision of some elements of the Covenant Code written during the late monarchic period. The intent of the revision would have been to overcome some of the problems inherent in the original formulation of the laws so that they might better serve the purposes for which they were written.

The only instance of the application of the Shabbat principle appears in Exodus 34:19–21, which calls for the people to present the first-born of cattle and sheep to YHWH for an offering. But the law addresses the problems inherent in the earlier formulation of Exodus 22:28–29 by specifying that the first-born of an ass is to be redeemed with a sheep; otherwise, its neck is to be broken. No rationale for the redemption of an ass is apparent; indeed, asses were routinely offered in the ancient Near Eastern world, although asses are not included among the animals that may be eaten by human beings insofar as they do not chew the cud or have a cloven hoof. Likewise, the first-born son is redeemed, although the text does not specify the purpose other than to present an offering to YHWH, presumably in thanks for the birth of a first-born son. As was the case in Exodus 23:12, the legal paragraph in Exodus 34:21 concludes with a restatement of the command to observe the Shabbat to provide the basis for the preceding legal instructions, although the present text makes sure to specify that the rest takes place during plowing and harvest times.

As in the case of the Covenant Code, the supplement in Exodus 34 appears designed to ensure the sanctification of the herds, flocks, and human beings in keeping with the principles articulated in relation to the Shabbat.

IV

The next laws to be considered are those of Exodus 25–30; 31; 35–40; Leviticus; and Numbers.

We may begin with the instructions concerning the construction of the Tabernacle, its furnishings, and the ordination of the priesthood that will serve in it in Exodus 25–30; 31; and 35–40.[14] These narratives are assigned to the Priestly stratum of the Pentateuch and point to the construction of the Tabernacle not only as the pattern for the Temple to be built for YHWH in the land of Israel but as the culmination of creation as well.[15] Exodus 25–30 presents the instructions to build the Tabernacle; Exodus 31 presents statements concerning the builders and the observance of Shabbat; and Exodus 35–40 presents an account of Israel's compliance with the instructions. Franz Rosenzweig and Martin Buber noted the parallels between the account of creation and the account of the construction of the Tabernacle, indicating that the account of the Tabernacle, with its portrayal of the introduction of the Divine Presence

---

[14] Antony J. Campbell and Mark A. O'Brien, *Sources of the Pentateuch: Texts, Introductions, Annotations* (Minneapolis: Fortress Press, 1993), 44–61.

[15] Jon D. Levenson, "The Temple and the World," *JR* 64 (1984): 275–298.

of YHWH in the form of a pillar of cloud and smoke into the Tabernacle, would constitute completion of creation.[16] Fishbane summarizes the observations of Rosenzweig and Buber, who noted that statements from Genesis 1:1–2:3 were echoed in Exodus 39:43 (Gen 1:31); Exodus 39:32 (cf. Gen 2:1); Exodus 40:33b–34 (cf. Gen 2:2); and Exodus 39:43 (Gen 2:3).[17]

Evidence of the concern with the Shabbat is apparent within Exodus 25–30; 31; and 35–40. The *menorah* or "lampstand" of the Tabernacle is constructed with three lights branching out from both of its sides to signify the six days of labor, and a seventh lamp in its center to signify the Shabbat (Exod 25:31–40; 35:17–24). The account of the ordination of the priests in Exodus 29 likewise shows concern with the Shabbat by positing a seven-day process for the consecration of the priests who would serve in the holy Tabernacle and Temple. Following the account of the instructions to build the Tabernacle, Exodus 31 presents YHWH's statements to Moses concerning Bezalel ben Uri ben Hur and Oholiab ben Ahisamach as the architects and artisans who will oversee the construction. Immediately following in Exodus 31:12–17 is the account of YHWH's statements to Moses concerning the observance of the Shabbat as a *berit olam*, "eternal covenant" or "covenant of creation," which provides the theological foundation for the building of the Tabernacle, i.e., it provides the means to sanctify and complete creation by observance of the Shabbat and other holy observances that will take place at the

---

[16] Sweeney, *Tanak*, 101–104.
[17] Fishbane, "Genesis 1:1–2:4a," esp. 11–13.

Tabernacle and Temple. Indeed, the account of the compliance with the instructions to build the Tabernacle in Exodus 35–40 begins with instructions to observe the Shabbat in Exodus 35:2–3, which once again provides the rationale for the construction of the Tabernacle and Temple.

Leviticus 1–16 presents instructions concerning the offerings to be presented to YHWH at the Tabernacle and Temple, and various other instructions concerning the priesthood and the sanctity of the people. These chapters are clearly the work of the P stratum.[18] We may note another account of the seven-day ordination of the priests in Leviticus 8 and various instructions in Leviticus 12–15 concerning the seven-day purifications of those who have become unclean by reason of childbirth, skin disease, bodily emissions, leprosy, etc., and culminating in the purification of the sanctuary in Leviticus 16, which among other things requires the sprinkling of the blood of the sin offering on the altar seven times.

The Holiness Code in Leviticus 17–26 is generally considered to be a Priestly work, although many scholars argue that it dates to a much earlier period than the rest of the P stratum.[19] Interpreters have noted that the Holiness Code elaborates upon the laws that appear in both the Covenant Code in Exodus 20–24 and the Deuteronomic Law Code.[20] It is fundamentally concerned with the holiness of the people, beginning with the treatment of blood and sexual

---

[18] See Campbell and O'Brien, *Sources*, 61–67.

[19] Campbell and O'Brien, *Sources*, 61, n. 76.

[20] Jeffrey Stackert, *Rewriting the Torah: Literary Revision in Deuteronomy and the Holiness Legislation* (FAT 52; Tübingen: Mohr Siebeck, 2007).

relations in Leviticus 17, 18, and 20. Leviticus 19 presents a combination of moral and ritual instruction that includes many of the elements found in the Ten Commandments. Following the initial command to be holy in v. 2, v. 3 turns to commands to revere one's parents and to observe YHWH's Shabbats. A second presentation of the instruction to observe YHWH's Shabbats appears in v. 30, which emphasizes the importance of Shabbat observance in the Holiness Code. Leviticus 23 presents instruction concerning the observance of holidays in ancient Israel and Judah. This calendar begins with the observance of the Shabbat in v. 3. It specifies the times for the observance of Passover as seven days in Leviticus 23:4–8. The observance of Shavuot is calculated by counting seven weeks from Passover, thereby employing the Shabbat principle as the basis for calculation. The festival of Sukkot is observed for seven days like Passover. The Covenant Code in Exodus 20–24 did not mention these times, and so Leviticus 23 represents a specification of the times of observance for these holidays. The festival calendar in Deuteronomy 16:1–17 does mention the times, but Leviticus 23 presents a far more elaborate discussion. The presentation of the bread of the presence in Leviticus 24:5–9 likewise follows a seven-day pattern defined by Shabbat.

Perhaps the most elaborate use of the Shabbat principle in the Holiness Code appears in Leviticus 25, which discusses the observance of the Jubilee year. The Jubilee year is determined by counting off seven weeks of years for a total of forty-nine years and then observing the fiftieth year as the Jubilee year. It is a development out of the

72

previously discussed seven-year agricultural cycle in Exodus 23:10-12 and the laws concerning the release of debts in Deuteronomy 15:1-18. Leviticus 25 instructs the people to work their land for six years and allow it to lie fallow in the seventh year as in Exodus 23:10-12, but it builds upon both Exodus 23:10-12 and Deuteronomy 15:1-18 by envisioning a Jubilee year of the release of all debts and the return of property. According to vv. 13-17, any land sold by an Israelite to another Israelite to raise capital returns to its original owner. The transaction actually functions as a form of lease. The seller will retain only those funds applied to the years that the buyer had control of the land, and the buyer will be obligated to pay only for those years that he actually held control of the land. The law presumes in vv. 18-22 that YHWH will grant greater fertility in the land so that the people may harvest more food that will last them through the seventh year when the fields lie fallow. Verses 23-28 require that all land may be reclaimed by its original owner. He may redeem his land when he has sufficient funds, but his land will be returned to him in the Jubilee year even if he lacks funds.

Leviticus 25:29-34 specifies that a house sold in a city may be redeemed up to a year following the sale, but afterwards, it may not be redeemed. A house in a village which lacks a wall may be redeemed and is released in the Jubilee year. The city houses of the Levites are an exception in that they may be redeemed and returned to the Levites in the Jubilee years. Houses owned by Levites in an unwalled village may not be sold.

Leviticus 25:35–46 forbids Israelites to lend money to their kinsmen at interest. A kinsman is not to be treated as a slave, but is considered a hired hand who will serve only until the Jubilee year, after which he is released. Only Gentile slaves may be purchased and retained following the Jubilee year. An Israelite who becomes a servant of a resident alien may be redeemed by his kinsmen. The price for his redemption is calculated according to the number of years left until the Jubilee year. If he is not redeemed, he is released in the Jubilee year.

Leviticus 26 concludes the Holiness Code with a presentation of blessings and curses that will come upon the people depending on whether or not they observe YHWH's expectations. If the people do not observe the seventh year in which the land lies fallow or the Jubilee year, they will be exiled from the land so that the land may make up its lost Shabbat time. By contrast, the blessings and curses in Deuteronomy 28–30 envision an exile that will continue until the people repent from their failure to observe divine expectations.

Although Leviticus 27 is not considered to be a part of the Holiness Code, it builds upon the provisions of the Holiness Code by stipulating the value of land consecrated to the Temple is calculated in relation to the Jubilee year. Anyone who redeems land consecrated to the Temple must add one-fifth of its value at the time of its redemption. Likewise, animals and tithes consecrated to the Temple may be redeemed by an additional one-fifth of their value.

The laws of Numbers are rather disparate when compared with Leviticus and appear first in the Sinai narrative in Numbers 1–10 and then in the Wilderness narratives in Numbers 11–36. Most are considered P, but there may be reason to challenge this assessment in some cases.

The Nazirite law in which a person may consecrate him- or herself to divine service in Numbers 6 envisions a seven-day purification period in case of contact with the dead or other defilement. Numbers 8 once again envisions *menorot* with seven lamps each. Although it portrays an ordination for the Levites, it does not specify a seven-day period.

Whereas the manna and quail narratives in Exodus 16 note that the food does not appear on Shabbat, the corresponding narrative in Numbers 11 makes no mention of the Shabbat. There is no mention of the Shabbat throughout Numbers 12–18, which includes the selection of Aaron and the tribe of Levi to serve as priests. Numbers 19 calls for sprinkling the blood of the red heifer seven times to purify the Tent of Meeting. Likewise, someone subject to contact with a corpse requires a seven-day purification period. Numbers 23–24 indicates that Balaam builds seven altars to offer seven bulls and seven rams when he attempts to curse Israel. The discussion of offerings for holy times in Numbers 28–29 includes instructions concerning Shabbat offerings in Numbers 28:9–10. Numbers 28:16–27 calls for offerings and the eating of unleavened bread on the seven days of Passover, Numbers 29:17–34 specifies the offerings for the seven days of Sukkot, and Numbers 29:35–38 calls for an observance on the eighth day. Numbers 31:19–20 requires a seven-day purification period for those who killed Midianites or came into contact with the dead.

V

The last law code to consider is the book of Deuteronomy, which functions synchronically within the literary structure of the Pentateuch as Moses's repetition of the laws previously revealed at Sinai. But a diachronic reading of the book indicates that these laws are not repetitions at all. Instead, they represent revision of many of the laws of the Covenant Code examined above.[21] The book of Torah discovered during Josiah's Temple renovation according to 2 Kings 22–23 appears to be a version of Deuteronomy insofar as Josiah's reforms coincide with many of Deuteronomy's requirements. Many scholars have consequently argued that Deuteronomy must have been written in the northern kingdom of Israel during its last years, but Deuteronomy's principle of cultic centralization suggests that it was actually composed in Judah. The revised versions of the laws found in Deuteronomy give greater rights to the poor and to women, which would suggest that the laws were revised to address the needs of the Judean rural farming class or *am ha'aretz*, the very group that placed the eight-year-old Josiah on the throne in 640 BCE following the assassination of his father, Amon ben Manasseh, during

---

[21] Bernard M. Levinson, *Deuteronomy and the Hermeneutics of Legal Innovation* (Oxford and New York: Oxford University Press, 1997); cf. Bernard M. Levinson, *Legal Revision and Religious Renewal in Ancient Israel* (Cambridge and New York: Cambridge University Press, 2008); and Marvin A. Sweeney, *King Josiah of Judah: The Lost Messiah of Israel* (Oxford and New York: Oxford University Press, 2001), 137–169.

a failed coup against the House of David. The laws of the Holiness Code in Leviticus 17–26 appear to revise those of Deuteronomy as well as the Covenant Code, indicating ongoing attempts to revise earlier laws in order to ensure a just legal system in ancient Israel and Judah that would evolve in keeping with the emerging needs of the nation.

Like the Covenant Code, Deuteronomy 5 includes a version of the Ten Commandments which serves as a statement of the principles that come to expression in the Deuteronomic law code. The commandments are quite similar to those of Exodus 20, although the wording often differs in an effort to clarify the meaning of the text or offer a different understanding of the commandment in question. Thus the command concerning the Shabbat in Deuteronomy 5:12–15 begins with "observe the Shabbat day to sanctify it just as YHWH your G-d commanded you" in contrast to the command to "remember the Shabbat day to sanctify it" in Exodus 20:8. Apparently, the Deuteronomic version aims to emphasize the people's action to observe the Shabbat, and the qualification that YHWH had commanded such observance adds incentive to the command. The Deuteronomic text also adds the bull and the ass to the list of animals who will rest on the Shabbat as well as reference to male and female servants, all of which are added to ensure that all in the Israelite or Judean households are recognized as having the right to observe the Shabbat. The additional reference to the male and female servants also serves as a basis to provide a different rationale from that of Exodus 20. Whereas Exodus 20 justified the Shabbat by pointing to YHWH's creation of the universe in six days and rest on the seventh, Deuteronomy 5:15 calls upon the people to remember that they were slaves in Egypt and that YHWH freed them from slavery, thereby justifying their observance of Shabbat. Indeed, the Exodus from Egypt plays an important role in the theology of Deuteronomy, whereas Shabbat, although present, appears to play a lesser role.

The key expression of the Shabbat as an epistemological legal principle in the Deuteronomic law code appears in the laws concerning the year of release and the treatment of Israelite and Judean slaves in Deuteronomy 15:1–18.

The law concerning the year of release appears in Deuteronomy 15:1–11. It refers to the seventh year as a year of *shemittah*, which refers to release or the remission of debts. It appears to presuppose the Covenant Code slave law of Exodus 21:2–11, which allows male debt slaves to go free in the seventh year of service, and the law concerning the use of agricultural fields in Exodus 23:9–11, which requires Israelite and Judean farmers to allow their fields to lie fallow in the seventh year so that they might be replenished through rest and so the poor might glean from them to support themselves. The Deuteronomic law extends the principle to the remission of debts for Israelites and Judeans, i.e., any debt owed by Israelites or Judeans is forgiven in the seventh year as a means to give aid to the poor among the people and ensure fulfillment of the principle stated in v. 4 that there shall be no poor in the land among the people of Israel and Judah. In case one might decline to grant loans as the year of remission approaches, vv. 9–11 calls upon the people to make the loans anyway, although no mechanism is included to ensure the observance of such practice. The debts owed to Israelites or Judeans by Gentiles, however, are not remitted.

The laws concerning treatment of a Hebrew, i.e., Israelite or Judean, slave, then follow in Deuteronomy 15:12–18. The Deuteronomic laws differ substantively from those of Exodus 21:2–11 in a manner that gives greater rights and support for the slave. Deuteronomy 15:12–18 continues to envision a six-year period of service with release in the seventh year, but it differs from the Covenant Code by stipulating that the master is required to grant to the newly freed slave a share of the flock, threshing floor, and vat, which ensures that the slave will have at least some capital to make a fresh start following his period of service. Such a grant helps to cut down the rates of recidivism that would have been inherent in the Exodus version of the law, in which slaves were freed with nothing, practically ensuring that they would not be able support themselves once freed and would likely choose perpetual service as a slave. Unlike the Exodus version of the law, women are also granted the right to go free in Deuteronomy 15:12, which again provides incentive for slaves who otherwise might remain in slavery because their wives are not freed with them. Nothing is said about the children, however. Nevertheless, Deuteronomy 15:16–18 continues to allow a slave to choose perpetual slavery if he or she so desires. Again, the rationale for these laws is Israel's experience of having been slaves in Egypt and YHWH's redemption of the nation from Egyptian bondage.

Otherwise, the Shabbat principle appears in relation to the observance of the major holidays as stated in

Deuteronomy 16:1–17. Passover appears to be one festival which combines Passover and Matzot, and it is observed for seven days, during which the people eat no leavened bread. As one would expect, the festival is justified by YHWH's redemption of the nation from Egyptian bondage. Likewise, the festival of Shavuot is celebrated seven weeks after Passover. The law very deliberately states that sons and daughters, male and female slaves, Levites, resident aliens, orphans, and widows will take part in the celebration, and it justifies the celebration because YHWH redeemed the nation from Egyptian bondage. Finally, the festival of Sukkot is celebrated for seven days like Passover. YHWH's blessing of the people in the land provides the rationale for the observance.

VI

Overall, the preceding survey demonstrates that that the Shabbat serves as a holy epistemological principle for the formulation of law in the Pentateuch. Specifically, the Shabbat appears as a holy principle of creation itself in Genesis 1:1–2:3, and it thereby serves as the template for conceptualizing the character of land and creation at large and the basis for Israelite and Judean life within that creation and land. It serves as the basis for the covenant between Israel/Judah and YHWH, and it provides the foundations for the laws of festival observance and socio-economic justice in ancient Israel and Judah. Although the Shabbat appears to provide a foundation for the synchronic reading of the Pentateuch, it also functions as a basic epistemological foundation for diachronic readings, insofar as it informs the formulation of Israelite law codes from the time of the northern kingdom of Israel in the eighth century BCE, the Judean kingdom of King Josiah in the seventh century BCE, the post-Josian Judean kingdom in the late seventh and early sixth century BCE, and the post-exilic restoration of Nehemiah and Ezra in the fifth–fourth centuries BCE. The Shabbat's principle of rest and holiness for all creation thereby provides a basis for conceiving the need and reality of the replenishment of creation as an inherent element of creation and human life within creation itself and as a basis for ensuring socio-economic justice for Israelite and Judean life within creation. Such an agenda has implications for the contemporary world as well.

Can Homer Be Read with Profit?
A Delightful Response — and Then Some

Richard I. Pervo

Profit or Delight

Plutarch's essay "How to Study Poetry," (*Mor.* 14e–37b)[1] is a manual for teaching young men Homer without ruining them.[2] On the principle that it is never too late to repent, I am bringing this text to the attention of Dennis R. MacDonald.[3] The presumably Homer-imitating author of the *Acts of Andrew* may have admired Plato,[4] but Plato did not admire Homer. In terms not completely unfamiliar to us, Plato viewed poetry as damaging to (young, in particular) minds and would have preferred to banish it from the properly managed state.[5] The tenth book of the *Republic* has Socrates challenge poetry's admirers to defend the medium

---

[1] The treatise is divided into fourteen readily distinguishable chapters. References here are to the more readily locatable page numbers.

[2] Note the useful edition of Richard Hunter and Donald Russell, eds., *Plutarch: How to Study Poetry* (CGLC; Cambridge: Cambridge University Press, 2011), which has an introduction and detailed commentary. The standard English translation is Frank C. Babbitt, LCL.

[3] An honor this is for one who has learned from his friend for more than four decades. MacDonald's most important contributions to scholarship are a willingness to challenge conventional solutions and the invention of a new discipline: the impact of mimesis upon early Christian writings.

[4] Dennis R. MacDonald, *Christianizing Homer: The* Odyssey, Plato, *and the* Acts of Andrew (New York: Oxford University Press, 1994).

[5] *Resp.* 2–3.

in prose by showing that poetry provided not only delight (ἡδύς) but also profit (ὠφέλιμος). This invitation generated both a long-standing debate and the terms of that debate. In short, Plutarch did not enter the discussion early in the opening period. Plato's objections inspired Aristotle to compose his *Poetics*. Subsequent Peripatetics offered additional comment. Stoics also contributed. Finally, the ongoing criticism and discussion of Homer had much to offer.[6]

By Plutarch's time the idea that culture should be taken straight might have elicited admiration, but it did not dictate curriculum.

> From the earliest age, children beginning their studies are nursed on Homer's teaching. One might say that while we were still in swathing bands we sucked from his epics as from fresh milk. He assists the beginner and later the adult in his prime. In no stage of life, from boyhood to old age, do we ever cease to drink from him.[7]

Homer was in the syllabus to stay.[8] The task and object for Plutarch were to make the best of a poor choice. The governing presumption was that moral formation was

---

[6] See, for a concise summary of the tradition, Hunter and Russell, 3–7, who devote much of their commentary to the helpful identification of Plutarch's sources and predecessors.

[7] Ps.-Heraclitus Homeric Questions 1.5–6, tr. D. R. MacDonald, *Mythologizing Jesus: From Jewish Teacher to Epic Hero* (Lanham, MD: Rowman & Littlefield, 2015), 3.

[8] The victory was not perpetual. In the standard curriculum considered age-old sixty years ago, the first Latin author read was Caesar. Not until the fourth year did a poet—Virgil—appear. Likewise, Greek reading began with the *Anabasis* of Xenophon. Few imagined that one might *enjoy* the *Gallic Wars*.

the goal of *paideia*.[9] Students were not assigned texts whose sole purpose was entertainment. Poetry was, Plutarch maintained, to serve as a propaedeutic to philosophy.[10] The problem was not as we might initially frame it: that Homer's ethic suits a heroic era. His competitive ethos remained vital. The problem was that poets lied. They also aroused sympathy for bad characters and portrayed many unworthy actions by those from whom more should be expected. The issue, in our terms, is that readers might view the epics as giving impressionable readers permission to behave badly. The strongest challenge was Homer's portrayal of the gods, who were by and large excellent role models for those who wished to spend their lives in maximum security prisons, if you will pardon the anachronism. Olympian antics gave Christian apologists a field day.[11]

At first Plutarch's suggestions seem less than profound, the obvious decked out with tropes, quotes, and figures. Upon further reflection (or rereading) it transpires that Plutarch views education as a triangular relationship involving teacher, student, and text. Correct exegesis is the responsibility of both student and teacher. Were it the latter alone, one could label the activity instruction. The

---

[9] Our Renaissance (presumably) forebears labeled all of Plutarch's nonbiographical writings *Moralia*.

[10] This raises a question for MacDonald's mimesis criticism: was Homer taught differently in non-elite schools, i.e., for those who would not go on to study philosophy?

[11] "Far be it from every sound mind to entertain such a concept of the deities as that Zeus, whom they call the ruler and begetter of all, should have been a parricide and the son of a parricide, and that moved by desire of evil and shameful pleasures he descended on Ganymede and the many women whom he seduced...." Justin *1 Apology* 21 (Hardy LCL)

involvement of both parties makes it education, learning how to engage texts critically. The process begins, reasonably enough, with examples for teachers, but the thrust is toward getting students to think. A discontinuity for us is that the object of criticism is entirely moral.[12] Genuine "lit crit" emerges during the Christian empire.[13] On these grounds MacDonald's arguments for mimesis of Homer are not controverted, for the episodes he studies have no marks of questionable morality in their proposed Christian transformations.

Scholars have wisely been studying the progymnastic literature because it shows how students were taught composition, how to organize projects, and what topics to treat.[14] These can be useful clues. If an encomiastic biography was expected to include antecedents, education, and youthful formation, one may ask why Mark omitted these features. Reflection on "How to Study Poetry" can reveal ideals about teaching young people how to read. To place this within the framework provided by our honoree, one might take a relevant Homeric episode, interpret it

---

[12] The concern remains in the objections of conservatives to reading matter in public schools. They, too, presume that description implies recommendation.

[13] Jaeger, *Paideia* 1:35, observes that Christians could read Homer aesthetically because they did not believe his theology. A contemporary parallel would be "the Bible as Literature." In the fourth century ethical questions remained for Christians. Basil wrote an imitation of Plutarch's treatise, on which see Johannes Quasten, *Patrology* (Westminster, MD: Newman, 1960), 3: 214–15. N. G. Wilson has produced a current edition: *Saint Basil on Greek Literature* (London: Duckworth, 1998).

[14] See, for example, Todd C. Penner, "Reconfiguring the Rhetorical Study of Acts: Reflections on the Method in and Learning of a Progymnastic Poetics," *PRS* 39 (2003): 425–39.

through the criteria proposed in this treatise (which are, to reiterate, typical), and seek to show if this exegesis might throw any light upon the proposed retelling or other uses of literature.

One presupposition that Plutarch does not introduce—and that we should not expect him to develop—is that the epics are set in the long ago and feature people who held values and followed codes that would make life in a polis all but impossible; the different ethos noted earlier. Historical distance and the relativism it entails are not in the picture. The dominant and nearly insufferable presupposition is that poets lie (16a). For Plato that was unqualifiedly insufferable. Perhaps a route to understanding this problem for many readers of this essay is the difficulty students may have with the concept of fiction in the Bible. Even calling the parables of Jesus "fictitious stories" will raise some hackles. Behind this is the unstated assumption that God would not inspire fiction, which is naughty, because it amounts to lies, which good little girls and boys do not tell. I am not seeking to equate Homer with Scripture, but to identify the penumbra that clouds fiction.[15] To say that poets lie is, of course, a moral judgment, quite different from saying that they make up stories. Note also that the statement means that poets are viewed primarily as narrators, since it is difficult to condemn dactyls or metaphors as mendacities.

> "Many the lies the poets tell," some intentionally and some unintentionally; intentionally, because for the

---

[15] On the subject see Christopher Gill and T. P. Wiseman, eds., *Lies and Fiction in the Ancient World* (Austin: University of Texas Press, 1993).

purpose of giving pleasure and gratification to the ear (and this is what most people look for in poetry) they feel that the truth is too stern in comparison with fiction. For the truth, because it is what actually happens, does not deviate from its course, even though the end be unpleasant; whereas fiction, being a verbal fabrication, very readily follows a roundabout route, and turns aside from the painful to what is more pleasant. (16a–b, trs. Babbitt, 83)

What causes delight is not diction, meter, and image but "fabulous narrative" (διάθεσις μυθολογίας).[16] Plutarch does not approve of fictitious plots and happy endings.[17] Students are to train themselves to seek out the wheat from among the tares.[18] Reading is therefore a critical art. Rather than protect students from works containing questionable passages, they are to be taught to distinguish good from bad and absorb the former while shunning the latter.[19] If one allows critical thinking to be transferable—that learning to distinguish good and evil facilitates other types of critical reflection—this is a step in the right direction.[20]

The other chief objection to poetry is that it is imitative. In Platonic terms this imitation of the phenomenal world is third hand, a dream of shadows on the wall of the

---

[16] On this phrase consult Hunter and Russell, 85.

[17] I should issue a consumer warning to any who might plunge into the *Iliad* and Aeschylus in quest of happy endings. One is tempted to ask what Plutarch had in mind. These words would constitute an apposite critique of romantic novels. On happy endings see *Callirhoe* 8.1.4.

[18] Plutarch's own simile is to bees, which, in accordance with the then-current science, seek out honey from malodorous plants and troublesome thorns (32e–f).

[19] Note, however, the comments on censorship below.

[20] The moral orientation did not expire with Plutarch or antiquity. Popular culture has not long been emancipated from the requirement to demonstrate that crime does not pay.

cave, doubly removed from reality. For Plutarch the issue is moral: one can have good imitations of bad persons or ugly objects.[21] To understand the issue we must recall the Greek preference for identifying the good and the beautiful. That may require some reflection, as in the somewhat notorious example of Paris, consoled by his wife in bed after a discreditable departure from the field of combat.[22] By this means Homer shows, rather than tells, that only bad people have sex in the daytime.[23]

Immediately following elucidation of this debatable principle, he urges readers to look for hints, i.e., telling, of the poet's views (19). Epic is more subtle than drama; Homer can often judge in silence.[24] This challenges readers, and might even provide them excessive interpretive scope, for Plutarch immediately (19e–f) opposes the quests for underlying meanings (ὑπόνοια) and allegory.[25] Plutarch was not a committed despiser of allegory, as is apparent

---

[21] See §18. One inevitably thinks of Hellenistic art, which produced some grotesque representations of various social types. See Christine M. Havelock, *Hellenistic Art: The Art of the Classical World from the Death of Alexander the Great to the Battle of Actium* (rev. ed.; New York: Norton, 1981), nos. 83, 132–36, for examples.

[22] *Iliad* 3.369–447.

[23] The same principle is used by Christian exegetes. For example, in his comments on the death of John the Baptist, Jerome condemned the observance of birthdays by noting that in the Bible only bad guys—Pharaoh and Herod—observed them: *Commentariorum in Matheum Libri IV* (CCSL 77; D. Hurst and M. Adriaen, eds.; Brepols: Turnhout, 1969), 116–19. See also Plutarch 26a–b. The well-trained will admire the good and disdain the bad.

[24] See Hunter and Russell, 110.

[25] As Robert Lamberton, for example, stresses, ancients used the vocabulary of allegory rather generally. See *Homer the Theologian: Neoplatonist Allegorical Reading and the Growth of the Epic Tradition* (Berkeley: University of California Press, 1986), 20–21. Pp. 10–43 discuss the rich exegetical tradition up to Plutarch's era.

from his treatise on Isis and Osiris.[26] The Stoics played a large role in the allegorical interpretation of Homeric theology, but Plutarch is not consistently hostile to them here.[27] I suspect that he regards the quest for deeper meaning both beyond the mental capacity of the young and too easy a dodge from the challenges that poetry raises.

He does, on the other hand, encourage students to observe how the names of gods are employed, for they sometimes are literal but can also be tropes (23a–24c). Hephaestus may mean "fire," Ares "war," and Zeus "fate." By good fortune (or fate or Zeus) no pedant intervenes to label this practice as insidious poetic mendacity. In the balance between allegory and metonymy Plutarch appears to have recognized the need to find age-appropriate critical tools.

Much of his advice urges countering the morally objectionable with better sentiments. If necessary, one may introduce citations from other authors (e.g., 20e, 21d). When this takes the form of supporting Homer's statements with sayings of the philosophers, the author can call it "demythologizing."[28] By such means students are directed toward consideration of context rather than isolated fragments. A useful criterion appears in the admonition to eschew stereotypes. Not all kings are noble or ladies of high standing virtuous (25e). Homer can be shown to dismiss the

---

[26] *Mor.* 351c–84c.

[27] See Hunter and Russell, index *s.v.* "Stoics," 221.

[28] 34d: "This method of conjoining and reconciling such sentiments with the doctrines of philosophers brings the poet's work out of the realm of myth and impersonation...." tr. Babbitt, 193. "Myth and impersonation" refer to lies and mimesis.

external as unworthy of attention (35a). On the broader level reading poetry (drama would be especially suitable here) teaches humility and moderation. Reversals instruct one not to despise those battered by misfortune and not to be overwhelmed by personal setbacks (35d). These examples indicate that, beneath the surface, as it were, of his relentless moralism, such as the quest for texts promoting cardinal virtues (e.g. 29–31), Plutarch envisions equipping pupils with resources for critical thinking and for achieving some distance from the ups and downs of life.[29] His program is not narrowly moralistic, for he moves ultimately toward a broadly humanistic appreciation of literature.

Another enduring contribution of the ancients was to deal with objectionable parts of texts through censorship.[30] The story of how Hephaestus trapped his wife Aphrodite and Ares *en flagrante* by enclosing them in invisible bonds (*Odyssey* 8.266–369) contains an excellent cautionary theme and a useful saying (v. 329), but the subject was unsuitable. A portion was omitted in some mss. Hunter and Russell suggest that teachers may not have had students read beyond v. 332.[31] Not until recent decades has the practice of bowdlerizing come to an end.[32]

---

[29] Much Greek formation dealt with self-control, mastery of anger and lust, the temperate use of alcohol, and related qualities. This should not be confused with repression. Plutarch's moral program is not bad; to us it appears to be too narrow.

[30] On the problem in general, see Hunter and Russell, 10. Some material has been lost from various Homeric mss.

[31] Hunter and Russell, 108. See Alfred Heubeck, Stephanie West, and J. B. Hainsworth, *A Commentary on Homer's Odyssey* (Oxford: Clarendon, 1988), 1: 363–72 on the episode, 369–70 on vv. 333–42.

[32] Outside of changes in mores, students who read Latin and Greek are likely to be older than in previous generations. For examples see

At 30d–e, the beginning of chap. 11, Plutarch steps away from his primary task to venture into reader-response criticism, identifying three types of readers: the *philomythos*, who attends to the story and its development, including plot and structure; the *philologos*, more a rhetorical reader than a philologist, as this person focuses on language, tropes, and figures; and, in pride of place, the *philokalos kai philotimos*, the moral/philosophical reader, who looks to poetry for *paideia* rather than entertainment.[33] The order is hierarchical, from entertainment to what we should call "philology" to philosophical analysis. Real reading requires all three, of course; Plutarch's types are in part abstractions, but they do represent strategies.[34]

"The passages rejected on moral grounds are most easily defended on those same moral grounds, by reasoning from the text of Homer and reaching conclusions different from those reached by Socrates."[35] Lamberton's comment could serve as a summary of Plutarch's endeavor. Students would enjoy Homer, no doubt. The task of the teacher was to lead them toward serious concerns, in large part by developing various critical skills, grounded, to be sure, on

---

the changes in the Loeb Library, which once refused to translate some poems, rendered some Greek passages into Latin, and Latin into Italian. The school editions of Aristophanes I used in college eliminated the passages dealing with bodily functions, including sex. (No discernible voices were then raised in condemnation of passages glorifying violence, of which Homer has more than a few.)

[33] See Hunter and Russell, 171 and David Konstan, "The Birth of the Reader: Plutarch as a Literary Critic," *Scholia* 13 (2004): 3–27.

[34] Note also 34b (the beginning of chap. 13), which cites Chrysippus on giving Homer's statements broader application. Tasks like this may begin with teachers, but responsibility is placed upon the reader.

[35] Lamberton, *Homer the Theologian*, 19.

moral principles. Communication was not merely one-way, from master to disciple. To read Homer as preparation for philosophy involved learning how to think and becoming an active, inquiring, even, from time to time, resisting reader.

Plutarch does not mention rhetorical education. If this were the only available information about Greek education c. 100 CE, one might imagine his students leaving the study of poets and marching straight into Philosophy 101. `Twas not so, we well know. One might argue that would-be rhetors should study poetry so that they can learn how to lie. If we are to presume that Mark and Luke, among others, had a modicum or more of Greek education, what would their study of Homer contained? Dare we imagine teachers who would follow, however crudely and distantly, the kind of path represented in "How to Study Poetry?"

The general consensus of learned antiquity was toward balance and moderation, along the line of "all work and no play make Jack a dull boy." The wise educator sugarcoats a bitter pill. This is the advice of the author of the treatise in the Plutarchian corpus preceding that just surveyed: "As physicians, mixing bitter drugs with sweet syrups, have found that the agreeable taste gains access for what is beneficial, so fathers should combine the abruptness of their rebukes with mildness...."[36]

Plutarch's approach to profit with delight is in part developmental: serious persons should move beyond the need for a mixture, at least in theory, but the pleasurable, i.e., poetry, always provides a challenge to look for the

---

[36] Ps.-Plutarch, *The Education of Children* 13d (tr. Babbitt, *Plutarch's Moralia* I, 63–65.

philosophical gold amidst the dross of entertainment. He hovers between "a little delight is acceptable so long as it does not corrupt or interfere with profit" and "profit in spite of delight." Everyone agreed that poetry brimmed with delight. The issue was management of it. For prose the question should never have, in theory, arisen, but it did. That discussion occupies the next section of this essay.

Profit *and* Delight

When I began my dissertation research in the fall of 1973, there was widespread agreement that the Apocryphal Acts were mainly entertaining, while the canonical book was purely edifying. That contrast highlighted the differences in genre. To facilitate communication, I have reduced this to a table, in which 0 indicates absence and X presence:

Table 1

Canonical Acts		Apocryphal Acts	
Profit	X	Profit	0
Delight	0	Delight	X

To this consensus I took firm exception. That debate is essentially finished. Consensus now recognizes that Acts is entertaining and that the Apocryphal Acts are edifying.[37] In antiquity poetry was supposed to be attractive.

---

[37] "Pervo's main contention is correct: Acts is entertaining and edifying." David E. Aune, *The New Testament in Its Literary Environment* (LEC 8; Philadelphia: Westminster, 1987), 80. For the general shift on the Apocryphal Acts see the relevant contributions in Wilhelm Schneemelcher, ed., *New Testament Apocrypha* (2 vols.; rev. ed.; tr. and ed. Robert McL. Wilson; Louisville: Westminster/John Knox, 1991–92), vol. 2, in contrast to the preceding editions of that standard handbook.

Subsequent discussion focused on whether it could also possess utility.[38] That prose history was useful may be taken as a given. The question that arose was whether it might also be pleasant and, if so, the nature of that pleasure.[39]

As Plutarch indicates, the useful and the entertaining formed the two opposing poles of the Hellenistic and Roman debate. The most famous synthesis is in the so-called *Ars Poetica* of Horace, 333–46:[40] *Omne tulit punctum qui miscuit utile dulci, / Lectorem delectando pariterque monendo.*[41] It is customary to call the synthesis a "Peripatetic

---

[38] Loveday Alexander, *The Preface to Luke's Gospel: Literary Convention and Social Context in Luke 1.1–4 and Acts 1.1* (SNTSMS 78; Cambridge: The University Press, 1993), 97, lists a number of prefaces of quite varied works, most of which are technical, promising usefulness.

[39] Major resources for the following include: Paul Scheller, *De hellenistica Historiae conscribendae Arte* (Leipzig: Noske, 1911); Eduard Norden, *Die antike Kunstprosa* (2 vols.; Stuttgart: Teubner, 1995 [reprint of 1915]), 1:91–95; G. Avenarius, *Lukians Schrift zur Geschichtsschreibung* (Hain: Meisenheim am Glan, 1956); Alexander Scobie, *Aspects of the Ancient Romance and Its Heritage: Essays on Apuleius, Petronius, and the Greek Romances* (Hain: Meisenheim am Glan, 1969); C. O. Brink, *Horace on Poetry: The 'Ars Poetica'* (Cambridge: Cambridge University Press, 1971); F. W. Walbank. *Polybius* (Berkeley University of California Press, 1972); Charles W. Fornara, *The Nature of History in Ancient Greece and Rome* (Berkeley: University of California Press, 1983); R. L. Hunter, *A Study of Daphnis and Chloe* (Cambridge: Cambridge University Press, 1983); James S. Romm, *The Edges of the Earth in Ancient Thought* (Princeton: Princeton University Press, 1992); Alexander, *Preface to Luke's Gospel*; André Hurst, *Lucien de Samosate: Comment écrire l'histoire* (Paris: Les Belles Lettre, 2010); and Robert Doran, *2 Maccabees: A Critical Commentary* (Hermeneia; Minneapolis: Fortress Press, 2012).

[40] See the comments of Brink, *Horace*, 352–60, who identifies its Greek roots and shows the relation between Greek and Latin terms, along with much other useful information.

[41] The one who combines profit with delight, equally pleasing and admonishing the reader, captures all the plaudits. Horace *Ars Poetica* 343–44 (author's tr.).

compromise."[42] Strabo, of Stoic leanings, is a good representative:

> Since Homer devoted his stories to the principle of education, he largely occupied his mind with facts; "but he set therein" fiction (*pseudos*) as well, using the latter to win popularity and marshall the masses while still giving sanction to the former. "And just as when some workman pours gold overlay onto silver," so the poet set a mythical element into his true events, sweetening and ornamenting his style.[43]

Like Plutarch, Strabo makes his case attractive by lacing it with Homeric citations (in quotes). As a Stoic Strabo strongly defends the utilitarian value of poetry.[44] What must be justified is entertainment. Poets of various intellectual orientations were inclined to agree. Few authors wish to boast that their creations are useless,[45] reserving such judgments for the compositions of others.

The historical tradition strove to maintain the line announced by Thucydides. In 1.22 he rejects the "mythical" (*mythōdes*) and promotes the useful (*ōphelimon*). By the time of Lucian the expression of this ideal has become rather shrill:

> Now some think they can make a satisfactory distinction in history between what gives pleasure (*terpnon*) and what is useful (*chrēsimon*) and for this reason work eulogy into it as giving pleasure and enjoyment to its readers... the distinction they draw is false. History has

---

[42] Horace *Ars Poetica* 352.

[43] Strabo, *Geog.* 1.2.9, tr. James Romm, *Edges,* 189. See his comments, 186–94.

[44] On the importance of utility in Stoic discussions of poetry see Romm, *Edges,* 179 n.20.

[45] Here also "myth" refers to narrative, stories.

one task and one end—what is useful—and that comes from truth alone.[46]

Too shrill. Lucian is shrieking at the waves to calm down. Polybius, the other admired exponent of truth, stressed utility, but he was not prepared to banish the attractive absolutely from history's salons.[47] As this small sample indicates, which does not even touch the Hellenistic debates or the "tragic history" tempest, something has changed. The cause of that shift was rhetoric and its impact (ignored by Plutarch in "How to Read") upon education. Rhetoric had three goals: *docere, movere,* and *delectare.*[48] To the pair of teaching and pleasing has been added persuading, how to move an audience. Pleasing is a component of persuading. Rhetoric transformed the two dialectical opponents into a cooperative trinity. One might also recall that rhetoric did not place truth at the summit of its moral platform. The rhetorically formed could admire Thucydides *ad infinitum,* but when they took up historiography, they would not produce good imitations of him.[49] One can follow the path by observing how ψυχαγωγία moved from its concrete sense of "leading souls" to "persuading/seducing" to becoming a synonym for

---

[46] *Quomodo Historia* 9 (Kilburn LCL). Sections 9–13 develop Thucydides 1.22.

[47] Cf. I.4.11; VII 7.8; IX.2.6; XI.19a. 1–3; XV.36. XXXI.30.1, upholding utility over pleasure. At I.4.11 (cf. III.31.2), however, he allows for both.

[48] Heinrich Lausberg, *Handbook of Literary Rhetoric* (tr. and ed. D. Orton and R. Anderson; Leiden: Brill, 1998), §257, pp. 113–17.

[49] For the transformation of historiography through rhetoric, see Clare K. Rothschild, *Luke-Acts and the Rhetoric of History* (WUNT 175; Tübingen: Mohr Siebeck, 2004), 1–23.

"entertaining."[50] Forty years ago conservative exegetes, in particular, viewed Luke as a representative of the Thucydidean standard. That is no longer the case. The current challenge is to locate him on the spectrum of rhetorical historiography, at best.[51] To stimulate this conversation I shall offer parts of two prefaces and an extract from an epistle:

> 2 Macc 2:24–25: For considering the flood of statistics involved and the difficulty there is for those who wish to enter upon the narratives of history because of the mass of material, we have aimed to please (ψυχαγωγίαν) those who wish to read, to make it easy for those who are inclined to memorize, and to profit (ὠφέλειαν) all readers.
>
> *Daphnis and Chloe* Prol. 3: I... have carefully fashioned four books, an offering to love and the Nymphs and Pan, a delightful (τερπνὸν) possession (κτῆμα) for all persons that will heal the sick and encourage the depressed, that will stir memories in those experienced in love and for the inexperienced will be a lesson (παιδεύσει) for the future.[52]

Loveday Alexander says that 2 Macc 2:24 is "a seductive cocktail of 'entertainment'... 'ease'... and 'usefulness'.... This is a neat expression of the 'profit with delight' *topos*..."[53] Longus promises lots of usefulness and delight, and—cruel blow!—plays with Thucydides' (1.22)

---

[50] See LSJ *s.v.*, 2026. Romm, *Edges,* 185, speaking of Eratosthenes, glosses *psychagogia* as "a species of aesthetic pleasure (perhaps 'entertainment')." Doran, *2 Maccabees* 69–70, has an excellent discussion. He declines to abandon the rhetorical sense.

[51] See Thomas E. Phillips, "The Genre of Acts: Moving Toward a Consensus," *Acts within Diverse Frames of Reference* (Macon: Mercer University Press, 2009), 46–77.

[52] *Longus: Daphnis and Chloe* 13–15, *alt* (Henderson LCL).

[53] Alexander, *Preface*, 149.

claim to have produced an everlasting possession.[54] 2 Maccabees is normally ranked as an example of rhetorical history, *Daphnis and Chloe* a romantic novel, yet both make similar campaign promises.

What kind of pleasure was deemed legitimate in history? If one peruses 2 Maccabees for examples, she will find the splendid epiphany, punishment, and conversion of Heliodorus (ch. 3), speeches, martyrdoms, reversals of fortune, and, if found appealing, thrilling military engagements. This is not utterly unlike what can be found in Polybius, let alone Livy. Would the reader of Acts believe that the two represented the same genre? The answer is not obvious, even if those who say "yes" may have a steeper climb before them.

In his review of the question Charles Fornara proposes to understand the important historian Duris of Samos as taking a page from Aristotle on tragedy and asserting that "the *pleasure* of history is produced through the *imitation* of the emotions raised by history."[55] Needless to say, an old charge raised against poetry was its mimetic quality. The result was a roller coaster, aptly, as Fornara notes, portrayed in Cicero's modest proposal that Lucceius compose a monograph on his consulship and subsequent adventures:

> Moreover, what has happened to me will supply you with an infinite variety of material, abounding in a sort of pleasurable interest which could powerfully grip the attention of the reader — if you are the writer. For there is nothing more apt to delight the reader than the

---

[54] See Hunter, *A Study*, 46–47.
[55] Fornara, *Nature*, 120–34. On Duris see 124 and n. 47.

manifold changes of circumstance, and vicissitudes of fortune, which, however undesirable I found them to be in my own experience, will certainly afford entertainment in the reading; for the placid recollection of a past sorrow is not without its charm.

The rest of the world, however, who have passed through no sorrow of their own, but are the untroubled spectators of the disasters of others, find a pleasure in their pity.[56]

The author of Acts knows something about the pleasures of ups and downs, even if his audience was not likely to be composed of "untroubled spectators of the disasters of others," but I should hesitate to argue that Cicero, reading Acts, would exclaim: "By Jove, this is precisely what a well-designed and properly crafted historical monograph should contain!"[57]

---

[56] Cicero, *ad fam.* 5.12.4–5 (Williams LCL); Fornara, *Nature,* 133–34.

[57] Alan J. Bale, in his recent monograph *Genre and Narrative Coherence in the Acts of the Apostles* (LNTS 514; London: Bloomsbury T&T Clark, 2015), 9, considers classifying Acts as Hellenistic historiography as "a leap too far." Richard Pervo, *Acts: A Commentary* (Hermeneia; Minneapolis: Fortress Press, 2009), 17–18, notes ten features in which Acts differs from historiography in general.

James 3:7–8, Genesis 1:26, and the Linguistic Register of the Letter of James

John S. Kloppenborg

Throughout his career, Dennis MacDonald has insistently argued that contexts matter to interpretation. This principle, of course, is admitted by most critical scholars of Christian origins. But stipulating what those contexts are is a much more contested issue. It is often imagined that the Jesus movement and Christ cults were carefully bounded such that, while they existed in the multi-ethnic and cosmopolitan environments of the ancient Mediterranean, their cultural and intellectual resources were drawn primarily from the culture of ancient Israel. This is a deeply improbable approach, but one that draws its life from Christian apologetics and the need to set Christianity apart from its various environments — Protestants from Catholics, Christians from Enlightenment learning, Christianity from 'secularism,' and so forth. 'Judaism' — at least as it is constructed by Christian scholars — has proved a convenient foil for distinguishing the earliest Christ cults from their Greek and Roman contexts and thus for preserving a putative purity of 'biblical religion,' analogous to the apologetic urge to defend the purity of more recent christianities in the face of contemporary challenges.[1]

MacDonald has conceived of context in a much broader sense, and this context includes many of the principal cultural resources of Greek civilization, including Homer and the classical poets — the kinds of resources that formed the basis of classical education, rhetoric, and moral argument. This is to conceive of context not in a manner that threatened the intellectual integrity of Christ cults, but rather as a resource. In several important monographs, MacDonald has worked out not only the criteria for discerning *mimesis* of classical (and other) texts in the literary production of the Christ cults, but has also identified a number of stories and literary motifs that seem indebted to stories from Homer and others.[2] It is fair to say that the gains of this approach have been hard won, and there remains much opposition to thinking of context in any more than the limited way in which it has in the past been conceived. But as more scholars, some of whom were trained by MacDonald, demonstrate the exegetical value of his models of *mimesis*, this situation will no doubt change. This essay is offered as an *hommage* to MacDonald's work.

---

[1] See Jonathan Z. Smith, *Drudgery Divine: On the Comparison of Early Christianities and the Religions of Late Antiquity* (Jordan Lectures in Comparative Religion 14; Chicago: University of Chicago Press, 1990).

[2] Dennis R. MacDonald, *The Homeric Epics and the Gospel of Mark* (New Haven and London: Yale University Press, 2000); *Mimesis and Intertextuality in Antiquity and Christianity* (Harrisburg, Pa.: Trinity Press International, 2001); and *Does the New Testament Imitate Homer? Four Cases from the Acts of the Apostles* (New Haven and London: Yale University Press, 2003).

The letter ascribed to "James" offers many puzzles to the interpreter. Ostensibly the work of the brother of Jesus, whose level of literacy was likely not much above craftsman literacy, the letter represents some of the best Greek found in the early Christian writings. The letter pretends to be from a distinguished figure of the earliest Jesus movement who was killed in 62 CE, but its first clear citation in the East is not until the early third century, by Origen after his move to Caesarea in 231 CE,[3] and by the Pseudo-Clementine *Epistula de virginitate* (early III CE),[4] while the earliest attestation in the West is Hilary of Potiers in the mid-fourth century (*de Trinitate*, 4.8, ca. 356 CE).[5] The late appearance of the letter seems hardly consistent with an early date for the composition of the letter, still less had the real author in fact been the influential brother of Jesus.

The content of James is equally puzzling. Although it was transmitted as a document belonging to Christ groups and eventually found its way into the Eastern and Western canons, James is noticeably devoid of the most obvious

---

[3] Origen, *Comm. in Joh.* 19.23 (ed. Preuschen, *Origens Werke* Bild 4, GCS; Leipzig: J. C. Hinrichs, 1903. 325): ὡς ἐν τῇ φερομένῃ Ἰακώβου ἐπιστολῇ ἀνέγνωμεν, "as we read in the letter James that is in circulation."

[4] The *Epistula de virginitate* cites Jas 1:5 (1.11.10); 1:26 (1.3.4); 1:27 (1.12.1); 3:1 (1.11.4); and 3:2 (1.11.4) and alludes to 2:1 (1.12.8); 2:17–18 (1.2.2); 3:1 (1.11.8); 3:15 (1.11.9); and 4:6 (1.8.3), but nowhere identifies the source as "James."

[5] Hippolytus (170–235 CE), in a commentary on the Apocalypse (4:7–8), preserved only in a fifteenth-century Arabic manuscript, refers to "the tribes [that] were dispersed, as the saying of Jude in his first letter to the twelve tribes proves: 'which are dispersed in the world.'" See G.N. Bonwetsch, et al., *Hippolytus Werke* (2. Aufl.; GCS 36; Leipzig: J.C. Hinrichs, 1897–1929), 1: 231. It is not clear whether Hippolytus has confused Jude with James, but the late date of this manuscript renders any conclusions drawn from it extremely tenuous.

appeals to the beliefs, language, and practices of those groups: there are no allusions to baptism, the Lord's Supper, or the Holy Spirit; *kyrios* is used mainly in reference to God; there are no other christological titles apart from the formula *kyrios Iesous Christos* in 1:1 and 2:1; and the examples of faithfulness, patience, and prayer are not drawn from figures known from the Jesus movement, but are instead from the Hebrew Bible: Abraham, Rahab, Job, and Elijah.

Perhaps even more curious is the fact that the letter is peppered with allusions to the Jesus tradition — mostly the sayings that are usually thought to come from Q,[6] but none of these sayings is marked as a saying of Jesus or as a quotation at all. Even more interestingly, the sayings of Jesus that are present are not cited verbatim, but are heavily paraphrased and adapted to the argumentative texture in which James uses them. This, in fact, finds an explanation if the author of James, surely not a semi-literate Galilean artisan, but rather a writer with at least modest literary pretensions, employed the rhetorical practice of *aemulatio* — the technique of rhetorical paraphrase, whereby an author evoked a predecessor text but intentionally paraphrased and recast it in a way appropriate to his or her intended audience. *Aemulatio* (in Greek, *zēlos*), was widely practiced in rhetoric and literary composition, and depended on the orator or writer knowing that the audience would both recognize the allusion to the predecessor text, and would

---

[6] For varying assessments of the number of allusions to the Jesus tradition, see Dean B. Deppe, "The Sayings of Jesus in the Epistle of James," D.Th. diss.; Free University of Amsterdam (Chelsea, MI: Bookcrafters, 1989) and Patrick J. Hartin, *James and the "Q" Sayings of Jesus* (JSNTSup 47; Sheffield: Sheffield Academic Press, 1991).

then appreciate the artistry involved in redeploying that text in a new context.[7] As Quintilian says, the duty of *aemulatio* is to "rival and vie [*aemulatio*] with the original in the expression of the same thoughts" (10.5.5).

There is, for example, general agreement that James 1:5, εἰ δέ τις λείπεται σοφίας, αἰτείτω παρὰ τοῦ διδόντος θεοῦ πᾶσιν ἁπλῶς καὶ μὴ ὀνειδίζοντος καὶ δοθήσεται αὐτῷ ("if anyone lacks wisdom, let them ask from the God who gives to all, singly and without reproach, and it will be given to them") evokes and paraphrases Q 11:9–13. But the paraphrase takes up only Q's 'ask/give' pair, ignoring the 'seek/find' and 'knock/open' binaries. Moreover, James's paraphrase elaborates the character of God, especially as one who 'gives,' taking up and condensing Q's homely illustrations of what earthly fathers are inclined to do (Q 11:11–13) into the single notion that God gives gifts ἁπλῶς and without reproach. Second, the elaboration that follows in James 1:6–8 turns its attention to the problem of the interior conditions that attend 'asking,' insisting that just as God gives gifts 'singly' (ἁπλῶς), the one who asks cannot be 'double-souled' (δίψυχος) and expect to receive anything. The principal good to be sought, moreover, is wisdom (σοφία), rather than some lesser good. In other words, James takes up Q's rather extraordinary and unqualified assurance, αἰτεῖτε καὶ δοθήσεται, and paraphrases it in order to explain *what* is to be sought, and *how* it is to be sought. At

---

[7] See John S. Kloppenborg, "The Reception of the Jesus Tradition in James," *The Catholic Epistles and the Tradition* (ed. Jacques Schlosser; BETL 176; Leuven: Peeters, 2004), 93–139. For explorations of the use of literary imitation more widely, see MacDonald, *Homeric Epics*.

4:3 James returns to the aphorism, now explaining αἰτεῖτε καὶ οὐ λαμβάνετε, διότι κακῶς αἰτεῖσθε, ἵνα ἐν ταῖς ἡδοναῖς ὑμῶν δαπανήσητε. This effectively reverses the assurance when the conditions of the petitioner are not conducive to its fulfillment. These kinds of paraphrase betray an interest on the part of the author of James in Stoic psychagogy and other popular philosophical reflections on the cultivation of a self such that one is not subject to the passions and pleasures, but is on the contrary, singly oriented to τὸ καλόν.[8]

There is yet another puzzle about James. On the one hand, the style and syntax of James are relatively good. Eduard Norden noticed the diatribe-like characteristics of James, especially in 2:14–26, and the use of ἄγε in constructing apostrophes in 4:13 and 5:1.[9] James, moreover, observes the distinction between οὐ and μή more strictly that does Hebrews;[10] in compound phrases the "law of correlation" is observed;[11] ἄγε is used correctly with the

---

[8] This is further illustrated in John S. Kloppenborg, "James 1:2–15 and Hellenistic Psychagogy," *NovT* 52.1 (2010): 37–71.

[9] Eduard Norden, *Die antike Kunstprosa vom 6. Jahrhundert v. Chr. bis in die Zeit der Renaissance* (2 Aufl.; Leipzig: B.G. Teubner, 1909 [repr. Darmstadt: Wissenschaftliche Buchgesellschaft 1981]), 556–57. Norden followed Adolf von Harnack (*Die Chronologie der Litteratur bis Irenäus nebst Einleitenden Untersuchungen* [vol. 1 of *Geschichte der altchristlichen Litteratur bis Eusebius. Zweiter Theil: Die Chronologie*; Leipzig: J.C. Hinrichs, 1897–1904], 485) in suggesting a late second-century date for James, which Norden argued was consistent with the use of the diatribe form (455, n. 2).

[10] Joseph B. Mayor, *The Epistle of St. James: The Greek Text with Introduction, Notes and Comments* (3rd ed.; London: Macmillan & Co., 1910), ccxliv.

[11] Georg Benedikt Winer, *A Treatise on the Grammar of New Testament Greek* (3rd ed.; Edinburgh: T&T Clark, 1882), 174; James Hope Moulton, Wilbert Francis Howard and Nigel Turner, *A Grammar of New*

plural, in contrast to all of the instances of ἄγε in the LXX[12] and in 2 Tim 4:11; and there are various dislocations of normal sentence order — the separation of a genitive from its noun by the verb, and the advancing of the subject of an interrogative sentence before the interrogative particle, all for emphasis.[13] The author also employs alliteration and word plays possible only in Greek.[14]

Conceding that some of James's Greek "belongs to the higher reaches of the literary *Koine*," Nigel Turner also noted a number of failings, including the lack of care to avoid hiatus (six times in 1:4 and at various other points throughout) and concludes that the author had "only moderate pretensions (or none) to classical Greek style."[15] There are only two periodic sentences in the letter (2:2–4; 4:13–15), no instances of an absolute genitive, and a few odd phrases.[16] Genitives almost always follow rather than precede their substantives.[17]

Testament Greek (Edinburgh: T&T Clark, 1963–85), 3: 180 citing Apollonios Dyskolos. Philo violates the rule, Plato keeps it.

[12] Judg 19:6; 2 Kgs 4:24; Tobit 9:2; Sir 33:32; Isa 43:6 (*bis*).

[13] Genitive-noun order: 1:1, 17; 3:3; separation of genitive from its governing noun by intervening verb: 3:8; subject of interrogative sentence is advanced for emphasis: 2:21, 25; 4:12.

[14] Dale C. Allison, *A Critical and Exegetical Commentary on the Epistle of James* (ICC; New York and London: Bloomsbury, 2013), 82.

[15] Moulton, Howard, and Turner, *MHT*, 4:115. But see 1:17: παρ' ᾧ; 2:7: ἐφ' ὑμᾶς; 2:17: καθ' ἑαυτήν; 2:18: ἀλλ' ἐρεῖ; 3:9: καθ' ὁμοίωσιν; 4:7: ἀφ' ὑμῶν; 5:4: ἀφ' ὑμῶν; 5:7: ἐπ' αὐτῷ; 5:9: κατ' ἀλλήλων; 5:14: ἐπ' αὐτὸν.

[16] Mayor, *James*, ccxlv.

[17] The exceptions are 1:1, 17; 3:3.

On the other hand, examination of the lexical frequency profile of James is also telling.[18] Of the sixty-three words that appear only in James and not in any other New Testament writing, forty-five are also attested, unsurprisingly, in the LXX. If one looks at the distinctive linguistic tokens in James that occur 0–3 times elsewhere in the NT, another profile emerges: James displays striking agreement with the singular vocabulary of later NT writings: Luke–Acts,[19] 1–2 Timothy,[20] and 1–2 Peter;[21] with the later books of the LXX: 1–4 Maccabees, Wisdom of Solomon, and Sirach;[22] and with Philo. That is, James's linguistic register seems to belong to that of Hellenistic Judaism. Just as importantly, James employs a number of words that are among the *least* common words in use in Greek prior to the second century CE. For example, James uses philosophical terms such as ἀδιάκριτος (undecided), ἀκατάστατος (unstable), and ἀπείραστος (untempted) which are attested only five to thirty-three times in six centuries of Greek literature prior to James—that is, they do not belong to the most basic tiers of ordinary vocabulary but rather to much

---

[18] On Lexical Frequency Profile, see Batia Laufer and Paul Nation, "Vocabulary Size and Use: Lexical Richness in L2 Written Production," *Applied Linguistics* 16.3 (1995): 307–22 and Batia Laufer, "Lexical Frequency Profiles: From Monte Carlo to the Real World: A Response to Meara (2005)," *Applied Linguistics* 26.4 (2005): 582–88.

[19] ἀνάπτειν, ἀτμίς, βραδύς, εὐθυμέω, εὐχή, θρησκεία, καταδυναστεύω, κλύδων, μακαρίζω, οἰκτρίμων, ὁρμή, περιπίπτω, πηδάλιον, πορεία.

[20] ἄγε, κακοπαθέω.

[21] δελεάζω, δοκίμιον, ἐμπορεύομαι, καταλαλέω.

[22] ἀλαζονεία, ἁπλῶς, ἀποκυέω, ἀποτελέω, ἔμφυτος, ἐπιλησμονή, ἐπιτήδειος, ἔσοπτρον, θανατηφόρος, θρησκεία, κακοπάθεια, κατιόομαι, μετατρέπω, ὕλη, φιλία.

more specialized linguistic registers.[23] Other words such as βρύω (*to gush*) and ἐνάλιος (*maritime*) are uncommon in prose but create resonances in classical poets such as Homer, Aeschylus, Euripides and Sophocles. These and other markers point to an author who wishes to create the impression of learned and sophisticated discourse, in spite of the fact that his sentence construction is quite simple.

James 3:7 and Maritime Creatures

A case in point is found in James's discourse on the tongue (3:1–12). The overall discourse draws on several classical psychagogic metaphors of the control of the self and the dangers of speech: the equestrian image of 'bridling' (χαλιναγωγέω) the passions,[24] the nautical metaphor of the pilot or the rudder controlling the entire ship by the application of small quantities of force (3:3),[25] and the tongue

---

[23] On the concept of linguistic register, see Michael A. K. Halliday, Angus McIntosh, and Peter Strevens, *The Linguistic Sciences and Language Teaching* (London: Longmans, 1964), 87–98.

[24] Philo often uses the cognates χαλινός, χαλινόω (7x), ἀχάλινος (14x), ἐγχαλινόω (5x) and ἀχαλίνωτος (8x) as a metaphor for the control of the passions and desires, the tongue, and anger—in a way that is comparable to James's use of these equestrian metaphors. See *Agr.* 69, 70 (cf. 73); *Mut.* 240 (on bridling the tongue as a way to control speaking falsely, swearing falsely, deceiving, practicing sophistry, and giving false information); *Spec.* 1.235; 4.79; *Det.* 53; 44 (people with an unbridled tongue [ἀχαλίνῳ γλώττῃ] displaying folly); *Deus* 47 (contrasting animals, which have yokes and bridles to control them, with humans, who are self-controlled); *Leg.* 3.155; *Praem.* 154; and many examples of the "unbridled" tongue/mouth: *Her.* 110; *Abr.* 29, 191; *Spec.* 1.53, 241; *Det.* 174; *Somn.* 2.132; *Jos.* 246; *Mos.* 2.198; *Legat.* 163.

[25] Philo uses the metaphor of the rudder (πηδάλιον) or pilot (κυβερνήτης) for the wise person's control of the passions, anger, and the rational direction of the body, comparable to James's argument that control of the tongue is a kind of rudder on the entire self. See *Leg.* 2.104; 3.80, 118,

as a dangerous and fiery instrument.[26] The peroration of the discourse underscores the dual character of speech, and how it is used for both beneficial and destructive ends.[27] In this context James contrasts the ease with which animals are tamed with the impossibility of taming the tongue:

πᾶσα γὰρ φύσις θηρίων τε καὶ πετεινῶν ἑρπετῶν τε καὶ ἐναλίων δαμάζεται καὶ δεδάμασται τῇ φύσει τῇ ἀνθρωπίνῃ· τὴν δὲ γλῶσσαν οὐδεὶς δαμάσαι δύναται ἀνθρώπων· ἀκατάστατον κακόν, μεστὴ ἰοῦ θανατηφόρου. (3:7–8)

For every species of beast and bird, reptile and sea-creature is tamed and has been tamed by the human species; but no one is able to tame the tongue of humans; it is a disorderly evil, full of death-dealing poison.

Dale Allison is no doubt right that James 3:7 evokes Genesis 1:26 and its division of the animal kingdom into four groups. The allusion to Genesis is inescapable not only because James 3:7 concerns the domination of animals — James prefers the verb δαμάζειν to Genesis's ἀρχέτωσαν — but also because in v. 9 James refers to "those who are in the likeness of God" (τοὺς καθ' ὁμοίωσιν θεοῦ γεγονότας), recalling Genesis 2:26a, ποιήσωμεν ἄνθρωπον κατ' εἰκόνα

223–224; Sacr. 45, 51; Det. 141; Agr. 69; Conf. 22; Migr. 67; Somn. 2.201; Abr. 272. See also Plutarch, Garr. 507A–B.

[26] Plutarch. Cohib. ira 454E: "Just as it is an easy matter to check a flame which is being kindled in hare's fur or candle wicks or rubbish, but if it is ever takes hold of solid bodies having depth, it quickly destroys and consumes «with youthful vigor lofty craftsmen's work» [Nauck, Tragicarum Graecarum Fragmenta, no. 357]"; Diogenes of Oenoanda, frag. 38 (ed. Chilton, p. 17).

[27] Compare Plutarch, Garr. 50eE: "Pittacus did not do badly when the king of Egypt sent him a sacrificial animal and asked him to cut out the best and the worst meat, when he cut out and sent him the tongue, as being the instrument of both the greatest good and the greatest evil (ὄργανον μὲν ἀγαθῶν ὄργανον δὲ κακῶν τῶν μεγίστων)."

ἡμετέραν καὶ καθ' ὁμοίωσιν.[28] Allison observes, however, that the naming of the divisions and their sequence in James does not correspond to any of the divisions of the animal kingdom attested in the biblical and parabiblical literature:[29]

Jas 3:7	θηρίων	πετεινῶν	ἑρπετῶν	ἐναλίων
Gen 1:26	ἰχθύων	πετεινῶν	κτηνῶν	ἑρπετῶν
Gen 1:28	ἰχθύων	πετεινῶν	κτηνῶν	ἑρπετῶν
Gen 7:14	θηρία	κτήνη	ἑρπετόν	πετεινόν
Gen 7:21	πετεινῶν	κτηνῶν	θηρίων	ἑρπετόν
Gen 8:1	θηρίων	κτηνῶν	πετεινῶν	ἑρπετῶν
Gen 8:19	θηρία	κτήνη	πετεινόν	ἑρπετόν
Gen 9:2	θηρίοις	ὄρνεα	κινούμενα	ἰχθύας
Dt 4:17-18	κτήνους	ὀρνέου	ἑρπετοῦ	ἰχθύος
3 Kgs 5:13	κτηνῶν	πετεινῶν	ἑρπετῶν	ἰχθύων
Ps 148:10	θηρία	κτήνη	ἑρπετά	πετεινά
Ez 38:20	ἰχθύες	πετεινά	θηρία	ἑρπετά
Hos 4:3	θηρίοις	ἑρπετοῖς	πετεινοῖς	ἰχθύες
1 En. 7:5	πετεινοῖς	θηρίοις	ἑρπετοῖς	ἰχθύσιν
Acts 10:12	τετράποδα	θηρία	ἑρπετά	πετεινά (v.l)
Acts 11:6	ἰχθύων	πετεινῶν	κτηνῶν	ἑρπετῶν
Gk LAE 29.11	θηρία πετεινά ἑρπετά ἐν τῇ γῇ καὶ θαλάσσῃ			

Other divisions of the animal kingdom are attested, and some use a triadic division: Genesis 1:30, Hosea 2:14, 2:20; and Theophilus, *Ad Autolycum* 2.11 propose τὰ θηρία – πετεινὰ – ἑρπετά.[30]

---

[28] Dale C. Allison, "The Audience of James and the Sayings of Jesus," *James, 1 & 2 Peter and the Early Jesus Tradition* (ed. Alicia Batten and John S. Kloppenborg; LNTS 478; London and New York: Bloomsbury T&T Clark, 2014), 58–77, 59 and *James*, 542–43.

[29] This table is adapted from Allison, "Audience of James," 60.

[30] Theophilus, *Ad Autolycum* 1.10 lists five types of animals worshipped by Egyptians: ἑρπετῶν τε καὶ κτηνῶν καὶ θηρίων καὶ πετεινῶν καὶ ἐνύδρων νηκτῶν, 'serpents, sea monsters, beasts, birds, and swimming things.'

What is perhaps noteworthy is that in none of these lists does ἐνάλιος occur. Nor does it appear in other Christian literature before Theophilus of Antioch in the later part of the second century CE[31] and then much later, in Epiphanius.[32] One wonders why James had not been satisfied with ἑρπετῶν τε καὶ ἰχθυῶν or ἑρπετῶν τε καὶ τῶν πελαγίων or ἑρπετῶν τε καὶ τῶν ἐν τῇ θαλάσσῃ, any of which would have conveyed the sense of maritime creatures and have done so with ordinary vocabulary.

While the term ἐνάλιος is not attested in any of the other allusions to Genesis 1:26, it does have a distinguished literary profile. It appears in the *Odyssey* only three times,[33] but nineteen times in Pindar to describe maritime gods and monsters, sea-faring ships, coastal cities,[34] and especially in Euripides, Sophocles (5x) and Callimachus's Hymn 4 *to Delos* (3x). Of the eighty occurrences of forms of ἐνάλιος prior to James, the majority are in poetic and dramatic works, and the term appears with special frequency in relation to Poseidon and other δαίμονες ἐνάλιοι.[35]

---

[31] At *Ad Autolycum* 1.6 Theophilus uses a four-fold classification (τετραπόδων – πετεινῶν – ἑρπετῶν – νηκτῶν), but then subdivides water creatures into river and sea creatures (ἐνύδρων τε καὶ ἐναλίων).

[32] Epiphanius, *Haer.* 3.26 (ed. Holl, 374): οὕτω καὶ ἐπὶ τῶν ζῴων καὶ ἐπὶ τῶν πετεινῶν, οὕτω καὶ ἐπὶ τῶν κτηνῶν καὶ ἑρπετῶν καὶ ἐναλίων....; also Haer. 2.162; 3.74.

[33] *Od.* 4.443; 5.67; 15.479.

[34] Pindar, *Pythia* 2.79; 4.27; 4.39; 4.204; 11.40; and *Olympia* 9.99.

[35] Poseidon: Pindar, *Pythia* 4.204; Sophocles, *Oedipus Coloneus* 888; Oracula Sibyllina, 5.157; Philo *Decal.* 54; Aristonicus, *De signis Iliadis* on *Il.* 1.404; maritime gods and monsters: Pindar, *Pythia* 12.12; Euripides, *Iphigenia Aulidensis* 976; Philo, *Decal.* 54; Oppianus, *Halieutica* 5.421; Lucian, *Verae historiae* 1.33; and Claudius Aelianus, *De natura animalium* 9.35.

James's treatment of Genesis 1:26 is an example of *aemulatio*: it is not a citation but a rewriting of the text that makes both vocabularic and stylistic adjustments; the allusion is typically not marked as to its ultimate source, although the audience is expected to perceive the predecessor text; and the style of the paraphrase is geared to the audience that is being addressed.

An instance of this kind of emulation is found in Dio's first discourse on kingship. In the course of enumerating the characteristics of a good ruler, including the ruler's ability to control anger, pain, fear, pleasure and desire and to attend both to himself and his subjects, Dio says of the ruler (1.13),

ἀλλ' οἷον οὐδὲ καθεύδειν αὐτὸν ἀξιοῦν δι' ὅλης τῆς νυκτός, ὡς οὐκ οὖσαν αὐτῷ σχολὴν ῥᾳθυμεῖν

but he ought to be just the sort of person who would suppose that he should not sleep the entire night, for he has no leisure to be lazy.

Although Dio mentions Homer in the immediate context (1.12, 14), he does not indicate that this statement is in fact a paraphrase of *Il.* 2.2.24, 61, οὐ χρὴ παννύχιον εὕδειν βουληφόρον ἄνδρα, "A man who is a counselor should not sleep throughout the night." Dio's paraphrase substitutes better Attic equivalents for two of Homer's uncommon words,[36] and then elaborates on the reason for not sleeping the entire night. So extensive is the paraphrase that not a single lexeme of the original remains. Nevertheless, the

---

[36] The Homeric βουληφόρος and παννύχιον were evidently not common in the first and following centuries; they appear, respectively, in Apollonios's *Lexicon Homericum* 52.30 [I CE] and Julius Pollux's *Onomasticon* 1.64 [II CE].

audience would immediately see Homer standing in the background, especially since this Homeric verse was widely quoted elsewhere in the first and second century CE in a chreia concerning Alexander the Great and Diogenes of Sinope.[37]

James's paraphrase of Genesis 1:26 likewise departs from its predecessor text in a variety of ways: the paratactic construction of Genesis 1:26 is avoided in favour of parallel τε καί constructions. This is not only better Greek, but also identifies within Genesis's unorganized division of animals into two pairs of closely related animals, beasts and birds, on the one hand, and reptiles and maritime creatures on the other.[38] The substitutions of θηρία for κτήνη (usually used of domestic animals), and ἐνάλιοι for ἰχθύες are probably an effort to make the description more comprehensive of terrestrial and aquatic life. This division could be seen as a proto-scientific impetus towards classification.

James's paraphrase of Genesis 1:26 is also unmarked. That is, unlike the citation of Leviticus 19:18 and the Ten Words in James 2, marked by κατὰ τὴν γραφήν or ὁ γὰρ εἰπών, James 3:7 simply assumes that the reader or auditor will perceive the allusion to Genesis 1:26. The role of *aemulatio*, as Quintilian says, is to "rival and vie with the original" (10.5.5) for beauty and appropriateness and James

---

[37] See Epictetus, *Diss.* 3.22.90; Theon, *Progymnasmata* (ed. Spengel 2.98). The verse is also quoted in Cornutus, *De natura deorum* 37.9 and in Hermogenes, *Progymnasmata* (ed. Rabe, 10).

[38] τε καί is used infrequently in translations of the Hebrew Bible: only 6x in the LXX Pentateuch; but 8x in 1 Esdras, 3x in the more idiomatic LXX rendering of Esther. It is used 12x in 1–4 Maccabees and once in Matthew, but 32x in Luke-Acts, 8x in Paul and 10x in Hebrews.

does this both by his stylistic reformulation, and by his gestures in the direction of nuancing the classificatory system of Genesis.

The transformations that James effects on Genesis 1:26 provide some insight into the nature of his intended or ideal reader. James accommodates the syntax of the phrase to a higher level of Koinē and his more extensive coverage of the animal kingdoms appeals, presumably, to sophisticated and analytic propensities in his audience. But in order to render his prose even more elevated in its cultural register, he includes a poetic word, ἐνάλιος, from the classical past, rather than avoiding poetic terms as Dio did. James's usage of a word drawn from epic and lyric vocabulary, along with the various rare philosophical words he uses elsewhere, is designed to lend to his prose the impression of erudition, apt of course, in a small discourse that is focused on the qualities of good teachers (3:1–2).

James 3:7–8 Taming and Training

Another vocabularic item in this discourse has resonances with Homeric vocabulary. The same sentence that we have been discussing, 3:7, and the next, 3:8, contain the verb δαμάζειν, used both in the present and the perfect:

> πᾶσα γὰρ φύσις θηρίων τε καὶ πετεινῶν ἑρπετῶν τε καὶ ἐναλίων δαμάζεται καὶ δεδάμασται τῇ φύσει τῇ ἀνθρωπίνῃ· τὴν δὲ γλῶσσαν οὐδεὶς δαμάσαι δύναται ἀνθρώπων· ἀκατάστατον κακόν, μεστὴ ἰοῦ θανατηφόρου

> For every species of beast and bird, reptile and sea-creature is tamed and has been tamed by the human species; but no one is able to tame the tongue of humans; it is a disorderly evil, full of death-dealing poison.

The *aemulatio* of Genesis 1:26 continues in the notion of the 'training' or domination of animals by humans. Genesis 1:26 uses the cohortative, ἀρχέτωσαν, "and let them [humans] rule." Genesis 1:28 reiterates the statement in 1:26 by adding κατακυριεύσατε ('dominate') in relation to the earth, and ἄρχετε ('rule') in relation to animals. These are unexceptional choices: Aristotle (*Pol.* 1.2.8 [1254a.20–27]) uses ἄρχω both in its active and passive senses to describe the practice of rule:

> τὸ γὰρ ἄρχειν καὶ ἄρχεσθαι οὐ μόνον τῶν ἀναγκαίων ἀλλὰ καὶ τῶν συμφερόντων ἐστί ... καὶ εἴδη πολλὰ καὶ ἀρχόντων καὶ ἀρχομένων ἔστιν καὶ ἀεὶ βελτίων ἡ ἀρχὴ ἡ τῶν βελτιόνων ἀρχομένων, οἷον ἀνθρώπου ἢ θηρίου....

> For to rule and to be ruled are not only inevitable but also advantageous.... And there are many species of both ruling and being ruled, and the rule that is exercised over the loftier subject is always the better type, as for example to rule a human being is a better thing than to rule a wild animal.

The other common verbs for 'to tame' are ἡμερεῖν, attested in Wis 16:18, meaning 'to restrain [a flame]' (ἡμεροῦτο φλόξ), and its adjective, ἥμερος, (4 Macc 2:14; 14:15),[39] and ὀχμάζειν, 'to grip,' but used of horses to mean 'to make horses obedient to the bit.'[40]

James's use of δαμάζειν is striking because of the 552 occurrences of the verb before the second century CE, fully one-third are in Homer (mostly the *Iliad*), and if one includes Hesiod (22x), Theognis, Pindar (16x), Euripides, Aeschylus (18x), Euripides (17x), Sophocles, and the citations of Homer

---

[39] The verb is used in Plato, *Resp.* 493β and the noun in Plato, *Sophist* 222b; Aristotle, *Historia animalium* 488a29.

[40] Euripides, *Electra* 817; Sophocles, *Antigone* 351.

in Aristonicus's *De signis Odysseae, De signis Iliadis,* and Apollonius's *Lexicon Homericum,* the percentage of occurrences of the verb in pre-fourth century literature rises to over sixty percent. Thus, although the verb is not restricted to epic, lyric and tragic vocabularies, it is strongly identified with poetry of the fifth century BCE and earlier. The verb often means 'to overpower,' 'to subdue' and even 'to kill,' but it is used of taming animals at *Il.* 23.665 and *Od.* 4.637 and later in Xenophon, *Mem.* 4.1.3 and 4.3.10, Diodorus Siculus *Bibliotheca historica* (5.69.4), Philo, *De congressu* 159; *Leg. all.* 2.104 and the *Testament of Abraham* A 2.29.

As with James's paraphrase of Genesis's list of animals and his use of ἐνάλιος, the paraphrase of ἄρχω with δαμάζειν is an instance of an *aemulatio* of the predecessor text. But while *aemulatio* often involved invoking a Homeric text and substituting more common Attic or Koinē words for Homeric vocabulary, as Dio Chrysostom had done in the case of *Il.* 2.2.24 (see above), James invokes a text from Genesis and substitutes vocabulary whose resonances are with Homer and classical poets. We must ask, why does James do this?

Homer used the verb δαμάζω in its literal sense to describe broken (tamed) and unbroken mules:

ἡμίονον ταλαεργὸν ἄγων κατέδης᾽ ἐν ἀγῶνι ἐξέτε᾽ ἀδμήτην,
ἥ τ᾽ ἀλγίστη δαμάσασθαι · (*Il.* 23.655)

He led a labor-bearing mule and tethered in the place of the context, a mule six years unbroken, the worst of all to tame.

and

Ἀντίνο᾽, ἦ ῥά τι ἴδμεν ἐνὶ φρεσίν, ἦε καὶ οὐκί,
ὁππότε Τηλέμαχος νεῖτ᾽ ἐκ Πύλου ἠμαθόεντος;
νῆά μοι οἴχετ᾽ ἄγων· ἐμὲ δὲ χρεὼ γίγνεται αὐτῆς
Ἤλιδ᾽ ἐς εὐρύχορον διαβήμεναι, ἔνθα μοι ἵπποι

117

δώδεκα θήλειαι, ὑπὸ δ' ἡμίονοι ταλαεργοὶ
ἀδμῆτες· τῶν κέν τιν' ἐλασσάμενος δαμασαίμην. (*Od.* 4.632–637)

Antinoüs, have we any idea when Telemachus will return from Pylos? He has a ship of mine, and I want it to cross over to Elis, where I have twelve brood mares and labor-bearing mules yet unbroken, and I want to bring one of them and break it.

Homeric usage of δαμάζω, however, became the occasion for psychagogic discourse, in particular about the control of the self. In Book 4 of the Odyssey, the bard describes Odysseus:

All things I cannot tell or recount, even all the labours of Odysseus of the steadfast heart; but what a thing was this which that mighty man wrought and endured in the land of the Trojans, where you Achaens suffered woes! Marring his own body with cruel blows (αὐτόν μιν πληγῇσιν ἀεικελίῃσι δαμάσσας), and flinging a wretched garment about his shoulders, in the fashion of a slave he entered the broadwayed city of the foe, and he hid himself under the likeness of another, a beggar, he who was in no wise such an one at the ships of the Achaeans. In this likeness he entered the city of the Trojans, and all of them were but as babes. (*Od.* 4.240–250; Murrary LCL)

Odysseus's 'marring' or 'taming' (δαμάζειν) himself and the practice of taming animals came to serve as a metaphor of the taming of the self, both controlling anger and controlling the tongue. In *Oration* 33 Dio Chrysostom attacks the people of Tarsus for their interest in what philosophy has to offer, but their unwillingness to receive the harsh correction of philosophy. He contrasts speakers who simply flatter and praise their audiences with the one who rebukes and upbraids his hearers, revealing their sins by his words. He invokes Odysseus entering Troy as an example, but reconfigures Odysseus not as one who destroys, but one who has tamed his body and in order that "he may unobtrusively do them some good" by harsh and stubborn words (33.15.4).

The taming of animals came to be a standard psychagogic metaphor for the control of the self. Philo, in *Legum Allegoria* (2.104), invokes the example of the training of horses in order to make them more compliant as a metaphor for the 'taming' of the passions (δαμάζων τὰ πάθη) so that the rider is not drowned in the sea — the sea serving as a metaphor for the unruly and unstable self. Plutarch (*De virtute morali* 451D) compares the taming of horses and oxen to eliminate their 'rebellious kicking and plunging' (τὰ πηδήματα καὶ τοὺς ἀφηνιασμοὺς) with the 'taming of the passions' (τοῖς πάθεσι δεδαμασμένοις) by Reason. As a Platonist, Plutarch did not think that Reason could or should extirpate the passions, but it makes the passions, once tamed, the servant (τὸ ὑπηρετικόν) of Reason.

The control of the self for Plutarch is also a way to control anger, with which James is also concerned (James 1:19–20; 3:9). For Plutarch all of the passions, especially anger, must be tamed and trained (δαμάζοντος καὶ καταθλοῦντος), since without such taming, the power of anger can easily destroy the subject (*De cohibenda ira* 459B).[41]

---

[41] See the Homeric notion of "taming anger" *Od*. XI. 560–64: "Yet no other is to blame but Zeus, who bore terrible hatred against the host of Danaan spearmen and brought on you your doom. Yes, come here, prince, that you might hear my word and my speech; and *tame your anger* [δάμασον δὲ μένος καὶ ἀγήνορα θυμὸν] and your proud spirit."

In the second century Maximus of Tyre repeatedly cited *Od.* 4.242 in order to illustrate the self-discipline used by Diogenes of Sinope,

> Nor did he spare himself but punished [his body] subjected it to many things,
>> he tamed himself by ignominious blows [αὐτόν μιν πληγῇσιν ἀεικελίῃσι δαμάσσας]
>
> and throw rags over his shoulders carelessly.
>
> I omit to mention that a good man when he engages in active pursuits without drawing back or yielding to the depraved, will both preserve himself and turn others to a better life. (*Dissertatio* 15.9.20)

and

> it is also necessary that a champion from Pontus [Diogenes] should engage in a strenuous contest against bitter antagonists, poverty and infamy, cold and hunger. But I praise his exercises:
>> "He tames himself with ignominious blows and throws rags over his shoulders carelessly."
>
> He did not however, on this account vanquish with difficulty. I crown the men, therefore, and proclaim them conquerors in the cause of virtue. (*Dissertatio* 34.9.13)

The Homeric verb δαμάζειν and Homer's story of Odysseus 'taming' himself achieved widespread currency as a metaphor for the philosophical discipline of control of the self. Thus James's paraphrase of Genesis 1:26 with δαμάζειν in place of ἄρχειν exploits the semantic range of the δαμάζειν, which in the first part of James 3:7, πᾶσα γὰρ φύσις... δαμάζεται καὶ δεδάμασται τῇ φύσει τῇ ἀνθρωπίνῃ,[42]

---

[42] Mayor (*James*, 120) notes that James's use of the present passive and perfect (δαμάζεται καὶ δεδάμασται) is also attested in Juvenal *Sat.* 3.190 *quis timet aut timuit gelida Praeneste ruinam aut positis nemorosa inter iuga Volsiniis aut simplicibus Gabiis aut proni Tiburis arce?* "Who at cool Praenest

has the connotation of 'to subdue or dominate,' while the second part, τὴν δὲ γλῶσσαν οὐδεὶς δαμάσαι, evokes the psychagogic model of Odysseus as one who 'tamed' himself through self-discipline. The semantic range of this Homeric verb was the ideal tool for the purpose, and at the same time, lifted the linguistic register of James 3:7 into the range of learned and cultured discourse.

What does James's use of language indicate about the author and the actual audience to whom the letter is addressed? The author employs the rhetorical practice of *aemulatio* throughout the letter, and structures the core argumentative units in the form of the "perfect argument" described in Ps-Cicero's *Rhetorica ad Herennium*.[43] The suite of concerns that are evident in the document, which include the pursuit of wisdom as the highest good, the suppression of desire (ἐπιθυμία) and control of the tongue, the avoidance of both *hybris* and rivalry, the fundamental unity of the Law (2:10) and the indivisibility of πίστις and ἔργα, point to an author interested in the control of the self and the production of moral subjects. The Judaean texture of the letter, with its appeals to *exempla* drawn from the Hebrew Bible, suggest a location in the same general orbit as that of Philo, Pseudo-Phocylides, and the Wisdom of Solomon.

James's appeals to philosophical and epic/lyric vocabulary should not be thought of as forced or artificial,

---

or at Volsinii amid its leafy hills was ever afraid of his house tumbling down?" and 8.70 *qos illis damus ac dedimus quibus omnia debes*, "in addition to those honours which we pay, and have paid, to those to whom we owe your all."

[43] See Patrick J. Hartin, *James* (SP 14; Collegeville, MN: Michael Glazier Books; Liturgical Press, 2003), 124–28, 181–83, 203–07.

but instead reflect a linguistic register common to psychagogic discourses that drew their *exempla* from the heroes of the past and turned them into models who exemplified the virtues of prudence, justice, self-restraint, courage and piety.

To suggest that the linguistic register of James is related to that of Hellenistic psychagogy is not to suggest that this is the only linguistic register in which its author functioned. Speakers (and audiences) typically function in multiple registers, depending on the kinds of activities in which they are engaged, whether it is marketplace transactions, or dinner repartee, or child rearing, or sports or other activities, each with its own register. The choice of a register is likely largely unconscious. "*All* language functions in contexts of situation, and is relatable to those contexts," says Michael Halliday.[44]

> We do not, in fact, first decide what we want to say, independently of setting, and then dress it up in a garb that is appropriate to it in the context.... The 'content' is part of the total planning that takes place. There is no clear line between the 'what' and the 'how'; all language is language-in-use, in a context of situation, and all of it relates to the situation, in the abstract sense in which I am using the term here.[45]

If this is so, the author of James performs in a linguistic register that is peppered with both philosophic and Homeric vocabulary because this is the register appropriate to the audience in view, and appropriate to the kind of psychagogic discourse he envisages. It is a register in

---

[44] Michael A. K. Halliday, *Language as Social Semiotic: The Social Interpretation of Language and Meaning* (London: Edward Arnold, 1978), 32.

[45] Halliday, *Language as Social Semiotic*, 33.

which learned paraphrase of predecessor texts is expected and appeal to moral exemplars, both Greek and Jewish, only adds to the persuasive force of his words.

Irony and Interpretability
in Mark's Passion Narrative

Margaret Froelich

The earliest written account of Jesus's death comprises seventeen verses, and for all its terseness it is one of Mark's more detailed passages; Matthew and Luke found little to add and some to omit. A careful reading reveals a tightly packed narrative that asks its audience to recall particulars of the foregoing Gospel and hold in tension the text itself and the expectations of subsequent christology, history, and tradition. Mark's account is thick with irony, obvious and subtle, much of it lost on later readers who read into the text their own theologies.

This study approaches Mark's Passion with an eye toward the narrative unity of the entire Gospel. This does not preclude acknowledgement and discussion of the evangelist's sources. The question is not *whether* Mark used sources and models, but *how, why,* and, maybe most contentiously, *which ones*. The goal is to discover what we can about Mark's text as a worthy piece of tradition in its own right.

To that end, this paper will tackle several points. First, I analyze the synoptic tradition to show how subsequent writers received Mark, and whether they understood and approved of his portrayal. Second, I highlight some of the ways in which modern scholarship, including MacDonald, has interpreted the text, with particular emphasis on considerations of historicity, source redaction, and literary models. Finally, I will make a case that Mark's Passion narrative relies heavily on multiple levels of irony in order to emphasize the coming Kingdom of God.

For my purposes, the narration of Jesus's death begins at Mark 15:16 and ends at 15:39. I have excluded the women at the cross, burial, and scene at the tomb largely for expediency, but also because these final scenes have a dramatic arc somewhat separate from the death scene, relying more heavily on tension and mystery than irony and pathos (though not to the exclusion of the latter). In her landmark commentary, Adela Yarbro Collins begins the Passion narrative at 14:1 and carries it to the original ending of the Gospel.[1] The section Collins titles "The Crucifixion and Death of Jesus" is 15:21–39.[2] Verses 16–20, the mockery by the soldiers before the crucifixion itself, inhabits an ambiguous position in the narrative, not a part of the trial

---

[1] Adela Yarbro Collins, *Mark: A Commentary*, Hermeneia, (Minneapolis: Fortress Press, 2007), 620. See also Joel Marcus, *Mark 8–16: A New Translation with Introduction and Commentary*, Anchor Bible 27a (New Haven: Yale University Press, 2009). Marcus separates chapter 16 from the Passion narrative, terming it an epilogue. Bas M. F. van Iersel (*Mark: A Reader-Response Commentary* [tr. W. H. Bisscheroux; London: T&T Clark International, 2004]) ends the Passion at 15:39, regarding the burial as part of the epilogue. I find the idea of an "epilogue" unhelpful for thinking about Mark's story. It implies aftermath, perhaps important to tie up loose ends or to look forward in the story world, but not a part of the story proper. Anticlimax is an important part of Mark's storytelling, and the designation "epilogue" artificially pulls the author's punch.

[2] Collins, *Mark*, 730.

but not quite all the way to the execution. In scholarship it is something of a structural orphan, joined to whichever scene a commentator finds most useful. Collins comments on it separately, but Marcus and van Iersel include it in the crucifixion scene.[3] I have chosen ultimately to follow Marcus and van Iersel. The mockery scene sets up an ironic image of Jesus as king, without which the visual of Jesus on the cross is incomplete.

Matthew and Luke alter very little of Mark's narrative, but some of their changes are telling. Both of the later synoptic evangelists omit the names Alexander and Rufus (Mk 15:21//Mt 27:32//Lk 23:26), presumably because they were meaningless to them. The reference to the third hour (Mk 15:25) is also absent from the later texts, though they both keep the references to the sixth and ninth hours (Mk 15:33//Mt 27:45//Lk 23:44). Matthew closely redacts Mark's text. Most of his changes are minor rewordings, including the alternate spelling of the cry of dereliction (Mk 15:34//Mt 27:46), and the change from πορφύραν (Mk 15:17) to χλαμύδα (Mt 27:28), perhaps to add to the realism by substituting a soldier's cloak, which would be on hand.[4] Matthew's single major addition to the text is 27:51b–53 (~Mk 15:38). To the rending of the temple veil he adds an earthquake and the resurrection of "many bodies of saints who had died."

Luke was far less satisfied with Mark's narrative. Aside from general wording changes that we expect from Luke's redactions of Mark, he omits a number of details: the

---

[3] Collins, *Mark*, 722; Marcus, *Mark*, 1038; van Iersel, *Mark*, 465–66.
[4] Marcus, *Mark*, 1040.

praetorium and battalion (Mk 15:16); the wine with myrrh (Mk 15:23); the mockery of the crowd (Mk 15:29); the cry of dereliction; and the names of the women at the cross (Mk 15:40). Luke's additions are also more extensive. He adds a four-verse lament for the women of Jerusalem to the procession to Golgotha (Lk 23:27–31); additional mockery by the soldiers once Jesus is on the cross (Lk 23:36–7); an extended exchange between Jesus and the two others crucified alongside him (Lk 23:39–43); and a cry of submission as Jesus dies (Lk 23:46). In both of the later synoptics we see a dissatisfaction with Mark's tone. By the time he dies, Mark's Jesus is humiliated, broken, and abandoned. Matthew's apocalyptic-sounding earthquake and resurrection of the righteous dead do not diminish Jesus's suffering, but they flesh out and add a positive element to Mark's ambiguous scene. Ulrich Luz interprets this christologically: "God intervenes powerfully in what is happening.... Matthew allows not the slightest suspicion that Jesus could have suffered only for the sake of appearances."[5] Luke goes even farther: his changes downplay the suffering and portray a Jesus more accepting of his fate (though not so in control of it as John would have). The substitution of Psalm 30 for 21 (a cry of submission instead of dereliction) expresses a confidence that things are going to plan. As François Bovon puts it, "because he knows that God is stronger than the enemies and than death itself."[6]

---

[5] Ulrich Luz, *Matthew 21–28: A Commentary* (tr. James E. Crouch; Hermeneia; Minneapolis: Fortress Press, 2005), 571.

[6] François Bovon, *Luke 3: A Commentary on the Gospel of Luke 19:28–24:53* (tr. James Crouch; Hermeneia; Minneapolis: Fortress Press, 2012), 326.

So much for Mark as a source. The question of the earliest Gospel's own antecedents is quite a bit murkier, though there are a number of proposed solutions. Rudolph Bultmann took Mark's Passion narrative to be "a legendary editing of what is manifestly an ancient historical narrative to which we may trace back vv. [15:]20b–24a."[7] The form critic allowed little room for Markan redaction in the death account, let alone authorship. Most elements he ascribed to legend, frequently but not entirely based on prophetic literature and Psalms. Psalm 21 (LXX; Psalm 22 MT) is his most common target, with references throughout chapter 15. A short analysis of each of Bultmann's proposed antetexts will be helpful here.[8]

Mark 15:24 — Psalm 21:18[9]

Bultmann attributes the time references (vv. 25, 33, and 34) to Markan redaction. The Psalm citation here reads, "They divided my cloak among themselves, and cast lots for my clothing." The text certainly does seem to be a loose citation of scripture, sharing all the major vocabulary and differing only in the specifics of person and aspect to fit the narrative. Counter to Bultmann, Collins argues that this does not exclude historical occurrence, as it was a known custom for the executioner to take the property the condemned

---

[7] Rudolph Bultmann, *The History of the Synoptic Tradition* (2nd rev. ed.; tr. John Marsh; New York: Harper & Row, Publishers, 1968), 273.

[8] Bultmann, *History*, 273–74.

[9] Greek citations and reference for English translations of the LXX are from Lancelot C. L. Brenton, *The Septuagint with Apocrypha: Greek and English* (2nd printing; Peabody, MA: Hendrickson Publishers, 1986), which is primarily based on the fourth-century Vaticanus MS.

person had on hand, at least until the time of Hadrian.[10] Whether or not we can count this verse as an accurate depiction of Jesus's execution, it is a believable addition to the narrative, expressed poetically in terms of scripture.

MacDonald considers the *Iliad*'s death of Hector to be the primary literary model for Mark's Passion. He does not turn his attention to this verse in any particular detail, as it is a clear citation of Psalm 21 and as such is not directly salient to MacDonald's project. If mimesis criticism is able to show a direct relationship between Mark's Passion and Hector's, however, verse 24 maybe of some interest. Achilles strips Hector's armor (*Il.* 22.367–70) — perhaps in fact his own, since Hector stripped Patroclus of the purloined armor in book 16. This is a small detail, and little should be made of it on its own. If Mark had the Homeric custom in mind he was not concerned that the audience should recognize his use of it, except perhaps on a second reading, after having made the connections to *Iliad* 22 later in the chapter.

Mark 15:27 — Isaiah 53:12

This verse from Isaiah is more properly an antetext to verse 28, "And the scripture was fulfilled that says, 'And he was counted with the lawless,'" which is lacking in the earliest manuscripts and is likely a harmonization with Luke 22:37. Bultmann does "not presume to say" whether verse 27 exhibits the influence of Isaiah.[11] The connection is weak without 28 and requires a fairly literal reading of ἐν τοῖς ἀνόμοις that the prophetic text does not support. Collins

---

[10] Collins, *Mark*, 745.
[11] Bultmann, *History*, 273.

remarks that 27 "seems to evoke" the Isaiah passage, but her reasoning is unconvincing.[12] She lists several places in the Gospel where Jesus either interacts with or is compared to criminals, but with no direct citation to Isaiah there is nothing quite distinctive enough to be sure of a link. By the evidence of Luke and verse 28 we know that the connection between the two passages developed early in Christian tradition, and it is not impossible that the author had the LXX text in mind, but if he did he left no definite clue. I speculate whether modern commentators would have thought of the connection had Luke not.

The more obvious precursor to this passage is within the Gospel itself: in Mark 10:35–40 James and John ask to sit on Jesus's right and left hands in his glory. His response looks back to the passion prediction of 10:32–34: to sit on his right and left means to suffer. Later copyists, uncomfortable with the open-ended οἷς ἡτοίμασται, and who perhaps missed the imagery of 15:27, added ὑπὸ τοῦ πάτρος to 10:40, but the original reading gives no reason why the more immediate agent could not have been Pilate. Collins and Marcus both recognize this parallel;[13] Marcus suggests that the image in both cases is one of a royal retinue or bodyguard.

Mark 15:29–32 — Psalm 21:7–8; Lamentations 2:15

Both of these texts express mockery of a defeated one. There is quite a bit in common with the Markan text. In particular, all three passages contain some form of κινέω

[12] Collins, *Mark*, 748.
[13] Collins, *Mark*, 748; Marcus, *Mark*, 1051.

κεφαλὴν, and they are structurally similar: A declarative statement describes the actions of a group (πάντες in both LXX passages; οἱ παραπορευόμενοι and οἱ ἀρχιερεῖς in Mark) that derides the victim (first person in the Psalm, second in Lamentations, and third in Mark). A statement by the mockers follows, expressing sarcasm or belittlement. Mark also shares παραπορευόμενοι with Lamentations.

The object of scorn in Lamentations is Jerusalem, and the passersby ridicule the fallen state of the city. In that sense, Mark's line seems more closely related to the Psalmist's. The crowd's σῶσον σεαυτὸν which the high priests echo in the negative, reflects σωσάτο αὐτὸν in the Psalm, and, seeing the connection, Matthew quotes the LXX text explicitly in 27:43. Collins regards the Markan passage to be an expansion of a pre-Markan Passion source, and she presents a reconstruction of the "original" passage that is about half the length, omits characteristically Markan elements such as the high priests and the reference to the temple, and reads like an intentional paraphrase of the Psalm passage.[14] She does not state whether she regards this source as a historically reliable account of the crucifixion. Marcus does not deny the influence of the LXX here, but also does not believe it to exclude the possibility of historical memory, or at least early tradition: "Is it implausible that Jesus would have been mocked as a king both at the conclusion of his trial and on the cross?"[15]

---

[14] Collins, *Mark*, 749.
[15] Marcus, *Mark*, 1045.

Mark 15:34—Psalm 21:1

I am aware of no disagreement with this connection. Mark's wording of the Greek is different from that in the Vaticanus LXX, but this is not surprising. Mark may have cited directly from a version available to him, cited directly from an Aramaic source and translated it without recourse to a Greek text, or changed the wording to suit his needs. Vincent Taylor and others consider the cry of dereliction historical and originally in Hebrew, as Matthew has it, rather than Aramaic, to make more sense of the pun on "Elijah."[16] Collins's instinct is more correct: "We have no way of knowing what the historical Jesus actually felt as he died or what his last words on the cross, if any, were."[17] Instead she focuses on the fact that Mark avoids or subverts the trope of noble death, a topic that I will flesh out below.

Mark 15:36—Psalm 68:21

There is some difficulty in connecting these two verses. Both use ὄξος, but Collins makes a case that this was perhaps the most common type of wine in the ancient world, and cites a number of different contexts, including medicine, where it appears in literature.[18] In these various citations the most negative connotation is the wine's cheapness; it seems to occupy an otherwise neutral-to-positive place in ancient thought. Its inferior quality is most likely the reason it appears in the Psalm, and the negative tone there is more

---

[16] Vincent Taylor, *The Gospel According to St. Mark: The Greek Text with Introduction, Notes, and Indexes* (2nd ed.; Grand Rapids: Baker Book House, 1981), 593.

[17] Collins, *Mark*, 754.

[18] Collins, *Mark*, 756–57.

properly a function of the context than the wine itself — verse 19 reads, "For you know my blame, and my disgrace, and my shame." Mark's purpose seems to be remedial. The statement of the person offering the drink implies that the intent is to prolong Jesus's life in case Elijah comes for him. Though Jesus is certainly the object of scorn in Mark's text, and verse 36 may indeed be a part of general mockery, the ὄξος on its own does not seem a significant part of his humiliation. It is simply a common beverage, often used for medicinal reasons. The author could have easily used water without severely altering the meaning.

The examination of these five passages leads to the conclusion that Mark was familiar with at least Psalm 21 and found it a fitting source of language to describe parts of Jesus's death. Van Iersel suggests that the Psalm functions to trigger a larger realization: "what the reader of the Old Testament should have known all along, namely, that these things would happen to Jesus."[19] To some extent, then, the Psalm citations serve as proof to Jesus's own statements regarding what "is written about the Son of Man" (9:12). Vernon K. Robbins has observed that the allusions to and citations of Psalm 21 appear in reverse order in Mark.[20] In this he sees a "subversion" of the Psalmist's rhetoric, transforming a poem that is ultimately hopeful about the faithfulness and deliverance of God into a tragic and

---

[19] Van Iersel, *Mark*, 470.
[20] Vernon K. Robbins, "The Reversed Contextualization of Psalm 22 in the Markan Crucifixion," *Sea Voyages and Beyond: Emerging Strategies in Socio-Rhetorical Interpretation* (ESEC 14; Dorset: Deo Publishing, 2010), 258–281. My thanks to Michael Kochenash for alerting me to this piece.

inescapable death scene.[21] This elegant reading acknowledges Mark's adherence both to the popular Christian view that Jesus and his Passion were revealed in antiquity through the prophets and David, and to his own theme of the subversion of Messianic expectations. However, it is clear that Mark was not concerned with mining the Psalm for its quite distinctive and visceral descriptions of violence and death.

An even fuller interpretation of Mark's narrative can be had through MacDonald's recent work, *The Gospels and Homer*.[22] MacDonald argues that the shape of the scene is modeled on Homer's death of Hector in *Iliad* 22 and that such a reading brings the Gospel's irony into stark relief. He begins with a list of "traditional information" about the death of Jesus that would have been current in Christian communities before Mark, gleaned from the letters of Paul and from MacDonald's reconstruction of Q.[23] This reads as a sort of bare-bones summary of the Passion narrative, beginning with Jesus's predictions of his return and the destruction of the Jerusalem temple, and ending with post-resurrection appearances and the establishment of the apostolic church in Jerusalem. The list excludes specific details such as characters (other than Jesus), speech, and dramatic tension. Onto this frame MacDonald adds the LXX

---

[21] Robbins, "Psalm 22," 277–78.

[22] Dennis MacDonald, *The Gospels and Homer: Imitations of Greek Epic in Mark and Luke-Acts* (Lanham: Rowman & Littlefield, 2015).

[23] MacDonald, *Gospels and Homer*, 88. For MacDonald's construction of Q see *Two Shipwrecked Gospels: The* Logoi of Jesus *and Papias's* Exposition of Logia about the Lord (ECL 8; Atlanta: Society of Biblical Literature, 2012).

citations already discussed. However, quite a bit of Mark's narrative remains unaccounted for. In his words, "the LXX/OG cannot explain characterization, type-scenes, or plot development," and none of these things relevant to the Passion appear in Paul or the *Logoi of Jesus*.[24]

The death of Hector, MacDonald asserts, makes up some of the gap. The mockery, both after the trial and at the cross, conforms to a Homeric trope. "Deaths of combatants in the *Iliad* often begin with a threatening taunt that includes, somewhat ironically, an acknowledgement of the lofty pedigree or valor of the opponent."[25] In the epic this serves to elevate the glory of the mocker: Iliadic warfare is as much about individual competition as it is about putting cities under siege, and there is no honor to be had in an easy fight. Nobles go up against men of their own rank, and an earnest recitation of the opponent's pedigree and accomplishments is proof that the winner has conquered someone mighty. This is not the case in Mark. The soldiers, crowd, and high priests "honor" Jesus with tongues firmly in cheeks. They spit what they perceive to be his own claims back in his face, not to acknowledge his status as a worthy opponent, but to add verbal sting to his physical humiliation.

Nonetheless, not all of the taunts volleyed between Hector and Achilles are honorable. When Achilles misses a throw Hector responds with what MacDonald calls a "defiant imperative," declaring, "You will not plant your spear in my back as I flee; drive yours through my chest as I

---

[24] MacDonald, *Gospels and Homer*, 88–89.
[25] MacDonald, *Gospels and Homer*, 89.

charge straight ahead, if a god grants it!"[26] This is comparable to the taunts in Mark and also those in Psalm 22. In fact, the conditional taunt is so common ("Catch me if you can!") that it is difficult to make a case for direct literary imitation on the basis of this instance alone, without more distinctive features. However, this is not the only element of the passion scene that resembles the Homeric tale.

Jesus's refusal of wine in verse 23 also calls a Homeric precedent to MacDonald's mind. Hecuba, Hector's mother, offers him "honey-sweet wine" so that he can honor the gods with it and bolster his own strength, but Hector demurs, lest the alcohol numb him and lessen his courage and prowess.[27] Collins also suggests that Jesus's abstinence here is connected to portrayals of noble death, though she prefers to cite early Christian sources such as Tertullian, rather than Homer.[28]

There are two features possibly in MacDonald's favor, though neither comes directly from the text of Mark. Collins and others have noted that wine spiced with myrrh would have been a delicacy. Pliny the Younger mentions "savory" and "peppered wines," and says that "The finest wines in early days were those spiced with the scent of myrrh."[29] This will contribute to the discussion of irony later on, but for now it is distinctive in that it shows that Mark was describing the taste of the wine. Such a specific detail is unnecessary to the narrative, but could reflect μελιδέα in the

---

[26] *Il.* 22.283–84, tr. MacDonald, *Gospels and Homer*, 90.

[27] *Il.* 6. 242–65; MacDonald, *Gospels and Homer*, 50.

[28] Collins, *Mark*, 743–44.

[29] *Hist. nat.* 14.15.92; 14.19.107. Cited in Collins, *Mark*, 741.

Homeric text. Further, some commentators have noted that at one point it was the practice for Jerusalem noblewomen to distribute wine to those being executed, as an act of mercy. Collins rightly notes that all mentions of this practice are rabbinic and therefore not directly relevant to Mark,[30] but that does not exclude the possibility of the practice being current in the first century. If Mark expected his reader to see women — and specifically noble women — in the ambiguous subject of ἐδίδουν in verse 23, perhaps he meant it to reflect the queen of Troy.

The cry of dereliction may also find a reflection of itself in the *Iliad*. Although, as we have seen, Mark 15:34 is a citation of Psalm 22, it also could reflect Athena's abandonment of Hector at the crucial moment in the fight and the latter's cry of woe.[31] Mark's choice to cite the Jewish scriptures rather than the Greek epic obscures the possible connection, but, as we shall see, the irony and narrative arc of the scene lends itself to interpretation through the *Iliad* more satisfactorily than through the Psalm.

Interestingly, it is what happens after Jesus's death that gives MacDonald the distinctive trait he needs. There are a number of proposals to explain the rending of the temple veil in verse 38. Stephen Motyer reads it as the end of an inclusio together with Jesus's baptism in chapter 1.[32] He is not the first to see the parallels between the two passages, particularly on the basis of the shared verb σχίζω,[33] though

---

[30] Collins, *Mark*, 742.

[31] MacDonald, *Gospels and Homer*, 91–92.

[32] Stephen Motyer, "The Rending of the Veil: A Markan Pentecost?" *NTS* 33 (1987): 155–57.

[33] See Motyer, "Rending," 157 n.1.

Tom Shepherd's landmark dissertation on the topic of Markan inclusio does not seem to reference this connection.[34] Other scholars focus on the significance of the curtain itself and whether Mark's emphasis is on the destruction of the temple or the democratization of the Holy of Holies.[35] What has received little attention, however, is the enigmatic ἀπ᾽ ἄνωθεν ἕως κάτω, which is unusually descriptive for Mark. Howard M. Jackson argued that this detail was to signal the visibility of the event, so that the centurion could witness it from Golgotha and make his confession on that basis.[36] Even if one supposes that Mark was wholly unfamiliar with the geography of Jerusalem, this is a fantastic claim. At any rate, the expression "from top to bottom" does not connote visibility so much as completeness, which is where MacDonald's solution is most compelling.

MacDonald follows many others in saying that the tearing of the curtain "apparently anticipates the destruction of the temple and suggests that by killing Jesus those who had accused him of wishing to destroy it were the ones who doomed it."[37] What is new, though, is his connection of the prepositional phrase to κατ᾽ ἄκρης in the *Iliad*, noting of this unit, "whenever it appears in the epic it refers to the fall of Troy."[38] In both narratives, for different reasons, the death

---

[34] Tom Shepherd, *Markan Sandwich Stories: Narration, Definition, and Function* (AUSDDS 18; Berrien Springs, MI: Andrews University Press, 1993).

[35] See Collins, *Mark*, 759–64, for a summary of the discussion.

[36] Howard M. Jackson, "The Death of Jesus in Mark and the Miracle from the Cross," *NTS* 33 (1987): 23.

[37] MacDonald, *Gospels and Homer*, 92.

[38] MacDonald, *Gospels and Homer*, 92.

of the hero is connected with his city's destruction: Hector is Troy's greatest warrior and functions as its protector in the epic, and Mark's christology places the suffering and death of Jesus in complex relationships with both the Jerusalem temple and the Roman destruction of it.

I remarked above that Mark betrays his familiarity of Psalm 21 through clear citation of it. This is less obviously the case with the Homeric epic, as much of the shared material is fairly generic, and the closest literal similarity is ἀπ᾽ ἄνωθεν ἕως κάτω, a Koine paraphrase of the archaic line. Neither is Mark more indebted to Homer than to the Psalmist for his order: generally the death of Jesus follows the same sequence as that of Hector, but we should expect it to by definition, and the refusal of wine from *Iliad* 6 and the distribution of Jesus's clothing interrupt the sequence. Reading the *Iliad* as a literary model, however, adds to the interpretability of the scene.

Psalm 21 does not traffic in irony. Its shift from despair to hope operates completely in the open, and we have no sense that the narrator or the situation is anything other than the presentation suggests. Reading the crucifixion through the lens of this text produces a similar result: Jesus is humiliated and in misery, but the final result will be the glorification of God. A fine and legitimate christological interpretation, but from a narrative standpoint it does not satisfy the thick sarcasm about the scene. Robbins's reading, which inverts the order of the Psalm (from hope to despair) in order to emphasize Jesus's suffering, hits closer to the mark. Association with Hector, however, uncovers additional possibilities for interpretation. We see in Mark's text a reversal not of the sequence, but of the values in Homer's. Jesus tests the boundaries of a noble death, begging to be released from his fate in 14:36 and crying out in anguish on the cross. Hector's death is the doom of his people; Jesus's is the beginning of their salvation. The *Iliad* ends with the lavish funeral of the Trojan hero; the Passion ends with a lonely burial, and the Gospel with the ultimately uncommunicated news of the resurrection of Jesus Christ.

Aside from these reversals of significance, the irony in Mark's Passion operates on several levels. On the surface is the irony in the mouths of those witnessing the crucifixion; second is the irony of the reality of Jesus versus his followers' expectation, which the audience should remember from previous scenes and especially the Passion predictions; and finally the overarching dramatic irony of Mark's christology and his audience's knowledge, which turns the mockery of the soldiers, crowd, and priests into true honors of Jesus as king.

For Marcus, the crucifixion is "the climactic event in a sick parody of royal coronation."[39] This parody begins in verse 16 when the soldiers, after leading Jesus into the courtyard, clothe him in purple and crown him with thorny

---

[39] Marcus, *Mark*, 1051.

plants.[40] The inscription, the mockery of Jesus as King of the Jews, the attendants on his right and left, and even the image of crucifixion itself all contribute. Marcus presents several other cases in ancient literature that treat crucifixion in this manner. In a description of a particular Persian execution, Dio Chrysostom "concludes that the crucifixion of the Persian king pro tem was meant to show 'foolish and wicked people' that they would come to 'a most shameful and wretched end' if they insolently attempted to acquire royal power."[41] Collins also calls attention to the fact that though the soldiers remove the purple garment, the text does not mention whether they also take the crown off of Jesus before his crucifixion. This is a small detail, and we should not necessarily read into it, but she muses that if Mark does intend for us to imagine Jesus crucified with the crown (a common representation in later art), it adds to the irony of the scene.[42]

> Further, Marcus suggests that this dissonance was an intentional part of crucifixion in general: this strangely 'exalting' mode of execution was designed to mimic, parody, and puncture the pretentions of

[40] Collins (*Mark*, 726) questions the common translation of ἀκάνθινον, "thorns," suggesting that it properly refers to the actual Syrian acanthus (*Acanthus syriacus*). The leaves of this plant are quite spiny, but it does not bear the grisly, nail-like thorns common in artistic representations of the scene. In the context of the passage, she observes that the soldiers' intent in crowning him is mockery, rather than pure torture, so "they wove the crown out of the material that they found near at hand." My translation here attempts to honor this context and, at the same time, acknowledge the primary connotation of the Greek word, which indicates thorns and not necessarily a specific genus or species of plant. We lose nothing in our interpretation of this scene by imagining Jesus in more pain.

[41] Marcus, *Mark*, 1133.

[42] Collins, *Mark*, 728.

insubordinate transgressors by displaying a deliberately horrible mirror of their self-elevation.[43]

It does not take much imagination to ascribe this logic also to Jesus's execution. βασιλεύς is not an epithet for Jesus at all in Mark, but from the trial before Pilate to the end of the death scene it appears six times.[44] No one who speaks during the crucifixion, except for Jesus himself, believes the claims they attribute to him, but their ironic mockery is doubly so for the audience, who knows that Jesus is the Son of God, and likely expects him to take the crown of an eschatological king. Jerry Camery-Hoggatt refers to the mockery as "a perfect masque of the truth it parodies,"[45] a truth that the actors in the text cannot see, but that would be obvious to those reading Mark's Gospel. Jesus, for Mark, is of course a king.

The irony is not only a situation of who knows what. Mark's Gospel is full of conflicting expectations in preparation for this scene. The three Passion predictions and the responses they generate display the disconnect between the Messiah that Peter and his comrades expect and the Messiah that Jesus is. Verse 8:35 is the epitome of Jesus's paradoxical message, one that he demonstrates in full at the end of the Gospel. After all, the resurrection, that cornerstone of Pauline christology, would be impossible without the crucifixion.

---

[43] Joel Marcus, "Crucifixion as Parodic Exaltation," *JBL* 125 (2006): 78.

[44] Marcus, "Crucifixion," 73.

[45] Jerry Camery-Hoggatt, *Irony in Mark's Gospel: Text and Subtext* (SNTSMS 72; Cambridge: Cambridge University Press, 1992), 174.

The epitome of the scene's extended irony is the declaration of the centurion. It is generally, though by no means universally, assumed that this "confession" is in earnest and that the centurion, in Collins's words, "saw *rightly* in contrast to the other bystanders mentioned in vv. 35–36."[46] This position has led to a mass of investigation as to what the centurion saw and what should be read as the proper antecedent to ὅτι οὕτως ἐξέπνευσεν. As we have seen, Jackson considered it to be the rending of the veil, as, perhaps, did Bultmann.[47] Bultmann and others have also suggested the darkness of verse 33.[48] Collins and Marcus propose that the centurion's earnest confession is, ironically, in response to Jesus's suffering. Marcus focuses on the soldier's use of the term υἱὸς θεοῦ: "But the local representative of Roman power now sees that it is neither the emperor nor his revolutionary opponents but '*this* man,' who has just died in agony on a Roman cross, who is the true revelation of divine sonship and hence of royal sovereignty."[49] Collins arrives at a comparable conclusion, citing translation fables and Roman stories about the omens that accompany the death of a demigod.[50]

Others disagree. From a narrative standpoint it is important that no character has uttered a single earnest word since Pilate sentenced Jesus, except for the cry of

[46] Collins, *Mark*, 766, emphasis original.

[47] Bultmann, *History*, 274.

[48] See Collins, *Mark*, 765.

[49] Marcus, *Mark*, 1068.

[50] Collins, *Mark*, 766–67.

dereliction.[51] Robert Fowler sees this pattern, and the fact that the very last mention of soldiers in the Gospel had them dressing Jesus up in purple and crowning him with thorns, and concludes that 15:39 must be sarcastic.[52] MacDonald concurs, comparing this utterance with the gloat of Achilles after killing Hector, "whom the Trojans in the city prayed to as a god."[53] An earnest confession would carry its own irony—a previously unheard-of Roman declaring what Jesus's closest associates still fail to understand—but if it is insincere it preserves the level of irony already operational throughout the Passion scene. That is, the audience knows to be true what the characters only say in cruel jest.

Conclusion

Commentators often propose or assume "pre-Markan" sources, but are rarely explicit as to what these sources might be. There is no synoptic formula through which to tease out an earlier text, and those committed to such a text's existence rely ultimately on subjective clues from the language and structure, but often not the story, of the Gospel itself. The elements of the Passion scene that Bultmann most easily ascribes to Mark's invention are the time references, which have the least impact on the message of the narrative—source criticism is rarely concerned with

---

[51] There is even a reasonable christological argument that 15:34 is ironic, or at least wrong. The Passion predictions are clear that suffering is part of God's plan. In that light, the moment of greatest suffering cannot be a moment of divine abandonment.

[52] Robert M. Fowler, *Let the Reader Understand: Reader-Response Criticism and the Gospel of Mark* (Minneapolis: Fortress Press, 1991), 207.

[53] *Il.* 22.394; MacDonald, *Gospels and Homer*, 93.

narrative. The advent and popularity of narrative criticism and other literary-critical methods have legitimized Mark himself as an author to some extent, but have not eliminated speculation about sources. MacDonald is correct in referring to a pre-Markan Passion tradition, available to us through Paul and Q, for there surely was such a tradition. This study, however, has shown that Mark closely and intentionally weaves tradition with Jewish and Greek literature into a dense narrative that uses irony and imagery to express Jesus's kingship and to place blame on Jerusalem for his death and its own destruction.

The Forgotten Playground[1]

Matthew Ryan Hauge

Introduction

In the fall of 1999, I enrolled as a doctoral student in Religion (New Testament) at Claremont Graduate University. As fate would have it, Professor Dennis R. MacDonald had recently been appointed the John Wesley Professor of New Testament and Christian Origins at the Claremont School of Theology and was preparing for the publication of his watershed work, *The Homeric Epics and the Gospel of Mark.*[2] From the very beginning, his method, textual comparisons, and reframing of "gospel truth" captured my imagination and transformed my understanding of the purpose of early Christian composition.

Recent developments in the study of the New Testament have challenged the dominant scholarly tradition on Christian origins and literary composition. The hitherto clearly marked boundaries between the Christian community and the Greco-Roman environment have been successfully blurred; although Judaism remains an indispensable context for the study of early Christian

---

[1] Portions of this essay are adapted from Matthew Ryan Hauge, *The Biblical Tour of Hell* (LNTS 485; London: T&T Clark, 2013), and are included with the permission of Bloomsbury Publishing.

[2] Dennis R. MacDonald, *The Homeric Epics and the Gospel of Mark* (New Haven: Yale University Press, 2000).

literature, the interpretive relevance of the "pagan" world can no longer be ignored.

Over the past two decades, MacDonald has championed the mimetic-critical approach, investigating the literary relationship between the Homeric epics and the apocryphal Acts of Andrew, the Gospel of Mark, and Luke-Acts. Through his work and others, the stranglehold of form criticism is slowly losing its grip. The shift from historical criticism to literary criticism has succeeded in recasting the evangelists, not as mere collectors of pre-existent traditions, but rather as literary artists. MacDonald enabled, empowered, and inspired us all to rediscover the forgotten playground of pagan literature.

Greco-Roman Education and the Shadow of the Bard

MacDonald began his journey into the world of ancient epic and early Christian composition with the publication of *Christianizing Homer: The Odyssey, Plato, and the Acts of Andrew* in 1994.[3] In this controversial study, he argued the apocryphal *Acts of Andrew* was a mimetic transformation of Homer, Euripides, and several Platonic dialogues. His method, "mimesis criticism," was a relatively new approach for comparing texts, one which was based upon the mimetic ethos of Greco-Roman education and ancient composition.

---

[3] Dennis R. MacDonald, *Christianizing Homer: The Odyssey, Plato, and the Acts of Andrew* (Oxford: Oxford University Press, 1994). See also his earlier examination of this same apocryphal tradition, *The Acts of Andrew and the Acts of Andrew and Matthias in the City of the Cannibals* (Atlanta: Society of Biblical Literature, 1990).

At each curricular stage, primary, secondary, and tertiary students were taught to read and write through the practice of literary imitation (μίμησις; Lat. *imitatio*) of the canonical models of Greek literature, especially Homer. In advanced rhetorical and literary composition, pedagogues encouraged their students to borrow from multiple models, concealing and advertising their model so that the reader may benefit from the comparison. This literary practice involved both μίμησις and ζῆλος (Lat. *aemulatio*), a friendly rivalry in which the imitator strove to improve upon his model.

The classical treatments of Greek and Roman education drew primarily upon the elite educationalists, but more recent studies have incorporated the growing number of papyri, ostraca, and tablets from Greco-Roman Egypt that reflect the educational practices of more diverse strata of ancient society.[4] Greco-Roman education was largely a private enterprise, but there was remarkable consistency among educational practices from the fourth century BCE to

---

[4] For the classical treatments, see Henry Irénée Marrou, *A History of Education in Antiquity* (tr. George Lamb; New York: Sheed & Ward, 1956), 142–85; and Stanley Frederick Bonner, *Education in Ancient Rome: From the Elder Cato to the Younger Pliny* (Berkeley: University of California Press, 1977), 165–249. For the more recent discussions, see Teresa Morgan, *Literate Education in the Hellenistic and Roman Worlds* (Cambridge: Cambridge University Press, 1998); Rafaella Cribiore, *Writing, Teachers, and Students in Graeco-Roman Egypt* (*ASP* 36; Atlanta: Scholars Press, 1996); and *Gymnastics of the Mind: Greek Education in Hellenistic and Roman Egypt* (Princeton: Princeton University Press, 2001).

the fifth century CE.[5] Raffaella Cribiore comments on this unexpected phenomenon:

> Education was based on the transmission of an established body of knowledge, about which there was wide consensus. Teachers were considered the custodians and interpreters of a tradition and were concerned with protecting its integrity. Education was supposed to lead to a growing understanding of an inherited doctrine. Admiration for the past gave rise to the aspiration to model oneself on one's predecessors and to maintain the system and methods that had formed them.[6]

The static nature of education in antiquity was a reflection of its purpose as a "marker of Greek identity" and beyond the primary stage, a social indicator of the aristocrat; education served as a means to train children to become ideal Greek citizens.[7] And as Teresa Morgan notes in her study, *Literate Education in the Hellenistic and Roman Worlds*, cast over this ideal was the shadow of the bard: "Reading Homer is, among other things, a statement of Greek identity."[8]

---

[5] Peter Heather, "Literacy and Power in the Migration Period," *Literacy and Power in the Ancient World* (ed. Alan K. Bowman and Greg Woolf; Cambridge: Cambridge University Press, 1994), 177–97.

[6] Cribiore, *Gymnastics of the Mind*, 8.

[7] Rubén René Dupertuis, "The Summaries in Acts 2, 4 and 5 and Greek Utopian Literary Traditions" (Ph.D. diss., Claremont Graduate University, 2005), 52.

[8] Morgan, *Literate Education*, 75. For a thorough treatment of the role of Homer in Greco-Roman education, see the discussion by Ronald F. Hock, "Homer in Greco-Roman Education," *Mimesis and Intertextuality in Antiquity and Christianity* (ed. Dennis R. MacDonald; Studies in Antiquity and Christianity; Harrisburg, PA: Trinity International Press, 2001), 56–77.

Education in the Greco-Roman world was divided into roughly three stages: primary, secondary, and tertiary.[9] The first stage of education could be taught in the home or supervised in the classroom of a "teacher of letters" (γραμματιστής).[10] Students began by learning to identify and write the letters of the alphabet as well as copying and pronouncing increasingly difficult syllabic combinations.[11]

After mastering the alphabet, they turned to reading proper. The students would be asked to copy word lists arranged alphabetically or topically; it is at this early stage, they would be introduced to the model κατ' ἐξοχήν, Homer.[12] In her analysis of the extant word lists, Cribiore documents the overwhelming presence of Homeric names, especially those that figure predominantly in the epics.[13]

---

[9] For an excellent discussion of the historical development of the standard curriculum, see Morgan, *Literate Education*, 1–49.

[10] Alan D. Booth, "The Appearance of the 'Schola Grammatici'," *Hermes* 106 (1978): 117–25; also see "Elementary and Secondary Education in the Roman Empire," *Florilegium* 1 (1979):1–14 and Cribiore, *Writing*, 173–284.

[11] For more detailed treatments of the primary stage, see Marrou, *Education*, 150–54; Bonner, *Education*, 166–72; and Cribiore, *Writing*, 37–43 and 175–96; also *Gymnastics of the Mind*, 50–53 and 160–84.

[12] Pliny the Younger (61–112 CE) notes that Homer is the first lesson in school (*Ep.* 2.14.3). This statement is substantiated by Roger A. Pack's examination of the Egyptian papyri; according to his count, there are over six-hundred and seventy extant fragments of Homer, eighty of Demosthenes, over seventy of both Euripides and Hesiod, forty-three of Isocrates, forty-two of Plato, twenty-eight of Aeschylus, twenty-seven of Xenophon, and ten of Aristotle (*The Greek and Latin Literary Texts from Graeco-Roman Egypt* [2d ed., Ann Arbor: University of Michigan Press, 1965]).

[13] Cribiore, *Writing*, 42–43, 196–203, 269–70, 274–76, 280–81 and 283; see also Morgan, *Literate Education*, 101–04 and 275–87; Pack, *Literary Texts*, 137–40; and Janine Debut, "Les documents scholaires," *ZPE* 63 (1986): 251–78.

According to Janine Debut, these lists functioned not only as a tool for practicing reading, they were used to instruct students in the cultural heritage of antiquity, including mythology, history, geography, and philosophy.[14]

Word lists were then replaced with small pieces of poetry, maxims and χρεῖαι, and eventually longer passages, typically from Homer.[15] At this point, students were expected to learn to write not only with precision, but with speed.[16] In short, the primary level of education trained students to reproduce their literary models accurately and efficiently; along the way, however, a more profound lesson was absorbed: "A god, not man, was Homer" (Θεὸς οὐδ' ἄνθρωπος Ὅμηρος).[17]

For most students, their education would conclude after acquiring these basic scribal skills, but some would continue under the tutelage of a "teacher of language and literature" (γραμματικός).[18] At the secondary stage, students learned the fundamentals of grammar, following a more

---

[14] Janine Debut, "De l'usage des listes de mots comme fondement de la pédagogie dans l'antiquité," *REA* 85 (1983): 261–74; see also, Morgan, *Literate Education*, 77 and 101–02; cf. Cribiore, *Writing*, 42–43.

[15] The χρεία is a brief reminiscence that takes the form of an anecdote reporting a saying and/or an edifying action.

[16] Cribiore, *Writing*, 43.

[17] This line occurs on a waxed tablet and an ostracon; for the tablet, see D. C. Hesseling, "On Waxen Tablets with Fables of Babrius," *JHS* 13 (1892–1893): 296; for the ostracon, see *Papyri and Ostraca from Karanis* (ed. Herbert Chayyim Youtie and John Garrett Winter; Michigan Papyri 8; 2d series; Ann Arbor: University of Michigan Press, 1951), 206–07.

[18] Booth, "'Schola Grammatici'," 117–25. Most students would not advance to the secondary level, as Morgan notes in Greco-Roman Egypt (*Literate Education*, 163).

sophisticated progression introduced at the primary level.[19] They learned the difference between consonants and vowels, the metric value of syllables, and the eight parts of speech (i.e., noun, verb, participle, article, pronoun, preposition, adverb, and conjunction). In addition, longer passages from Homer, Euripides, and Menander were not only read, copied, and memorized, but also interpreted.

The primacy of Homer continued at this stage as well, though the early books of the *Iliad* appear as models more frequently.[20] Students were exposed to the epics by memorizing a set number of lines each day aided by *scholia minora*, reading paraphrases of the books known as catechisms, and in grammatical textbooks.[21] The standard grammar of Dionysius Thrax, for example, often used Homer to illustrate grammatical lessons.[22] As in the primary

---

[19] For more detailed treatments of the secondary stage, see Marrou, *Education*, 160–85; Bonner, *Education*, 189–249; and Morgan, *Literate Education*, 152–89.

[20] According to Morgan, of the ninety-seven Homeric texts used, eighty-six were from the *Iliad* and eleven from the *Odyssey* (*Literate Education*, 105). However, it should be noted prose authors imitated the *Odyssey* more than any other book in the ancient world; see further, MacDonald, *Homeric Epics*, 5.

[21] The *scholia minora* were glosses on words or phrases translated from poetic Greek into Koine; see further Cribiore, *Writing*, 50–51, 71–72, and 253–58; also *Gymnastics of the Mind*, 206; and John Lundon, "Lexeis from the Scholia Minora in Homerum," *ZPE* 124 (1999): 25–52.

[22] For the text, see *Dionysii Thracis Ars grammatica* (G. Uhlig, ed.; Grammatica graeci 1.1; Leibzig: Teubner, 1883), 3–100; for an English translation, see Alan Kemp, "The *Tekhnê Grammatikê* of Dionysius Thrax: English Translation with Introduction and Notes," *The History of Linguistics in the Classical Period* (ed. Daniel J. Taylor; Philadelphia: John Benjamins, 1987), 169–89. There are no known grammatical texts before the Roman period; see Morgan, *Literate Education*, 58 and 154–62.

curriculum, "facility with Homer was expected and frequently demonstrated."[23]

After completing their training under a γραμματικός, an even smaller number of students would advance to rhetorical or philosophical training.[24] As would be expected, most students chose rhetoric as the essential tool for success in literary composition, and more importantly, public life.[25] These elite students were introduced to the fundamentals of rhetorical argumentation through prerhetorical compositions known as the προγυμνάσματα.[26] The fourteen exercises from Aphthonius of Antioch became the standard curriculum; each exercise was a building block for the next, gradually providing students with the skills to compose advisory, judicial, and celebratory speeches.[27]

Like the previous stages of education, the tertiary curriculum was based on the imitation of the "canonical" authors.[28] As George C. Fiske notes in his study, *Lucilius and Horace*, the προγυμνάσματα were "designed to codify for the

---

[23] Hock, 67.

[24] For a more detailed treatment of the tertiary stage, see Marrou, *Education*, 186–216; and on rhetorical education proper, see Bonner, *Education*, 277–327.

[25] Marrou, *Education*, 194–96.

[26] Four examples of προγυμνάσματα survive from antiquity: Theon of Alexandria, Hermogenes of Tarsus, Aphthonius of Antioch, and Nicolaus of Myra. For a summative discussion of these materials, see George A. Kennedy, *Greek Rhetoric under Christian Emperors* (Princeton: Princeton University Press, 1983), 54–72; Ruth Webb, "The *Progymnasmata* as Practice," *Education in Greek and Roman Antiquity* (ed. Yoon Lee Too; Leiden: Brill, 2001), 289–316; and Cribiore, *Gymnastics of the Mind*, 221–30. For a recent English translation, see Kennedy, *Progymnasmata*, 3–72.

[27] Hock, 70.

[28] Marrou, *Education*, 162 and 200.

benefit of the student the practice of theory and good usage as illustrated by the great classical models in the genres of epic, drama, oratory, history, and other forms of prose and verse."[29] Once again, Homer was frequently used as a model, especially in three individual προγυμνάσματα: the διήγημα, the γνώμη, and the ἠθοποιία.[30]

After finishing with these prerhetorical exercises, students turned to rhetorical composition proper. At this point in the educational process, facility with Homer is simply assumed, and as a result, Homer appears less often in the rhetorical handbooks.[31] The kind of literate education expected at this stage is beautifully illustrated in the symposium narrated by Athenaeus, in which each diner participates in a game of wits, taking their turn citing Homeric lines.[32]

The preeminence of Homer as the model κατ' ἐξοχήν is unparalleled at each educational stage.[33] In her examination of ancient school texts, Morgan identified core and peripheral texts used in the classroom—at the heart of

---

[29] George C. Fiske, *Lucilius and Horace: A Study in the Classical Theory of Imitation* (New York: Herder and Herder, 1964), 35.

[30] The διήγημα is a specific incident set within a larger narrative (διήγησις). The γνώμη is an aphorism or maxim intended to offer instruction in a compact form. The ἠθοποιία is a speech that might have been spoken by someone on a specific occasion. For the special use of Homer in these προγυμνάσματα, see Hock, 71–75.

[31] On the assumed knowledge of Homer, see Aristotle, *Rhet.* 1.6.20–25, 7.33, 11.9 and 12, and 15.13; and Hermogenes, *On Ideas* 1.11 and 2.10.

[32] See Ronald F. Hock, "A Dog in the Manger: The Cynic Cynulcus among Athenaeus's Deipnosophists," *Greeks, Romans and Christians: Essays in Honor of Abraham J. Malherbe* (ed. David L. Balch, Everett Ferguson, and Wayne A. Meeks; Minneapolis: Fortress Press, 1990), 20–37.

[33] See further, MacDonald, *Christianizing Homer*, 17–34.

the ancient curriculum stood Homer alone.[34] The rhetorician, Dionysius of Halicarnassus, agrees—Homer is at the top of his recommended reading list for would-be rhetors (*De imit.* 9.1.1–5.6).[35]

For over eight hundred years, the educational practices of this private enterprise were anchored by the great poet.[36] In the fourth century BCE, the cultural influence of the bard led Plato to lament, "This poet has been the educator of Hellas" (*Resp.* 10.606e; Shorey LCL).[37] A few centuries later, the first-century Stoic philosopher and Homeric allegorist, Heraclitus, put it more poetically:

---

[34] According to her study of the educational papyri from Greco-Roman Egypt, fifty-eight texts are from Homer, twenty from Euripides, seven from Isocrates, and seven from Menander. At the core of the curriculum stood Homer alone; the second tier was occupied by Euripides, Isocrates, and Menander; the third tier represented a wide array of literature the teacher could use as supplementary material. In addition, Morgan discovered elite authors tend to cite more frequently these core texts and less frequently from those increasingly at the peripheral. See Morgan, *Literate Education*, 69, 97–100, 313, and 317–18.

[35] The list survives only in an epitome; for the text and French translation, see Germaine Aujac, ed., *Denys de Halicarnasse, opuscules rhétoriques*, vol. 5: *L'Imitation (fragments, épitomé), premiére lettre à Ammée à Pompée Géminos, Dinarque* (Collection Budé; Paris: Les Belles Lettres, 1992), 25–40. Dionysius refers to this corpus of acceptable models for rhetorical teaching as "the books" (τὰ βιβλία; *[Rhet.]* 298.1), the same phrasing used by Chrysostom in the fourth century CE to refer to the Christian testaments (Arthur G. Patzia, *The Making of the New Testament: Origin, Collection, Text & Canon* [Downers Grove: InterVarsity Press, 1995]), 118.

[36] See further, Tim Whitmarsh, *Ancient Greek Literature* (Cultural History of Literature; Cambridge: Polity Press, 2004), 18–32.

[37] Cf. Isocrates, *Paneg.* 159; Aristophanes, *Ran.* 1034. On Homer the educator, see Marrou, *Education*, 162; Werner Jaeger, "Homer the Educator," *Paideia: The Ideas of Greek Culture* (2d ed.; vol. 1; tr. Gilbert Highet; New York: Oxford University Press, 1945), 35–56; and Félix Buffière, *Les Mythes d'Homère et la pensée grecque* (Paris: Les Belles letters, 1956), 10–11.

> From the very first age of life, the foolishness of infants just beginning to learn is nurtured on the teaching given in his [i.e., Homer's] school. One might also say that his poems are our baby clothes, and we nourish our minds by draughts of his milk. He stands at our side as we each grow up and shares our youth as we gradually come to manhood; when we are mature, his presence within us is at its prime; and even in old age, we never weary of him. When we stop, we thirst to begin him again. In a word, the only end of Homer for human beings is the end of life (*All.* 1.5–7 [Russell and Konstan]).[38]

And a few centuries after that, the emperor Julian in an effort to quell the growing power of Christendom, banned the Christians from being instructed in poetry, rhetoric, and philosophy, over which Homer held court.[39] According to Theodoret, Julian lamented, "For we are, according to the old proverb, smitten by our own wings; for our authors furnish weapons to carry on war against us" (*Hist. eccl.* 3.8).

In sum, at each educational stage ancient students learned to read and write through the constant, repetitive imitation of the canonical models, especially Homer:

> Names from Homer were some of the first words students ever learned, lines from Homer were some of the first sentences they ever read, lengthy passages from Homer were the first they ever memorized and interpreted, events and themes from Homer were the ones they often treated in compositional exercises, and

---

[38] In a similar statement from Dio Chrysostom (I CE), he recommends that for the orator in training "Homer comes first and in the middle and last, in that he gives himself to every boy and adult and old man just as much as each of them can take" (*Orat.* 18.8; Cohoon LCL).

[39] See Robert Lamberton, *Homer the Theologian: Neoplatonist Allegorical Reading and the Growth of the Epic Tradition* (Transformation of the Classical Heritage 9; Berkeley: University of California Press, 1986), 138.

lines and metaphors from Homer were often used to
adorn their speeches and to express their self-
presentation.[40]

This poet educated not only Greeks, but Romans and
Christians alike — the shadow of the bard was indeed cast far
and wide.

Literary Mimesis and Ancient Composition

The term μίμησις does not appear until the sixth
century BCE and figures prominently in the later works of
Plato.[41] Plato used μίμησις broadly to speak of the imitative
nature of all human activities — "human, natural, cosmic,
and divine."[42] At the same time, however, he also applies the
term more narrowly to distinguish three types of poetic
styles: "pure narrative, in which the poet speaks in his own
person without imitation, as in the dithyramb; narrative by
means of imitation, in which the poet speaks in the person of
his character, as in comedy and tragedy; and mixed
narrative, in which the poet speaks now in his own person
and now by means of imitation" (*Resp.* 3.392d–94c; Shorey
LCL).[43] By the Hellenistic age, μίμησις was being used
widely in the context of rhetoric and literary composition —

---

[40] Hock, "Homer," 77.

[41] Gert J. Steyn, "Luke's Use of *ΜΙΜΗΣΙΣ*? Re-Opening the
Debate," *The Scriptures in the Gospels* (ed. C. M. Tuckett; Louvain: Louvain
University Press, 1997), 551–52.

[42] Richard McKeon, "Literary Criticism and the Concept of
Imitation in Antiquity," *MP* 34 (1936): 5; see also Hermann Koller, *Die
Mimesis in der Antike: Nachahmung, Darstellung, Ausdruck* (Bern: Francke,
1954); and Erich Auerbach, *Mimesis: The Representation of Reality in Western
Literature* (Princeton: Princeton University Press, 1953).

[43] See further, Gerald F. Else, "'Imitation' in the Fifth Century,"
CP 53 (1958): 73–90.

it became "μίμησις τῶν ἀρχαίων" — a poetic practice that revived the sacred past thorough imitation of the great masters.[44] The best surviving treatments of this poetic practice come from five ancient rhetoricians and pedagogues: Dionysius of Halicarnassus, Seneca the Elder, Seneca the Younger, "Longinus," and Quintilian.[45]

The Greek historian and teacher of rhetoric, Dionysius of Halicarnassus, flourished during the Augustan age. His work, *De imitatio*, is a fairly extensive treatment of μίμησις in three books: the first discusses the nature of the process, preserved only in fragments; the second lists desirable models; and the third explains how the process should be carried out, but it did not survive.[46] He is best known for the beloved parable of the ugly farmer, praising the benefits of imitating a range of models. This ugly farmer, out of fear of begetting children who would look like him, showed his wife beautiful pictures every day; he then lay with her and successfully fathered handsome children (9.1.2-3). In this allegory of literary μίμησις, the "ugly farmer" was the imitator, the "beautiful pictures" were the

---

[44] D. A. Russell, "*De Imitatione*," *Creative Imitation and Latin Literature* (ed. David West and Tony Woodman; Cambridge: Cambridge University Press, 1979), 2; and Fiske, *Lucilius and Horace*, 37.

[45] For fuller treatments of literary μίμησις, see Fiske, *Lucilius and Horace*, 25-63; Elaine Fantham, "Imitation and Decline: Rhetorical Theory and Practice in the First Century after Christ," *CP* 73 (1978): 102-116; Russell, "*De Imitatione*," 1-16; Brodie, "Greco-Roman Imitation," 17-46; and MacDonald, *Homeric Epics*, 3-7.

[46] According to Russell, the suggested literary models in book two served as the model for Quintilian; see Russell, "*De Imitatione*," 6. For a fuller treatment of *De imitatio*, see Tim Whitmarsh, *Greek Literature and the Roman Empire: The Politics of Imitation* (Oxford: Oxford University Press, 2001), 71-75.

desirable models, and conception was the process of literary creation. For Dionysius, "the importance of reading is to be found in the fact that it lays the spiritual foundation for imitation."[47]

Seneca the Elder (ca. 54 B.C.E–39 CE), a Roman rhetorician and writer, composed a treatise on deliberative oratory, the *Suasoriae*, in which he discusses what an orator should and should not do. He comments on Ovid's use of Virgil, "The poet [Ovid] did something he had done with many other lines of Virgil –with no thought of plagiarism, but meaning that his piece of open borrowing should be noticed" (3.7; Winterbottom LCL). In his estimation, a skilled rhetor must clearly advertise the model being imitated so that the oration achieves its desired effect.[48]

Seneca the Younger (4 BCE–65 CE), Roman philosopher and statesman, perhaps best describes the practice of literary μίμησις in one of his letters, *Epistula* 84.[49]

We should follow, men say, the example of the bees, who flit about and cull the flowers that are suitable for producing honey, and then arrange and assort in their

---

[47] Russell, "*De Imitatione*," 36.

[48] E.g., in a humorous account of a symposium that ended violently, the second-century satirist, Lucian of Samosata, wrote, "Histiaeus the grammarian, who had the place next him, was reciting verse, combining the lines of Pindar and Hesiod and Anacreon in such a way as to make out of them a single poem and a very funny one, especially in the part where he said, as though foretelling what was going to happen: 'They smote their shields together,' and 'Then lamentations rose, and vaunts of men'" (*Symp.* 17; Harmon LCL).

[49] For a fuller treatment of *Epistula* 84, see Thomas M. Greene, *The Light in Troy: Imitation and Discovery in Renaissance Poetry* (New Haven: Yale University Press, 1982), 70–74; and Karl Olav Sandnes, "*Imitatio Homeri? An Appraisal of Dennis R. MacDonald's 'Mimesis Criticism*'," *JBL* 124.4 (2005): 725–27

cells all that they have brought it.... It is not certain whether the juice which they obtain from the flowers forms at once into honey, or whether they change that which they have gathered into this delicious object by blending something therewith and by a certain property of their breath.... We should so blend those several flavours into one delicious compound that, even though it betrays its origin, yet it nevertheless is a clearly different thing from that whence it came (3–5; Gummere LCL).[50]

Seneca describes literary μίμησις as a mysterious process that is both concealing and revealing, recommending the eclectic use of multiple literary models to create something "clearly different."

The most celebrated pedagogical text of the Roman period, *De sublimitatae*, is attributed to "Longinus," an unknown author of the first century CE.[51] It is a discussion of the quality and thought that renders a composition sublime, including a compendium of over fifty works spanning over one thousand years. In *De sublimitatae* 13–14 he examines the role of literary μίμησις, which he considers the path to the sublime.

We too, then, when we are at looking at some passage that demands sublimity of thought and expression, would do well to form in our hearts the question, "How perchance would Homer have said this, how would Plato or Demosthenes have made it sublime or Thucydides in his history?" Emulation will bring those great characters before our eyes, and like guiding stars they will lead our thought to the ideal standards of perfection. Still more will this be so, if we give our minds the further hint, "How

---

[50] Seneca was not the only one to imagine the literary artist as a bee gathering honey; e.g., Macrobius, *Sat.* 1, *pref.* 4; Horace, *Carm.* 4, 2, 27.

[51] For a fuller treatment of *De sublimitate*, see Whitmarsh, *Politics of Imitation*, 57–71.

would Homer or Demosthenes, had either been present, have listened to this passage of mine? How would it have affected them?" (14.1–2; Fyfe LCL)

For "Longinus," literary μίμησις presumed a "generous rivalry," that is, imitation (μίμησις) and emulation (ζῆλος) were complementary aspects of the same creative process in which the masters were present in a spirit of competition.[52] The key to successful literary μίμησις lay in "the choice of object, the depth of understanding, and the writer's power to take possession of the thought for himself."[53]

The most comprehensive treatment of literary μίμησις comes from Quintilian (ca. 35–95 CE), the Roman rhetorician and head of the school of oratory in Rome for over twenty years. In his twelve-volume textbook on rhetoric, *Insitutio oratoria*, Quintilian outlines a comprehensive educational program, from boyhood to manhood, for the training of the *perfectus orator*. He divides his discussion of oratory into five canons: *inventio* (discovery of arguments), *dispositio* (arrangement of arguments), *elocutio* (style), *memoria* (memorization), and *pronuntiatio* (delivery).

In *Institutio oratoria* 10, Quintilian describes how the student can acquire a "firm facility" by reading, writing, and

---

[52] See also, "Longinus," [*Subl.*] 13.2–14.3. This rivalry is clearly expressed in Pliny the Elder, who describes the imitative process as a fight and competition (*Nat. pref.* 20–23; *De. Or.* 2.22.90–92; cf. Velleius Paterculus, *Res Gestae Divi Augusti*, 1.17.6–7. The relationship between the model and the imitator, however, should be characterized by respect and admiration, never jealousy. E.g., Aristotle carefully distinguished between emulation (ζῆλος) and envy (φθόνος) in his rhetorical handbook (*Rhet.* 1388ab).

[53] Russell, "*De Imitatione*," 10.

imitating good exemplars; imitation is necessary because few possess the natural abilities to equal the classical models (2.3). He writes to other teachers of rhetoric, "There can be no doubt, that in art no small portion of our task lies in *imitatio*, since, although invention came first and is all-important, it is expedient to follow whatever has been invented with success" (2.1; Butler LCL). *Imitatio* is not a mechanical affair; on the contrary, the student must understand why the model is worth imitating and be able to draw useful qualities from a range of models. Ideally, the *perfectus orator* will "speak better," rising above the achievements of his predecessors, but *imitatio* cannot supply the vital qualities of the rhetor—invention, spirit, and personality (5.5).[54]

These ancient treatments of literary μίμησις identify five markers of the mimetic ethos of Greco-Roman composition: intimate familiarity with the model(s), advertisement and concealment of the model(s), eclectic and creative use of multiple models, and most importantly, rivalry with the model(s). The most sophisticated form of literary μίμησις was an attempt to "speak better," a creative enterprise involving critical study and imitation of a plurality of models in which the imitator both concealed and revealed, and above all, graciously competed with the canonical authors.

---

[54] In his *Panegyricus*, Isocrates says that it is possible to speak about old things (τὰ παλαιά) in new ways (καινῶς): "it follows that one must not shun the subjects upon which others have spoken before, but must try to speak better than they" (8–10; Norlin LCL).

Mimesis Criticism and Early Christian Narrative

The first New Testament scholar to read biblical narrative in light of the mimetic ethos of Greco-Roman composition was Thomas L. Brodie. In a series of articles written over a span of twenty-five years, Brodie explored the role of literary μίμησις in the New Testament, especially the book of Acts.[55] He was particularly adept at identifying a range of mimetic techniques in the New Testament drawn from Greek and Roman poetry.[56] Brodie focused his considerable efforts almost exclusively on the Septuagint, but MacDonald re-cast the comparative net to include Greek literature as potential models of literary μίμησις in early Christian composition, especially the Homeric epics.

The mimetic ethos of ancient composition is now widely recognized, but determining the intentional use of one text by another is no easy task. The most significant obstacle to the detection of literary μίμησις is the disparity between two *mundi significantes*, the chasm that divides the conceptual world of the text and the modern interpreter.[57] Ancient readers were experts in detecting imitation, but this cultural expertise has naturally been lost with the passage of time. A range of relationships can exist between texts, and

[55] Brodie, "Greco-Roman Imitation," 17–46; "The Accusing and Stoning of Naboth (1 Kgs 21:8–13) as One Component of the Stephen Text," *CBQ* 45 (1984): 417–32; "Intertextuality and its Use in Tracing Q and Proto-Luke," *Scriptures in the Gospels* (ed. C. M. Tuckett; Louvain: Louvain University Press, 1997), 469–77; "Luke-Acts as an Imitation and Emulation of the Elijah-Elisha Narrative," *New Views on Luke-Acts* (ed. Earl Richards; Collegeville, MN: Michael Glazer, 1990), 78–85; and "Towards Unraveling the Rhetorical Imitation of Sources in Acts: 2 Kings 5 as One Component of Acts 8,9–40," *Bib* 67 (1986): 41–67.

[56] Dupertuis, "Summaries," 64.

[57] See further, MacDonald, *Homeric Epics*, 171–72.

therefore, each case of potential imitation should be tested and assessed individually.[58]

The second obstacle involves the problem of disguise. As Seneca the Younger illustrated through his wandering bees, imitation at its best creates something "clearly different." Students were taught to disguise their dependence upon a model through a variety of techniques (e.g., altering vocabulary; varying order, length, and structure of sentences; improving content; and formal transformations) to avoid charges of plagiarism and pedantry.[59] Identifying the range of mimetic possibilities is a monumental task, but an essential step toward improving the detection of literary μίμησις.[60]

In addition to the problem of disguise, how does one distinguish between an author's conscious evocation of a particular source and a chance combination of words, images, or concepts? Literary comparison is a subjective enterprise; thus, many scholars have proposed varying ways to assess literary parallels. Generally speaking, they can be

---

[58] Dupertuis, "Summaries," 68.

[59] In his discussion of hypertextual (imitative) practices, Gerard Genette distinguished between formal transpositions (e.g., translation), which affect meaning by accident, and thematic transpositions, which were deliberate in their alteration of the hypotext (model). As he notes, one of the most important types of thematic transposition is transvaluation, in which there is any operation of an axiological nature bearing on the value that is implicitly or explicitly assigned to an action or group of actions (*Palimpsests: Literature in the Second Degree* [tr. Channa Newman and Claude Doubinsky; Lincoln: University of Nebraska Press, 1997], 367–75).

[60] For a sophisticated taxonomy of literary μίμησις, see Genette, *Palimpsests*.

divided into three camps: philological fundamentalists, literary universalists, and those that vacillate between.[61]

Philological fundamentalists require unmistakable markers of dependence, such as shared vocabulary, similar genres, and distinctive grammatical or poetic constructions.[62] A textual parallel that does not meet their strict criteria is considered an accidental confluence (i.e., a literary τόπος). For example, in *Ovid's Art of Imitation*, Kathleen Morgan argued that clear philological criteria (e.g., choice of words, position of the words, metrical anomalies, and structural development) must be met in order to escape the pitfalls created by the thematic traditions of the genre.[63] Unless the potential parallel comes close to verbatim quotation, it must simply be a common literary τόπος.[64] These criteria provide a degree of certainty that is comforting for the mimetic critic, but they do not conform to ancient discussions of literary μίμησις nor to the vast majority of widely acknowledged imitations.

At the other end of the spectrum are literary universalists, who argue that meaning occurs in the act of reading. The reader is equipped with a treasury of information from many texts, making intertextual

---

[61] MacDonald, *Homeric Epics*, 7–8.

[62] Stephen Hinds, *Allusion and Intertext: Dynamics of Appropriation in Roman Poetry* (Roman Literature and its Contexts; Cambridge: Cambridge University Press, 1998), 19.

[63] Kathleen Morgan, *Ovid's Art of Imitation: Propertius in the Amores* (MnemosSup 47; Leiden: Brill, 1977), 3.

[64] See similarly, R. F. Thomas, "Virgil's *Georgics* and the Art of Reference," *HSCP* 90 (1986): 173.

associations regardless of authorial intention.[65] "Intertexuality" is a term associated with the fields of linguistic theory and literary criticism popularized by Julia Kristeva in the 1960s.[66] According to this theory, the author is hermeneutically irrelevant because all texts exist in an interconnected web of meaning. For example, in his intertextual study of Latin poets, Gian Biagio Conte concluded that identifying the traces of one particular text is impossible because poetic language already contains within it the memory of previous texts.[67] "Intertexuality" occurs when the reader chooses to see texts in relationship to one another.

The middle position is occupied by those who apply more flexible criteria and have not abandoned authorial intention.[68] A good example among Latinists is Stephen Hinds, who dismissed philological fundamentalism as unreflective of the mimetic ethos of ancient composition in

---

[65] For more detailed discussions of intertextuality in the field of biblical studies, see Timothy K. Beal, "Intertextuality," *Handbook of Postmodern Biblical Interpretation* (ed. A. K. M. Adam; St. Louis: Chalice Press, 2000), 128–30; Thomas B. Hatina, "Intertextuality and Historical Criticism in New Testament Studies: Is there a Relationship?" *Biblnt* 7 (1999): 28–43; and David R. Cartlidge, "Combien d'unités avez-vous de trios à quatre? What do we mean by Intertextuality in Early Church Studies?" *SBLSP 1990* (ed. David J. Lull; Atlanta: Scholars Press, 1990), 400–11.

[66] E.g., Julia Kristeva, *Desire in Language: A Semiotic Approach to Literature and Art* (ed. Leon S. Roudiez; tr. Thomas Gora, Alice Jardine, and Leon S. Roudiez; New York: Columbia University Press, 1980).

[67] Gian Biagio Conte, *The Rhetoric of Imitation: Genre and Poetic Memory in Virgil and Other Latin Poets* (tr. Charles Segal; Ithaca: Cornell University Press, 1986).

[68] E.g., Ellen Finkelpearl, "Pagan Traditions of Intertextuality in the Roman World," *Mimesis and Intertextuality in Antiquity and Christianity*, 78–90.

Allusion and Intertext.[69] There are many possible relationships between texts, some of which identify authorial intent (e.g., citation, reference, allusion, and echo) and some of which are more general in nature (e.g., shared τόποι and intertextual resonance).[70] He carefully distinguished between "source passages" and "modeling by code" in an effort to overcome the fine line separating direct allusion and the use of literary τόποι.[71] A literary τόπος is the result of the repeated imitation of a particular author or text; thus, according to Hinds, the allusion is intended to invoke a specific model within the mind of the reader, while the τόπος draws upon an intertextual tradition collectively.[72]

In New Testament studies, scholars who compare biblical literature with nonbiblical literature tend to apply the strict criteria characteristic of philological fundamentalism.[73] From their perspective, the only legitimate markers of literary μίμησις are direct, word-for-word parallels. It is important to note, however, that when comparing New Testament literature with materials from the Hebrew Bible, these same scholars apply more generous criteria.[74]

Literary comparison is a complex poetic task that requires criteria that can be consistently, yet flexibly applied.

---

[69] See Hinds, *Allusion and Intertext.* According to David Cartlidge, "Intertexuality in respect to the traditions of Late Antiquity must account for characteristics peculiar to the nature and operation of texts in that period" ("Intertextuality," 407).

[70] Dupertuis, "Summaries," 68.

[71] Hinds, *Allusion*, 40–49.

[72] Hinds, *Allusion*, 34.

[73] Brodie, "Intertextuality," 270–71.

[74] MacDonald, *Homeric Epics*, 169–71.

Brodie has suggested that these criteria be left undefined so that potential literary imitations are not rendered invisible because of methodological blinders.[75] The remarkable variety of mimetic practices in antiquity requires a certain degree of methodological flexibility, but set criteria need not inhibit the comparative vision of the interpreter. To this end, MacDonald has developed six criteria in his study of early Christian narrative: accessibility, analogy, density, order, distinctive traits, and interpretability.[76]

The first two criteria, accessibility and analogy, are environmental in nature and attempt to assess the cultural significance of the model in question. Accessibility is concerned with four issues: the physical distribution of the model; the popularity of the model in art, literature, and education; the dating of the model relative to the imitation; and the accessibility of the model to the intended audience of the imitation. On this last point, critics are quick to point out that while the Homeric epics were ubiquitous in the Greco-Roman world, they were not common among the

[75] Brodie, "Greco-Roman Imitation," 34–37.

[76] See especially *Christianizing Homer*, 302–27; *Homeric Epics*, 8–9; and *Does the New Testament*, 2–7. Richard Hays proposes seven criteria in his intertextual study of the Pauline letters and the Septuagint: availability, volume, recurrence, thematic coherence, historical plausibility, history of interpretation, and satisfaction (*Echoes of Scripture in the Letters of Paul* [New Haven: Yale University Press, 1989], 29–32). [Editor's note: More recently, MacDonald has added a seventh criterion: ancient and Byzantine recognitions. See Dennis MacDonald, *The Gospels and Homer: Imitations of Greek Epic in Mark and Luke-Acts* (The New Testament and Greek Literature 1; Lanham: Rowman & Littlefield, 2015), 6–7.]

New Testament authors (i.e., Palestinian Jews).[77] Even if they had written in Aramaic or Hebrew, Palestinian Jews were not exempt from the cultural impact of Hellenism.[78] Greek composition, however, was a skill that could only be acquired through Greco-Roman education, a curriculum based upon the imitation of the canonical authors, most notably Homer.[79] The New Testament is heavily indebted to Jewish literature and culture, but this does not exclude Greek influence.

The second criterion, analogy, asks whether the model was frequently imitated. The more often a model was the target of imitation, the more likely that other imitations exist. Needless to say, Homer was by far the most popular model of literary μίμησις in antiquity. In the *Saturnalia*, the Roman grammarian Macrobius (*fl.* 395–423 CE) recounts a series of historical, mythological, and grammatical discussions held at the house of Vettius Agorius Praetextatus during the Saturnalia festival. On the celebrity of the bard, he notes it is to the glory of Homer that he is copied by so

---

[77] For two critiques of MacDonald's criteria and application, see Sandnes, "*Imitatio Homeri?*" and Margaret Mitchell, "Homer in the New Testament?" *JR* 83 (2003): 244–60.

[78] See further, Hengel, *Judaism and Hellenism*; and Catherine Hezser, *Jewish Literacy in Roman Palestine* (TSAJ 81; Tübingen: Mohr-Siebeck, 2001).

[79] The role of Homer as the foundational text of Greco-Roman culture is highlighted in Philo's extensive discussion on encyclical education; see further, Peder Borgen, "Greek Encyclical Education, Philosophy and Synagogue: Observations from Philo of Alexandria's Writings," *Libens menito: Festshrift till Stig Strömholm* (ed. Olle Matson; Acta Academae Regiae Scientiarum Upsaliensis 21; Uppsala: Kungl. Vetenskapssamhället í Uppsala, 2001), 61–71.

many striving to compete with him and yet like an "ocean-rock" he stands unmoved (*Sat.* 6.3.1 [Davies]).

On this point, it has been argued that imitations of the epics are limited to highly cultured authors (e.g., Virgil), but the New Testament authors were not highly cultured. This objection fails on two counts. First, imitations of the epics can be found in literature intended for more popular audiences, such as Josephus, the book of Tobit, and the romances.[80]

Second, the presupposition that the New Testament authors were not well educated has been called into question, and in the case of "Luke," debunked. More than any other New Testament author, "Luke" quotes from Greek literature, including the didactic Greek poet Aratus (Acts 17:28) and the Athenian tragedian Euripides (Acts 21:39; 26:14)—he clearly possessed a literate education.[81] Two recent studies suggest "Luke" advanced to the early stages

---

[80] For Josephus, see Louis Feldman, *Josephus's Interpretation of the Bible* (Berkeley: University of California Press, 1998), 171–72; for Tobit, see Dennis R. MacDonald, "Tobit and the *Odyssey*," *Mimesis and Intertextuality*, 11–40; for the romances, see Ronald F. Hock, "The Educational Curriculum in Chariton's *Callirhoe*," *Ancient Fiction: The Matrix of Early Christian and Jewish Narrative* (ed. Jo-Ann A. Brant, Charles W. Hedrick, and Chris Shea; SBLSym 32; Atlanta: Society of Biblical Literature, 2005), 15–36.

[81] *Phaen.* 5, *Ion* 8, and *Bacch.* 795 respectively. For discussions of the relatively high level of education indicated by the evangelist's literary style and language and knowledge of Greek literature, see Eckhard Plümacher, *Lukas als hellenistischer Schriftsteller: Studien zur Apostelgeschichte* (SUNT 9; Göttingen: Vandenhoeck & Ruprecht, 1972); Gregory E. Sterling, *Historiography and Self-Definition: Josephos, Luke-Acts, and Apologetic Historiography* (NovTSup 64; Leiden: Brill, 1992); Richard Pervo, *Profit with Delight: The Literary Genre of the Acts of the Apostles* (Philadelphia: Fortress Press, 1987); and Robert Morgenthaler, *Lukas und Quintilian: Rhetorik als Erzählkunst* (Zurich: Gotthelf Verlag, 1993).

of a rhetorical education, but in any case, at each educational stage, primary, secondary, and tertiary students were trained in the art of copying, the fundamentals of grammar, and the complexities of rhetorical composition through "μίμησις τῶν ἀρχαίων."[82]

These two criteria clearly identify Homer as the most accessible and the most imitated model in antiquity, but they also introduce a more formidable obstacle. If the epics were in fact the cultural encyclopedia of the Greco-Roman world, it increases the likelihood that similarities are due merely to a shared Greek cultural identity. Also, it increases the possibility that the model is being imitated indirectly, that is, through another imitation. The comparative criteria that follow specifically address these potential pitfalls.

Density and order highlight the points of contact between texts, paying particular attention to the number and volume of the similarities and the relative sequencing of the

---

[82] On the rhetorical education of "Luke," see Todd C. Penner, "Civilizing Discourse: Acts, Declamation and the Rhetoric of the Polis," *Contextualizing Acts: Lukan Narrative and Greco-Roman Discourse* (ed. Todd C. Penner and Caroline Vander Stichele; SBLSym 20; Atlanta: Society of Biblical Literature, 2003), 65–104; and Mikael C. Parsons, "Luke and the *Progymnasmata*: A Preliminary Investigation into the Preliminary Exercises," *Contextualizing Acts*, 43–64. More recently: Osvaldo Padilla, "Hellenistic *paideia* and Luke's Education: A Critique of Recent Approaches," *NTS* 55 (2009): 416–37; M. W. Martin, "Progymnastic Topic Lists: A Compositional Template for Luke and other *Bioi?*" *NTS* 54 (2008): 18–41; and Sean A. Adams, "Luke and *Progymnasmata*: Rhetorical Handbooks, Rhetorical Sophistication and Genre Selection," *Ancient Education and Early Christianity* (ed. M. R. Hauge and A. W. Pitts; 2016), 137–54. They are more skeptical about Luke reaching the tertiary stage, but Adams in particular rightly emphasizes that the progymnastic exercises crept into the earlier stages by the Roman period.

proposed model and the proposed imitation. There is considerable disagreement over what constitutes a parallel, but examples include shared vocabulary, grammar, proper names, settings, characterizations, and motifs. In every case, the quality of the parallels is much more important than the quantity. Philological fundamentalists point out that density and order cannot be used as evidence of imitation because two texts of the same genre can share similar features without any kind of genetic relationship. The fifth criterion, distinctive traits, addresses this very problem by identifying mimetic flags.

A mimetic flag is a characteristic uncharacteristic of the genre as whole, such as a proper name, a telling word or phrase, literary context, or motif.[83] If present, the distinctive trait can be the most compelling evidence for binding two texts together. At its best, distinctive traits is a cumulative criterion in which a constellation of mimetic flags point to literary μίμησις, rather than form criticism. As with the criteria of density and order, not all interpreters agree on what constitutes a distinctive trait. Philological fundamentalists require a type of verbatim agreement that is discouraged by ancient rhetoricians, but a mimetic flag need only be unusual for that particular literary genre and context. Unfortunately for modern interpreters, these same rhetoricians encouraged their students to conceal their

---

[83] E.g., in his comparison of the casting of lots for Matthias in Acts 1:15–26 and the casting of lots for Ajax in *Iliad* 7, MacDonald notes the presence of Homeric vocabulary not found anywhere else in the New Testament; in addition, no known imitations of the Homeric scene exist, which eliminates the possibility of indirect influence (*Does the New Testament*, 105).

model; though desirable, this criterion is not always applicable.

The final criterion is interpretability, which examines the strategic differences between texts. Does the model help bring the imitation into interpretive clarity? This criterion is one of the most sharply criticized. If differences between texts are markers of imitation, what are indicators that imitation is not taking place? In her review of *The Homeric Epics and the Gospel of Mark*, Margaret Mitchell refers to this as the "have your cake and eat it too" methodology.[84] She complains that this final criterion renders any proposed imitation incapable of invalidation because parallels and divergences can be used as evidence of influence. This criterion must remain flexible, however, to account for the mysterious transformative process of literary μίμησις described by Seneca's wandering bees.

Together, these environmental and comparative criteria project an interpretive horizon for comparing texts bounded by five questions. (1) Was the model widely available? (2) Did other writers imitate the model? (3) How similar are the texts? (4) Are there any mimetic flags? And (5), does the model make sense of the imitation? The interpretive reward for detecting literary μίμησις is rich, but it is an exceedingly difficult task coupled by a lack of methodological agreement. Despite the challenges, it can be an invaluable contribution to the interpretation of any ancient text.

---

[84] Mitchell, "Homer," 252.

Conclusion

The unrivaled hegemony of Homer among grammarians, educationalists, and elite writers bears witness to the divine status of the epics in antiquity among Jews, Christians, and pagans alike.[85] Unfortunately, the interpretive relevance of the bard has been woefully neglected in modern biblical scholarship, as Brodie humorously notes,

> *The Anchor Bible Dictionary*, for instance, is a wonderful application—I treasure it—and one might expect it to be a good source from which to learn about one of the greatest writers of all antiquity, someone whose work was essentially complete before the Pentateuch: Homer. *The Anchor Bible Dictionary* does indeed have an entry under Homer: HOMER [Heb homer]. See WEIGHTS AND MEASURES. That entry, in so magnificent a work, is a symptom of the degree to which, as a group, we have lost our way. We have forgotten the priority of the literary.[86]

In addition, *The Encyclopedia of Early Christianity*, *The Encyclopedia of the Early Church*, and *The Oxford Dictionary of the Early Church* do not contain entries on Homer. Even the primary editions of the Greek New Testament, which include a compendium of possible citations and allusions, omit Homer entirely.

---

[85] See further, Margalit Finkelberg, "Homer as a Foundation Text," *Homer, the Bible, and Beyond: Literary and Religious Canons in the Ancient World* (ed. Margalit Finkelberg and Guy C. Stroumsa; Leiden: Brill, 2003), 75–96.

[86] Thomas L. Brodie, "Towards Tracing the Gospel's Literary Indebtedness to the Epistles," *Mimesis and Intertextuality*, 104–05, n. 1.

The absence of Homer in these critical tools projects an image (or lack thereof) of the bard in direct contradiction to the historical evidence, summed up nicely by Mitchell,

> This deficiency in English-language reference works is to some degree ameliorated by the collection of counterevidence provided in the article on Homer by G. J. M. Bartelink in the *Reallexikon für Antike und Christentum*. Bartelink documents the impressive aggregate of direct citations and allusions — positive and negative, and neutral — to Homer in the writings of authors such as Aristides, Justin, Tatian, Theophilus of Antioch, Athenagoras, Irenaeus, Tertullian, Minucius Feliz, Clement of Alexandria, Hippolytus, Gnostics (such as the Naasenes, the Simonians, and the Sethians), Origen, Ps-Justin, Methodius of Olympus, martyrological texts, Cyprian, the Cappadocians, Epiphanius, John Crysostom and Theodoret, Ambrose, Jerome, Augustine, and authors of Homeric centones on Christian narratives or themes, such as the empress of Eudocia. This list of Christians who grappled with Homer in a variety of ways read rather like "who's who" of patristic writers and thinkers. They could not, it seems, avoid Homer.[87]

The comprehensive discussion of Mesopotamian, Egyptian, and biblical metrology in the *Anchor Bible Dictionary* is impressive, but for those who seek the poet they will need to access the less known *Reallexikon für Antike und Christentum*.[88]

The chasm that separates the *mundi significantes* of the ancient author and the modern interpreter is wide and deep. Without question, the New Testament writings reflect

---

[87] Mitchell, "Homer," 244–45.
[88] See further, M. A. Powell, "Weights and Measures," *ABD* 6: 897–908.

a commitment, both culturally and religiously, to the Jewish Scriptures. Their literary commitments, however, are a natural by-product of a Greco-Roman education: they were wandering bees, gathering honey from the canonical models of antiquity. Literary comparison is an art, not a science; biblical scholars will continue to debate issues of literary comparison, influence, and dependence, but MacDonald has reminded us all of that which has been long forgotten — the playground of pagan literature.

When Did Paul Become a Christian?
Rereading Paul's Autobiography in Galatians and Biography in Acts

Thomas E. Phillips

Very early in my graduate training, I encountered Dennis MacDonald's marvelous little book, *The Legend and the Apostle*.[1] That volume opened up new worlds for me, providing for me, as it did, my first exposure to the apocryphal Acts and the rich world of early Christian fiction. Over time, as my own studies in Luke-Acts matured, I came to see that most of the New Testament narratives were — by modern standards — at least fictive, if not entirely fictional.[2] Although my convictions about the fictive nature of most New Testament narratives have often rendered me a bewildered spectator to scholarly debates about the "history" of early Christianity, my skepticism about the wisdom of deriving modern historical claims from the New Testament narratives seldom impacted my own scholarly work. Even while chairing the section on Acts at the Society

---

[1] Dennis R. MacDonald, *The Legend and the Apostle: The Battle for Paul in Story and Canon* (Philadelphia: Westminster, 1983).

[2] By "fictive," I mean that the narratives, even quite likely derived from historical events, are now cast in terms which render it impossible to create any more than the vaguest semblance of modern history from the ancient New Testament texts. By "fictional," I mean that the narratives have their origin entirely within human and community imagination and have no historical origin.

of Biblical Literature, I silently excused myself from discussions which presumed the historicity of Acts, and I confined my own work to other areas of inquiry.

My benign dismissal of the work of historical investigations and reconstructions came to an unceremonious end when a publisher invited me to write a volume comparing the Paul of Acts to the Paul of the letters.[3] When I initially accepted the invitation to write, I assumed that the book would take a pretty predictable form—I would present the "real Paul" of the seven undisputed letters, followed by a presentation of the "Paul of Acts." Standing as firmly as I did in the Knox tradition, which regarded the undisputed Pauline letters as our only primary sources about Paul's life,[4] I assumed that my task would simply be to summarize what other critical scholars had already said about the "real Paul." I was wrong, very wrong. I quickly came to believe that nearly all scholars, even the most widely respected critical scholars of the Pauline letters and Acts, tended to crossbreed the "real Paul" of the letters with the early church's memory of Paul in Acts, thus, creating a third sort of thing, a hybrid stepson of Paul and Luke. This scholarly *tertium quid* now looms large in New Testament scholarship. My purpose here, in the bold and daring spirit of Dennis MacDonald, is to strike a modest blow to this

---

[3] Thomas E. Phillips, *Paul, His Letters, and Acts* (Library of Pauline Studies; Peabody, MA: Hendrickson, 2009; Grand Rapids: Baker Academic, 2010).

[4] See John Knox, *Chapters in a Life of Paul* (rev. ed.; ed. Douglas R. A. Hare; Macon: Mercer University Press, 1987). Joseph B. Tyson was my Doktorvater; John Knox was his Doktorvater. Therefore, I am the intellectual grandson of Knox.

loathsome and omnipresent pseudo-Paul and its corrupting influence on New Testament scholarship by offering a rereading of Paul's autobiography in Galatians, a reading which is truly independent of Acts.

The Central Problem of Pauline Biography

Unfortunately, at least since the time of F. C. Bauer (if not since the time of Irenaeus), one of the most commonly discussed questions within Pauline scholarship has been the relationship between Paul's letters (particularly Galatians 1–2) and the Book of Acts (particularly Acts 9 and 15).[5] If we assume that Acts is either fictive or fictional, then parsing the correlations between Acts and Paul's letters becomes a pseudo-question, a mere red herring in a sea of misplaced concreteness. Rather, the actual problem to be solved should be the very different *Pauline* accounts of the origins of his message. The two key Pauline accounts regarding the origin of Paul's message are brief and can be quoted in their entirety.

First, within the combative context of Galatians, Paul insisted:

> [11]For I want you to know, brothers and sisters, that the gospel that was proclaimed by me is *not of human origin*; [12]for I did *not receive it from a human source, nor was I taught it*, but I received it through a revelation of Jesus Christ.

---

[5] Ferdinand Christian Baur, *Paul, the Apostle of Jesus: His Life and Work, His Epistles and His Doctrines: A Contribution to the Critical History of Primitive Christianity* (2 vols; 2nd ed.; ed. Eduard Zeller; London: Williams & Norgate, 1873–75; repr., Peabody, MA: Hendrickson, 2003). Irenaeus' arguments can be found in his treatise *Against Heresy*. See Robert M. Grant, *Irenaeus of Lyons* (New York: Routledge, 1997).

¹³You have heard, no doubt, of my earlier life in Judaism. I was violently persecuting the church of God and was trying to destroy it. ¹⁴I advanced in Judaism beyond many among my people of the same age, for I was far more zealous for the traditions of my ancestors. ¹⁵But when God, who had set me apart before I was born and called me through his grace, was pleased ¹⁶to reveal his Son to me, so that I might proclaim him among the Gentiles, *I did not confer with any human being*, ¹⁷nor did I go up to Jerusalem to those who were already apostles before me, but I went away at once into Arabia, and afterwards I returned to Damascus.

¹⁸Then after three years *I did go up to Jerusalem to visit Cephas and stayed with him fifteen days; ¹⁹but I did not see any other apostle except James the Lord's brother.* ²⁰In what I am writing to you, before God, *I do not lie!* ²¹Then I went into the regions of Syria and Cilicia, ²²and I was still unknown by sight to the churches of Judea that are in Christ; ²³they only heard it said, "The one who formerly was persecuting us is now proclaiming the faith he once tried to destroy." ²⁴And they glorified God because of me. (Gal 1:11–24, NRSV, emphasis added.)

Some years later, in the much less contentious context of his first letter to the Corinthians, the apostle explained:

³For I handed on to you as of first importance *what I in turn had received*: that Christ died for our sins in accordance with the scriptures, ⁴and that he was buried, and that he was raised on the third day in accordance with the scriptures, ⁵and that he appeared to Cephas, then to the twelve. ⁶Then he appeared to more than five hundred brothers and sisters at one time, most of whom are still alive, though some have died. ⁷Then he appeared to James, then to all the apostles. ⁸Last of all, as to one untimely born, he appeared also to me. ⁹For I am the least of the apostles, unfit to be called an apostle, because I persecuted the church of God. ¹⁰But by the grace of God I am what I am, and his grace toward me has not been in

vain. On the contrary, I worked harder than any of them—though it was not I, but the grace of God that is with me. [11]Whether then it was I or they, so we proclaim and so you have come to believe. (1 Cor 15:3–11, NRSV, emphasis added.)

Although critical scholars have long recognized the irreconcilable differences between these Pauline accounts (particularly Gal 1) and the Lukan accounts in Acts (particularly Acts 9–15), the incongruity between these primary sources in Paul's letters and the secondary sources in Acts is not my concern here.[6] Rather, my concern is *the significant incongruity between these two Pauline accounts*. In Galatians, Paul is emphatic that he did not "receive" (παρέλαβον) his gospel from any human being, including those who were apostles before him (1:11). He insists that he was not taught this gospel (1:11). In fact, Paul insists that he did not "confer with" (προσανθέμην, 1:16)—and he barely even saw (1:18–19)—the original apostles. Paul even vouched for the historical accuracy of these claims by exclaiming, "I do not lie" (1:20). In 1 Corinthians, in contrast, Paul claims to hand down what he had "received" (παρέλαβον, 15:3) from the apostles. Paul then continued by explaining that this message could be traced back to Cephas and James (vv. 5, 7), presumably the same Cephas and James with whom Paul had only marginal contact according to Galatians (1:18–19). Unfortunately, this striking incongruity *within Paul's letters* is often overlooked by scholars who are

---

[6] See Phillips, *Paul, His Letters, and Acts*, 50–82 for a comparison between the chronology and autobiography in Paul's letters and the chronology and biography in Acts.

preoccupied with the equally strong incongruity between Acts and Galatians.

Typical Readings of the Autobiography in Galatians

Scholars have traditionally interpreted Paul's autobiography in Galatians 1:13–17 as a conversion story. That is, the narrative in these verses is read as the story of how "Paul [or Saul] the Jewish Persecutor of Christianity" became "Paul the Christian Missionary." This interpretation is pervasive within scholarship from all confessional orientations. For example, from a conservative Evangelical perspective, Douglas Moo's comments on this autobiography claim that "God broke into Paul's life *as a Jew* and indeed persecutor of the risen Christ and his people, through an 'apocalyptic' transformative event."[7] From a Catholic perspective, Frank Matera, following the Jewish interpreter Alan Segal, explains, "it is undeniable that the course of [Paul's] life was inextricably altered by the revelation that he received in or near Damascus. Segal is not far from the truth that he was converted *from Pharisaic Judaism* to an apocalyptic form of Christianity."[8] From a liberal Protestant perspective, Hans Dieter Betz is reluctant to embrace the anachronistic categories of a Pauline

---

[7] Douglas J. Moo, *Galatians* (BECNT; Grand Rapids: Baker Academic, 2013), 104, emphasis added. Speaking as an Evangelical, Moo, not surprisingly, strongly defends the use of "conversion" language in his interpretation of this autobiography (pp. 98–99).

[8] Frank J. Matera, *Galatians* (SP 9; Collegeville, MN: Liturgical Press, 1992), 62, emphasis added. Note the subtle importation of Acts. When read independently of Acts, Galatians 1:13–17 would give no indication of Paul being in Damascus until well after the revelatory event in Galatians 1:16.

conversion from Judaism to Christianity. Betz prefers to speak of Paul's "so-called conversion," but he stills characterizes these autobiographical remarks as an account of how Paul "changed parties within Judaism *from Pharisaism* to Jewish Christianity."[9]

Moo, Betz, and Matera stake out different positions within the recent debate about whether this autobiography should be interpreted as a "conversion" or a "call."[10] On the one hand, the Evangelical Moo falls strongly on the "conversion" side of the debate, arguing that Paul's new commitment to Christ was so striking that it entailed conversion from one religion to another religion in Paul's mind. On the other hand, Betz argues equally strongly that Pauline autobiography should be understood as a "call" in the mode of the Hebrew Prophets. For Betz, Paul's experience was a move within Judaism. My concern here is not to determine whether Paul's initial belief in Christ should be interpreted as a move from Judaism to Christianity (Moo's position) or a move within Judaism (Betz's position). My concern is merely to illustrate that contemporary scholarship assumes — almost without exception — that the revelation described in Galatians 1:15–16 resulted in Paul's initial belief in Christ. But is this assumption justified?

---

[9] Hans Dieter Betz, *Galatians: A Commentary on Paul's Letter to the Churches in Galatia* (Hermeneia; Philadelphia: Fortress Press, 1979), 64, emphasis added.

[10] Most importantly, see Krister Stendahl, "Call Rather than Conversion," *Paul Among the Gentiles* (Philadelphia: Fortress Press, 1976), 7–23; and Alan F. Segal, *Paul the Convert: The Apostolate and Apostasy of Saul the Pharisee* (New Haven: Yale University Press, 1990).

I want to question this pervasive assumption and suggest that the revelatory event and Paul's response to that event in Galatians 1:16 should not be read as an account of Paul's initial acceptance of Jesus as Messiah. More specifically, I want to change the literary frames of reference within which Galatians 1:16 is read. Typically, scholars of all critical orientations equate the event in Galatians 1:16 with Saul/Paul's "Damascus Road" experience in Acts 9:4-6 — and they then read the autobiography in Galatians within frames of reference imported (consciously or unconsciously) from Acts. Even the most critical scholarly discussions of these verses in Galatians are littered with references to Acts and the Damascus Road account in Acts. *It is my contention that the autobiography in Galatians should be read in light of 1 Corinthians 15 (a primary source from Paul) and not in light of Acts 9 (a secondary source from decades later).* How would the revelatory event in Galatians 1:16 be interpreted if the Pauline text of 1 Corinthians 15:1-11 was employed as the primary frame of reference for shaping our interpretation of that revelatory event? What content would interpreters assign to the revelation discussion in Galatians 1:16 if that content was understood only in light of the Pauline letters — and without any reference to the content assigned to the revelatory event in Acts 9:1-10?

I understand that many scholars — particularly conservative scholars — will have ideological and methodological objections to removing Acts from the frames of reference for interpreting Galatians. However, it is my claim that even scholars who would have no procedural objections to interpreting Paul's letters without appeal to

Acts (like Betz, Matera, and Segal) have failed to adequately and vigorously explore readings of Galatians 1 which significantly diverge from Acts. I now want to offer such a reading and to argue that my rereading of Galatians is more faithful to the primary sources, Paul's letters.

Rereading Galatians 1

Because the influence of Acts so deeply permeates scholarly interpretation of Paul's letters, it is essential to begin with a negative project—to emphasize what the Pauline autobiography in Galatians does not say. First, Galatians says nothing about the location of this event. Scholarly references to the "Damascus Road" are clear evidence of reliance upon Acts. Second, Galatians says nothing about Paul opposing belief in Christ or the Christian message. Rather, in Galatians and elsewhere in Paul, Paul claims to have persecuted the "church of God" (1:13; 1 Cor 15:9; Phil 3:6). This distinction is important, because opposition to belief in Christ is a concern about the identity of Christ, while opposition to the church is a concern about the identity of the people of God. Third, despite a history of mistranslation culminating in the NRSV's extremely hyperbolic and completely unjustified "violently persecuting" (Gal 1:13), Paul's letters give no clear indication of Paul employing violence in his opposition to the "church of God." Neither of the verbs that Paul used to describe his opposition to the church (διώκω and ορθέω) necessarily entails violence.[11] As L. J. Lietaert Peerbolte has reminded

---

[11] It is noteworthy that *The Brill Dictionary of Ancient Greek* (ed. Franco Montanari; Boston: Brill, 2015) suggests that διώκω should be

readers of the Pauline letters, "[i]t is not very likely… that Paul actually used violence, and there is no solid proof in his letters to assume this."[12] Finally, nothing in Galatians ever states — nor even clearly suggests — that Paul was not already a follower of Jesus (a "Christian" in anachronistic categories) when the revelatory experience of Galatians 1:15–16 occurred.

How would our reading of the Pauline autobiography in Galatians be altered if we took these silences in Galatians seriously and we allowed ourselves to reread Galatians in dialogue with 1 Corinthians instead of in dialogue with Acts? Let me suggest that *we would read Galatians 1 as an account of how Paul, as a follower of Christ, nonviolently opposed Gentile inclusion into the church on the basis of his understanding of Judaism (and God's promises to the Jews regarding the Messiah), and of how Paul received a dramatic revelation from God which completely altered his views regarding Gentile inclusion into the people of God.* I will defend this thesis by addressing three related questions.

First, *how do Galatians and 1 Corinthians depict the origin of Paul's message and the content of his reported christophany?* According to 1 Corinthians 15:1–7, Paul

---

translated as "persecute" only in the New Testament. Outside of the New Testament, the meanings "drive away, chase off" and "chase, pursue" are suggested (s.v. διώκω). "Chase off" or "drive away" are probably better translations of διώκω in Paul's letters. Paul was trying to chase away those who espoused Gentile inclusion into the people of God.

[12] L. J. Lietaert Peerbolte, *Paul the Missionary* (CBET 34; Leuven: Peeters, 2003), 176. Also see Arland J. Hultgren, "Paul's Pre-Christian Persecutions of the Church: Their Purpose, Locale and Nature," *JBL* 95 (1976): 97–111 and J. Ashton, "Why did Paul Persecute 'the Church of the God?'" *Scripture Bulletin* 38 (2008): 61–68.

received the fourfold message of Jesus's death (v. 3), burial (v. 4), resurrection (v. 4), and post-resurrection appearances (vv. 5–7) from Peter [Cephas], James, and the other early disciples.[13] Although Paul insists upon being heir to his own post-resurrection christophany (vv. 8–9), the basic content of Paul's message about the crucifixion and resurrection is not attributed to that christophany in 1 Corinthians 15. Instead, Paul's initial reception of the message of Christ (vv. 3–7) clearly originated from — and is attributable to — those who were apostles before Paul. Eventually ("last of all" v. 8) Paul did encounter the risen Christ for himself, but the revelatory content which Paul drew from that event was related only to his own apostleship — and not to his acceptance of Jesus's resurrection and lordship (vv. 8–9; 1 Cor 9:1). Paul's letters never equate this christophany with his acceptance of Jesus as the Messiah. Thus, in Paul's letters, the content of the christophany has no clear relationship with Paul's initial belief in Christ; rather, the content of the christophany is associated with Paul's apostleship and mission to the Gentiles.

The typical, Acts-oriented reading of this Pauline account assumes that the christophany of 1 Corinthians 15:8–9 preceded the Christian instruction in verses 3–7, but what happens if Paul's account is read without appeal to Acts? Would one not assume that Paul came to accept the message of Jesus as it was taught to him by the original apostles and proven by their experiences with the resurrected Jesus (vv. 3–7), and that, *subsequent* to Paul's initial instruction about Christ and his appearances to the apostles, Paul also

---

[13] Note Paul's use of the four ὅτι clauses in vv. 3–5.

encountered the resurrected Christ and was called to apostleship by Christ (vv. 8–9)? In other words, apart from the influence of Acts, the most natural reading of 1 Corinthians 15 would be a sequential reading in which

- Paul heard the essential message of Jesus's death and resurrection from the apostles (vv. 3–7);
- Paul accepted this message on the basis of the witnesses from the apostles and "others;" and
- that Paul subsequently received a christophany, which called him to be an apostle (vv. 8–9).

Thus, it is quite plausible to read 1 Corinthians 15:1–11 (when taken in isolation from Acts) as an account of how Paul believed in Christ on the basis of the witnesses of other believers and how he *subsequently* experienced a christophany that called him to apostleship.

With that reading of the origins of Paul's message and apostleship in 1 Corinthians 15 in mind, let's consider the origins of Paul's message and apostleship in Galatians 1–2. As noted earlier, at first blush, the origin of Paul's message is quite different in Galatians than in 1 Corinthians. On the one hand, in Galatians, Paul claims complete independence for the gospel that the Galatians heard from him; it did not come from human origins (1:11–12). On the other hand, in 1 Corinthians, Paul claims to adhere to a message that originated from Peter, James, and others (15:3–7). This incongruity between the origins of Paul's message in Galatians and 1 Corinthians is striking. However, in spite of this incongruity, most interpreters correlate these Pauline revelatory experiences (Gal 1:15–16; 1 Cor 15:9–10) with the Damascus Road event in Acts 9 and conclude that the events in 1 Corinthians and Galatians should be interpreted as accounts of Paul's initial acceptance of Jesus as the Messiah. But could the event discussed in Galatians 1:15–16 be understood differently if the influence of Acts were set aside?

If we read Galatians 1 only in light of 1 Corinthians 15, would we not assume that Galatians 1:11–24 was simply an elaboration of the event in 1 Corinthians 15:8–11? Would we not assume that Galatians omits the beginning of Paul's "Christian" story — his initial Christian instructions regarding the crucifixion and resurrection — because that initial, faith-inducing, instruction discussed in 1 Corinthians 15:3–7 was irrelevant to the issue at hand in Galatians? Remember, *the issue at hand in 1 Corinthians 15 was the resurrection of Jesus*, an issue on which Paul and the other apostles agreed. Paul had no difficulty acknowledging his dependence upon the original apostles for the basic message of the resurrection. However, *the issue at hand in Galatians was Gentile inclusion into the people of God* as Gentiles (apart from circumcision), an issue on which Paul and the other apostles vehemently disagreed. Paul absolutely insisted that *his* gospel of Gentile inclusion was of divine origin (Gal 1:11–12), and Paul claimed to have gotten his message of Gentile inclusion through a direct christophany and not from any human source (Gal 1:15–17). It is significant to note that Paul routinely and characteristically both associated his christophany with his apostleship (1 Cor 15:8–11; Gal 1:15–17) and also associated his apostleship with Gentile inclusion

(Rom 1:5; 11:13; Gal 2:8). Paul never equated his christophany with his acceptance of Jesus's messiahship.

Put succinctly, Paul both insisted that he received a gospel message of the resurrection from those who were apostles before him (1 Cor 15:1–7), and also that he had received his gospel of Gentile inclusion directly from God — and not through any human intermediary (Gal 1:11–17). Scholars consistently overlook this important Pauline distinction between the elements of his message which were completely dependent upon the other apostles (i.e., the message of the resurrection) and the elements of Paul's message which were completely independent of the other apostles (i.e., Gentile inclusion). This scholarly failure to distinguish between the very different origins of these two key elements of the Pauline gospel is then compounded by an equally unfortunate failure to recognize that Paul always associates his christophany with the independently derived Gentile-inclusive part of his message.

When these distinctions are recognized and these failures overcome, and when the diverse origins of Paul's message are viewed apart from appeal to Acts, the following image appears. Paul received and accepted a basic Christian message regarding the resurrection from the earlier witnesses, including the original apostles (1 Cor 15:3–7). Then, Paul received a *subsequent* christophany, which called him to apostleship (1 Cor 15:8–11; Gal 1:15–17). The revelatory content of this christophany was not the messiahship of Jesus (that had already been decided by Paul's reception of the apostolic message). Instead, the revelatory content of this christophany was the message of

Gentile inclusion (Gal 1:16), the issue at hand in Galatians. Remember, Paul explains the divinely appointed outcome of his christophany as his proclamation of Christ among the Gentiles, not as his acceptance of Jesus as the Messiah (v. 16).

Before moving to the next question, a developmental observation is in order. The pervasive scholarly tendency to conflate Paul's acceptance of Jesus's messiahship with Paul's call to apostleship creates a narrative of Paul which is developmentally implausible at a *prima facie* level. The "Paul" of the prevalent scholarly reconstruction, the *tertium quid* that this "Paul" is, is introduced as a violently anti-Christian and ferociously ethnocentric Pharisee. This rigid ideologue is forced to make two massive ideological transitions *at the same time*: he must accept both that Jesus was the Messiah and also that Jesus's message should be inclusive of Gentiles. In developmental terms, scholars demand more immediate ideological conversion from Paul than even Luke demanded of Paul. In Acts, Saul's confrontation with Jesus results in Paul's acceptance of Jesus's lordship (9:5), and the reader is quickly informed of his importance for the forthcoming Gentile mission. However, Saul's role in the Gentile mission is *not* revealed to him in the Damascus Road incident; instead, Paul's future mission to the Gentiles is revealed to his would-be mentor, Ananais (9:15). Acts gives no clear indication of when Saul became aware of his role in the Gentile mission, but Acts 9 neither states nor implies any Pauline awareness of the Gentile mission. In fact, Saul's first sermon in Acts is in a distinctively non-Gentile context, a synagogue (9:20). Thus, not even Acts 9 supports the developmentally implausible image of a Paul who is capable of simultaneously accepting both Jesus's lordship and the inclusion of Gentiles. Ironically, therefore, the popular image in which Paul's "conversion and commission came together" is supported neither by Acts nor by Paul's letters.[14]

Thus, it is my contention that when 1 Corinthians 15 and Galatians 1 are read in isolation from Acts, the following, developmentally plausible, image of Paul arises. Paul received and believed the message of Jesus's resurrection from earlier witnesses, including the other apostles. Then, in a subsequent event, Paul received the message of Gentile inclusion through a revelatory christophany. At this point, many readers are likely to object that Paul's pre-christophanic behavior hardly seems consistent with a person who had already accepted Jesus as the resurrected Messiah. After all, the objection goes, Paul himself claimed to have persecuted the church of God. Again, the corrupting influence of Acts is leaching into our interpretation of Paul. The next question will address this objection.

Second, *according to Paul's letters, what does it mean for Paul to participate in "persecution?"* The Saul/Paul of Acts is clearly violent. He is not only introduced as an eager spectator of, and marginal participant in, the martyrdom of Stephen (8:1–3), but he also quickly takes on the role of "breathing threats and murder against the disciples" (9:1). As noted earlier, the Paul of the letters was not necessarily violent. Apart from Paul's reports about being the occasional

---

[14] Contra F. F. Bruce, *The Epistle to the Galatians: A Commentary on the Greek Text* (NIGTC; Grand Rapids: Eerdmans, 1982), 93.

victim of mob violence (2 Cor 11:21–12:10), none of Paul's accounts of persecution—neither as a victim (1 Cor 4:12; 2 Cor 4:9; Gal 5:11; 1 Thess 3:4, 7) nor as a perpetrator (1 Cor 15:9; Gal 1:13, 23; Phil 3:6)—clearly indicated the use of violence. In both Philippians and 1 Corinthians, Paul explicitly claims to have persecuted "the church," probably meaning that Paul—like his own opponents in Galatians—opposed Gentile inclusion into the church (Phil 3:6; 1 Cor 15:9). Likewise, it was "the faith" which Paul opposed (Gal 1:23). In Galatians, Paul was even "unknown by sight" to the people whom he is reported to have "persecuted" (Gal 1:21). Clearly, the account of Pauline persecution in Galatians cannot include acts of physical violence, or else Paul would have surely have been identifiable to those who had suffered under his literal blows. How could one "persecute" the church and the faith without ever being seen by one's victims? Clearly, only by engaging in a nonviolent, ideological struggle over one's perception of truth.

If the Pauline persecutions of the church were not fits of violence and despotic rage (as depicted in Acts), what were they? Galatians gives us solid guidance. In Galatians, Paul claimed to be a victim of persecution in two places (5:11; 6:12). Unfortunately, scholars have not given these Pauline references to persecution the attention which they deserve. In both cases, Paul claimed to have been "persecuted" over the issue of Gentile inclusion; that is, for proclaiming his message of the inclusion of all persons through the cross in contrast to the inclusion of elect persons through circumcision. In the first instance, Paul claimed to be persecuted for preaching Gentile inclusion (Gal 5:11–12); in the second instance, Paul claimed that other people insisted upon circumcision in order to avoid persecution (Gal 6:12). The same connection between persecution and Gentile inclusion appears in 1 Thessalonians, where the believers in Thessalonica have been persecuted (1 Thess 3:3), a persecution which is modeled after the earlier persecution experienced in Judea (1 Thess 2:14), a persecution of being pushed away or driven out (ἐκδιώκω, 2:15). The recurring pattern in the Pauline letters, therefore, is of "persecution" occasioned by the preaching of Gentile inclusion, but persecution which, though ideologically rigid in origin, is nonviolent in its delivery.

Clearly Paul was the repeated victim of violence. According to 2 Corinthians, he lived under the constant threat of hardship and violence (2 Cor 11:23–26), but Paul neither referred to such difficulties as "persecution" nor ever identified himself as the perpetrator of such activities. Paul did, of course, identify himself as involved in persecution of "the church" and "the faith," but in the context of Paul's letters (1) none of these Pauline persecutions was clearly identified as violent; (2) some of these Pauline persecutions could not possibly have been violent; and (3) all of these Pauline persecutions were associated with the message of Gentile inclusion. It therefore appears that the Pauline persecution of the church in Paul's letters was a nonviolent and intra-Christian opposition to the message of Gentile inclusion.

Third, *what did Paul mean by his "former life in Judaism" (Gal 1:13)?* My suggestion that Paul's persecution of the church was a part of a conflict within the Christian community over Gentile inclusion (i.e., Christians—like Paul—opposing other Christians over the issue of Gentile inclusion) will undoubtedly strike many readers as preposterous. However, before rejecting this suggestion out of hand, let me remind the reader of two important facts. First, as Paula Eisenbaum has reminded us, the primary classes of humanity in Paul's thought were never "Christian" and "Jewish." Rather, Paul's fundamental categories as witnessed in his letters were Jew and Gentile.[15] Thus, it is anachronistic in the extreme to interpret the reference in Galatians 1:13 in terms of a Jewish/Christian dichotomy. Paul never ceased being a Jew. The reference to Judaism must mean something other than "non-Christian."

Second, although it was once popular to assume that Paul's letter to the Galatians was arguing against "legalistic" Jewish persons who were advocates of "works of righteousness," the so-called "new perspective" on Paul has rendered such anti-Jewish interpretations of Paul completely untenable.[16] Rather, contemporary scholarship now widely recognizes that Paul's "opponents" in Galatians were persons who accepted Jesus as the Messiah, but who (unlike Paul) did not accept that Gentiles should be included within the people of God. Simply stated, the issue at stake in Galatians was not acceptance of Jesus as the Messiah; both

---

[15] See Pamela M. Eisenbaum, "Paul, Polemics, and the Problem of Essentialism," *BibInt* 13 (2005): 224–37, esp. 237. It is noteworthy that the term "Christian" never appears in Paul's letters.

[16] For a succinct introduction to the "new perspective" on Paul, see James D. G. Dunn, "The New Perspective on Paul," *Jesus, Paul and the Law: Studies in Mark and Galatians* (Louisville: Westminster/John Knox Press, 1990), 183–214. For more bibliography and analysis, see Phillips, *Paul, His Letters, and Acts*, 97–100.

Paul and his opponents accepted Jesus as the Messiah. The issue at stake in Galatians was Gentile inclusion within the people of God as Gentiles (and apart from circumcision); Paul and his opponents strongly disagreed over that issue. Remember, all of the people who are named as having fallen on the wrong side of issue in Galatians — Cephas [Peter], the people from James, and Barnabas — were "Christians" when they fell into this error (1:11-13). Paul's opponents agreed with him about the messiahship of Jesus, but they disagreed with him about the inclusion of Gentiles into the church.

In the context of the Galatian debate, it would have made no sense for Paul to appeal to his actions before accepting Jesus as Messiah; that period of Paul's (Jewish) life would have been irrelevant to the discussion at hand. Rather, it seems far sounder to interpret Paul's reference to his "former life in Judaism" as the period in Paul's life which was relevant to the current lives of his opponents. That is, Paul's reference to his former life was referring to his life as a Jew who accepted Jesus as the promised Messiah, but as the Messiah for the Jews alone. Thus, the "Judaism" of which Paul speaks is the "Judaism" which Paul once practiced and which his opponents still practice — a "Judaism" which accepts Jesus as the Messiah, but which insists the Messiah has come for the Jews and the Jews alone. For people practicing this kind of Messiah-accepting "Judaism," Gentiles could be incorporated into the people of God only by first becoming Jewish; that is, by accepting circumcision and the requirements of the Law.

Thus, the former life in Judaism to which Paul refers (Gal 1:13) was his former life as a Jewish follower of Jesus who had yet accepted the inclusion of Gentiles into the people. This period in Paul's life, the period after Paul's initial acceptance of the message of the resurrected Jesus (as taught by Peter, James, and others [1 Cor 15:3–7]) but before the life-altering christophany which revealed both his apostleship and the importance of Gentile inclusion to Paul (Gal 1:15–16), was the only period of Paul's "Jewish" life that was relevant to the discussion in Galatians. At that point — and only at that point — was Paul's experience and theological orientation comparable to that of Paul's Christian opponents in Galatians. Only at that point did Paul both accept the message of the resurrected Jesus as Lord, but also reject the message of Gentile inclusion — just like his current opponents. Only at that point in Paul's Jewish experience was his theological orientation comparable to the Jewish orientation of his theological opponents, Peter, James, and other Christian leaders.

When did Paul Become a Christian?

My answer to the lead question of this essay should now be clear. When Paul's letters are read in absolute isolation from the Book of Acts, the following biography of Paul emerges. Paul became a Christian before he began persecuting the church. Paul accepted the message of Jesus as the resurrected Lord from Peter, James, and other early Christian leaders. In keeping with the attitudes which he shared with other early Jewish/Christian leaders like Peter and James, Paul opposed Gentile inclusion into the church and persecuted (opposed) the Gentile-inclusive church in nonviolent ways. Eventually however, Paul experienced a life-altering christophany, which left him convinced both of the importance of including Gentiles within the church of God and of his role as an apostle of that message of Gentile inclusion. This christophany placed Paul in opposition to the very leaders (like James and Peter) who had brought him into the Christian faith and who had supported him in his persecution of the message of Gentile inclusion. Between Paul's acceptance of Jesus as the resurrected Lord and his Gentile-affirming christophany, Paul practiced a persecution of the church which paralleled the nonviolent, intra-Christian opposition which Paul ended up facing from Christian leaders like James and Peter. It was an opposition from Jewish Christians who accepted Jesus as the risen Lord, but who opposed the message of Gentile inclusion.

Bibliography

Adams, Sean A. "Luke and *Progymnasmata*: Rhetorical Handbooks, Rhetorical Sophistication and Genre Selection," *Ancient Education and Early Christianity*, 137–54. Edited by M. R. Hauge and A. W. Pitts; 2016.

Alexander, Loveday. *The Preface to Luke's Gospel: Literary Convention and Social Context in Luke 1.1–4 and Acts 1.1.* SNTSMS 78. Cambridge: The University Press, 1993.

_____. *Acts in its Ancient Literary Context: A Classicist Looks at the Acts of the Apostles.* LNTS 298. London: T&T Clark, 2005.

Allison, Dale C. "The Audience of James and the Sayings of Jesus." Pages 58–77 in *James, 1 & 2 Peter and the Early Jesus Tradition.* Edited by Alicia Batten and John S. Kloppenborg. LNTS 478. London and New York: T&T Clark, 2014.

_____. *A Critical and Exegetical Commentary on the Epistle of James.* ICC. New York and London: Bloomsbury, 2013.

Anderson, Gary A. *The Genesis of Perfection: Adam and Eve in Jewish and Christian Imagination.* Louisville: Westminster John Knox, 2001.

Ando, Clifford. *Imperial Ideology and Provincial Loyalty in the Roman Empire.* Berkeley: University of California Press, 2000.

Ashton, J. "Why did Paul Persecute 'the Church of the God?'" *Scripture Bulletin* 38 (2008): 61–68.

Auerbach, Erich. *Mimesis: The Representation of Reality in Western Literature.* Princeton: Princeton University Press, 1953.

Aujac, Germaine, ed. *Denys de Halicarnasse, opuscules rhétoriques.* Volume 5: *L'Imitation (fragments, épitomé), premiére lettre à Ammée à Pompée Géminos, Dinarque.* Collection Budé. Paris: Les Belles Lettres, 1992.

Aune, David E. *The New Testament in Its Literary Environment.* LEC 8. Philadelphia: Westminster, 1987.

Avenarius, G. *Lukians Schrift zur Geschichtsschreibung.* Hain: Meisenheim am Glan, 1956.

Bale, Alan J. *Genre and Narrative Coherence in the Acts of the Apostles.* LNTS 514. London: Bloomsbury T&T Clark, 2015.

Balch, David L. "The Cultural Origin of 'Receiving All Nations' in Luke-Acts: Alexander the Great or Roman Social Policy?" *Early Christianity and Classical Culture: Comparative Studies in Honor of Abraham J. Malherbe*, 483–500. Edited by J. T. Fitzgerald, T. H. Olbricht, and L. M. White. NovTSup 110. Leiden: Brill, 2003.

Barchiesi, Alessandro. *Homeric Effects in Vergil's Narrative.* Princeton: Princeton University Press, 2015.

Barr, James. *The Garden of Eden and the Hope of Immortality.* Minneapolis: Fortress Press, 1992.

Barrett, C. K. *A Critical and Exegetical Commentary on the Acts of the Apostles.* 2 volumes. ICC 34. Edinburgh: T&T Clark, 1994–1998.

Baur, Ferdinand Christian. *Paul, the Apostle of Jesus: His Life and Work, His Epistles and His Doctrines: A Contribution to the Critical History of Primitive Christianity.* Two volumes. Second edition. Edited by Eduard Zeller. London: Williams & Norgate, 1873–75.

Beal, Timothy K. "Intertextuality." *Handbook of Postmodern Biblical Interpretation*, 128–30. Edited by A. K. M. Adam. St. Louis: Chalice Press, 2000.

Betz, Hans Dieter. Galatians: *A Commentary on Paul's Letter to the Churches in Galatia*. Hermeneia; Philadelphia: Fortress Press, 1979.

Bonner, Stanley Frederick. *Education in Ancient Rome: From the Elder Cato to the Younger Pliny*. Berkeley: University of California Press, 1977.

Bonwetsch, G.N., H. Achelis, A. Bauer, and R. Helm, eds. *Hippolytus Werke*. 2. Aufl. GCS 36. Leipzig: J.C. Hinrichs, 1897–1929.

Bonz, Marianne Palmer. *The Past as Legacy: Luke-Acts and Ancient Epic*. Minneapolis: Fortress Press, 2000.

Booth, Alan D. "The Appearance of the 'Schola Grammatici'." *Hermes* 106 (1978): 117–25.

Borgen, Peder. "Greek Encyclical Education, Philosophy and Synagogue: Philosophy and Synagogue: Observations from Philo of Alexandria's Writings." *Libens menito: Festshrift till Stig Strömholm*, 61–71. Edited by Olle Matson. Acta Academae Regiae Scientiarum Upsaliensis 21. Uppsala: Kungl. Vetenskapssamhället í Uppsala, 2001.

Bovon, Francois. *Luke 3: A Commentary on the Gospel of Luke 19:28–24:53*. Translated by James Crouch. Hermeneia. Minneapolis: Fortress Press, 2012.

Brant, Jo-Ann A., C. W. Hedrick, and C. Shea, eds. *Ancient Fiction: The Matrix of Early Christian and Jewish Narrative*. Atlanta: Society of Biblical Literature, 2005.

Brenton, Lancelot C. L. *The Septuagint with Apocrypha: Greek and English*. Second printing. Peabody, MA: Hendrickson Publishers, 1986.

Brink, C. O. *Horace on Poetry: The 'Ars Poetica'*. Cambridge: Cambridge University Press, 1971.

Brodie, Thomas L. "Greco-Roman Imitation of Texts as a Partial Guide to Luke's Use of Sources." *Luke-Acts: New Perspectives from the Society of Biblical Literature Seminar*, 17–46. Edited by Charles H. Talbert. New York: Crossroads, 1984.

_____. "The Accusing and Stoning of Naboth (1 Kgs 21:8–13) as One Component of the Stephen Text." *CBQ* 45 (1984): 417–32.

_____. "Towards Unraveling the Rhetorical Imitation of Sources in Acts: 2 Kings 5 as One Component of Acts 8,9–40." *Bib* 67 (1986): 41–67.

_____. "Luke-Acts as an Imitation and Emulation of the Elijah-Elisha Narrative." *New Views on Luke-Acts*, 78–85. Edited by Earl Richards. Collegeville, MN: Michael Glazer, 1990.

_____. "Intertextuality and its Use in Tracing Q and Proto-Luke." *Scriptures in the Gospels*, 469–77. Edited by C. M. Tuckett. Louvain: Louvain University Press, 1997.

Bruce, F. F. *The Epistle to the Galatians: A Commentary on the Greek Text*. NIGTC. Grand Rapids: Eerdmans, 1982.

Buffière, Félix. *Les Mythes d'Homère et la pensée grecque*. Paris: Les Belles letters, 1956.

Bultmann, Rudolph. *The History of the Synoptic Tradition*. Translated by John Marsh. Second revised edition. New York: Harper & Row, Publishers, 1968.

Cairns, Francis. *Virgil's Augustan Epic*. Cambridge: Cambridge University Press, 1989.

Camery-Hoggatt, Jerry. *Irony in Mark's Gospel: Text and Subtext*. SNTSMS 72. Cambridge: Cambridge University Press, 1992.

Campbell, Antony J. and Mark A. O'Brien. *Sources of the Pentateuch: Texts, Introductions, Annotations*. Minneapolis: Fortress Press, 1993.

Cartlidge, David R. "Combien d'unités avez-vous de trios à quatre? What do we mean by Intertextuality in Early Church Studies?" *SBLSP 1990*, 400–11. Edited by David J. Lull. Atlanta: Scholars Press, 1990.

Clark, Raymond J. "The Reality of Hector's Ghost in Aeneas' Dream." *Latomus* 57 (1998): 832–41.

Collins, Adela Yarbro. *Mark: A Commentary.* Hermeneia. Minneapolis: Fortress Press, 2007.

Conte, Gian Biagio. *The Rhetoric of Imitation: Genre and Poetic Memory in Virgil and Other Latin Poets.* Translated by Charles Segal. Ithaca: Cornell University Press, 1986.

Coulson, Seana. *Semantic Leaps: Frame-Shifting and Conceptual Blending in Meaning Construction.* New York: Cambridge University Press, 2001.

Cribiore, Rafaella. *Writing, Teachers, and Students in Graeco-Roman Egypt. ASP* 36. Atlanta: Scholars Press, 1996.

_____. *Gymnastics of the Mind: Greek Education in Hellenistic and Roman Egypt.* Princeton: Princeton University Press, 2001.

Davies, Percival Vaughan. *Macrobius, The Saturnalia: Translated with An Introduction and Notes.* Records of Civilization, Sources and Studies 79. London and New York: Columbia University Press, 1969.

Debut, Janine. "Les documents scholaires." *ZPE* 63 (1986): 251–78.

_____. "De l'usage des listes de mots comme fondement de la pédagogie dans l'antiquité," *REA* 85 (1983): 261–74.

Dekel, Edan. *Virgil's Homeric Lens.* New York: Routledge, 2012.

Deppe, Dean B. "The Sayings of Jesus in the Epistle of James." D.Th. diss. Free University of Amsterdam. Chelsea, Mich.: Bookcrafters, 1989.

Doran, Robert. *2 Maccabees. A Critical Commentary.* Hermeneia. Minneapolis: Fortress Press, 2012.

Dozeman, Thomas B. and Konrad Schmid, eds. *A Farewell to the Yahwist? The Composition of the Pentateuch in Recent European Interpretation*. SBLSym 34. Atlanta: Society of Biblical Literature, 2006.

Dunn, James D. G. "The New Perspective on Paul." *Jesus, Paul and the Law: Studies in Mark and Galatians*. Louisville: Westminster/John Knox Press, 1990.

Dupertuis, Rubén René. "The Summaries in Acts 2, 4 and 5 and Greek Utopian Literary Traditions." Ph.D. dissertation. Claremont Graduate University, 2005.

Eisenbaum, Pamela M. "Paul, Polemics, and the Problem of Essentialism." *BibInt* 13 (2005): 224–37.

Else, Gerald F. "'Imitation' in the Fifth Century." *CP* 53 (1958): 73–90.

Fantham, Elaine. "Imitation and Decline: Rhetorical Theory and Practice in the First Century after Christ." *CP* 73 (1978): 102–116.

Fauconnier, Gilles and Mark Turner. *The Way We Think: Conceptual Blending and the Mind's Hidden Complexities*. New York: Basic Books, 2002.

Feldman, Louis. *Josephus's Interpretation of the Bible*. Berkeley: University of California Press, 1998.

Finkelberg, Margalit. "Homer as a Foundation Text." *Homer, the Bible, and Beyond: Literary and Religious Canons in the Ancient World*, 75–96. Edited by Margalit Finkelberg and Guy C. Stroumsa. Leiden: Brill, 2003.

Fishbane, Michael. "Genesis 1:1–2:4a: The Creation." *Text and Texture: Selected Readings of Biblical Texts*. New York: Schocken, 1979.

Fiske, George C. *Lucilius and Horace: A Study in the Classical Theory of Imitation*. New York: Herder and Herder, 1964.

Fitzmyer, Joseph A. *The Acts of the Apostles: A New Translation with Introduction and Commentary*. AB 31. New York: Doubleday, 1998.

Fornara, Charles W. *The Nature of History in Ancient Greece and Rome*. Berkeley: University of California Press, 1983.

Fowler, Robert M. *Let the Reader Understand: Reader-Response Criticism and the Gospel of Mark*. Minneapolis: Fortress Press, 1991.

Galinsky, Karl. "Vergil's *Aeneid* and Ovid's *Metamorphoses* as World Literature." *The Cambridge Companion to the Age of Augustus*. 340–58. Edited by K. Galinsky; Cambridge. Cambridge University Press, 2005.

Genette, Gerard. *Palimpsests: Literature in the Second Degree*. Translated by Channa Newman and Claude Doubinsky. Lincoln: University of Nebraska Press, 1997.

Gill, Christopher and T. P. Wiseman, eds., *Lies and Fiction in the Ancient World*. Austin: University of Texas Press, 1993.

Grant, Robert M. *Irenaeus of Lyons*. New York: Routledge, 1997.

Greene, Thomas M. *The Light in Troy: Imitation and Discovery in Renaissance Poetry*. New Haven: Yale University Press, 1982.

Haft, Adele J. "Odysseus' Wrath and Grief in the *Iliad*: Agamemnon, the Ithacan King, and the Sack of Troy in Books 2, 4, and 14." *Classical Journal* 85 (1990): 97–114.

Halliday, Michael A. K. *Language as Social Semiotic: The Social Interpretation of Language and Meaning*. London: Edward Arnold, 1978.

Halliday, Michael A. K., Angus McIntosh, and Peter Strevens. *The Linguistic Sciences and Language Teaching*. London: Longmans, 1964.

Harnack, Adolf von. *Die Chronologie der Litteratur bis Irenäus nebst Einleitenden Untersuchungen.* Volume 1 of *Geschichte der altchristlichen Litteratur bis Eusebius. Zweiter Theil: Die Chronologie.* Leipzig: J.C. Hinrichs, 1897–1904.

Hartin, Patrick J. *James and the "Q" Sayings of Jesus.* JSNTSup 47. Sheffield: Sheffield Academic Press, 1991.

_____. *James.* Sacra Pagina 14. Collegeville, MN: Michael Glazier Books; Liturgical Press, 2003.

Hatina, Thomas B. "Intertextuality and Historical Criticism in New Testament Studies: Is there a Relationship?" *BibInt* 7 (1999): 28–43.

Hauge, Matthew Ryan. *The Biblical Tour of Hell.* LNTS 485. London: T&T Clark, 2013.

Havelock, Christine M. *Hellenistic Art: The Art of the Classical World from the Death of Alexander the Great to the Battle of Actium.* Revised edition. New York: Norton: 1981.

Hays, Richard. *Echoes of Scripture in the Letters of Paul.* New Haven: Yale University Press, 1989.

Heather, Peter. "Literacy and Power in the Migration Period." *Literacy and Power in the Ancient World,* 177–97. Edited by Alan K. Bowman and Greg Woolf. Cambridge: Cambridge University Press, 1994.

Hesseling, D. C. "On Waxen Tablets with Fables of Babrius." *JHS* 13 (1892–1893): 293–314.

Heubeck, Alfred, Stephanie West, and J. B. Hainsworth. *A Commentary on Homer's Odyssey.* Oxford: Clarendon, 1988.

Hezser, Catherine. *Jewish Literacy in Roman Palestine.* TSAJ 81. Tübingen: Mohr-Siebeck, 2001.

Hiebert, Theodore. *The Yahwist's Landscape: Nature and Religion in Early Israel.* Oxford and New York: Oxford University Press, 1996.

Hinds, Stephen. *Allusion and Intertext: Dynamics of Appropriation in Roman Poetry*. Roman Literature and its Contexts. Cambridge: Cambridge University Press, 1998.

Hock, Ronald F. "A Dog in the Manger: The Cynic Cynulcus among Athenaeus's Deipnosophists." *Greeks, Romans and Christians: Essays in Honor of Abraham J. Malherbe*, 20–37. Edited by David L. Balch, Everett Ferguson, and Wayne A. Meeks. Minneapolis: Fortress Press, 1990.

Horsfall, Nicholas. "Aeneas the Colonist." *Vergilius* 35 (1989): 8–27.

Hultgren, Arland J. "Paul's Pre-Christian Persecutions of the Church: Their Purpose, Locale and Nature." *JBL* 95 (1976): 97–111.

Humphrey, Edith M. "Collision of Modes? — Vision and Determining Argument in Acts 10:1–11:18." *Sem* 71 (1995): 65–84.

Hunter, Richard and Donald Russell, eds. *Plutarch: How to Study Poetry*. CGLC. Cambridge: Cambridge University Press, 2011.

Hunter, R. L. *A Study of Daphnis and Chloe*. Cambridge: Cambridge University Press, 1983.

Hurst, André. *Lucien de Samosate: Comment écrire l'histoire*. Paris: Les Belles Lettre, 2010.

Hurst, D. and M. Adriaen, eds. *Commentariorum in Matheum Libri IV*. CCSL 77. Brepols: Turnhout, 1969.

Jackson, Howard M. "The Death of Jesus in Mark and the Miracle from the Cross." *NTS* 33 (1987): 16–37.

Jaeger, Werner. "Homer the Educator," *Paideia: The Ideas of Greek Culture*, 35–56. Second edition. Volume 1. Translated by Gilbert Highet. New York: Oxford University Press, 1945.

Johnson, Mark. *The Body in the Mind: The Bodily Basis of Meaning, Imagination, and Reason*. Chicago: University of Chicago Press, 1987.

Keener, Craig S. *Acts: An Exegetical Commentary*. 4 volumes. Grand Rapids: Baker Academic, 2012–2015.

Kemp, Alan. "The *Tekhnê Grammatikê* of Dionysius Thrax: English Translation with Introduction and Notes." *The History of Linguistics in the Classical Period*, 169–89. Edited by Daniel J. Taylor. Philadelphia: John Benjamins, 1987.

Kennedy, George A. *Greek Rhetoric under Christian Emperors*. Princeton: Princeton University Press, 1983.

Kleinknecht, Hermann. "Laokoon." *Hermes* 79 (1944): 66–111.

Kloppenborg, John S. "James 1:2–15 and Hellenistic Psychagogy." *NovT* 52.1 (2010): 37–71.

————. "The Reception of the Jesus Tradition in James." Pages 93–139 in *The Catholic Epistles and the Tradition*. Edited by Jacques Schlosser. BETL 176. Leuven: Peeters, 2004.

Knauer, Georg N. *Die Aeneis und Homer: Studien zur poetischen Technik Vergils mit Listen der Homerzitate in der Aeneis*. Hypomnemata 7. Göttingen: Vandenhoeck & Ruprecht, 1964.

Knox, John. *Chapters in a Life of Paul*. Revised edition. Edited by Douglas R. A. Hare. Macon: Mercer University Press, 1987.

Kochenash, Michael. "You Can't Hear 'Aeneas' without Thinking of Rome." *Journal of Biblical Literature* (forthcoming).

Koller, Hermann. *Die Mimesis in der Antike: Nachahmung, Darstellung, Ausdruck*. Bern: Francke, 1954.

Konstan, David. "The Birth of the Reader: Plutarch as a Literary Critic." *Scholia* 13 (2004): 3–27.

Kristeva, Julia. *Desire in Language: A Semiotic Approach to Literature and Art*. Edited by Leon S. Roudiez. Translated by Thomas Gora, Alice Jardine, and Leon S. Roudiez. New York: Columbia University Press, 1980.

Kuecker, Aaron. "Filial Piety and Violence in Luke-Acts and the *Aeneid*: A Comparative Analysis of Two Trans-Ethnic Identities." *T&T Clark Handbook to Social Identity in the New Testament*, 211–33. Edited by J. B. Tucker and C. A. Baker. London: Bloomsbury, 2014.

Lakoff, George. *Women, Fire, and Dangerous Things: What Categories Reveal about the Mind*. Chicago: University of Chicago Press, 1987.

Lakoff, George and Mark Johnson. *Metaphors We Live By*. Chicago: University of Chicago Press, 1980.

Lakoff, George and Mark Turner. *More than Cool Reason: A Field Guide to Poetic Metaphor*. Chicago: University of Chicago Press, 1989.

Lamberton, Robert. *Homer the Theologian: Neoplatonist Allegorical Reading and the Growth of the Epic Tradition*. Berkeley: University of California Press, 1986.

Laufer, Batia. "Lexical Frequency Profiles: From Monte Carlo to the Real World: A Response to Meara (2005)." *Applied Linguistics* 26.4 (2005): 582–88.

Laufer, Batia and Paul Nation. "Vocabulary Size and Use: Lexical Richness in L2 Written Production." *Applied Linguistics* 16.3 (1995): 307–22.

Lausberg, Heinrich. *Handbook of Literary Rhetoric*. Translated and edited by D. Orton and R. Anderson. Leiden: Brill, 1998.

Levenson, Jon D. *Creation and the Persistence of Evil: The Jewish Drama of Divine Omnipotence*. San Francisco: Harper and Row, 1988.

_____. "The Temple and the World." *JR* 64 (1984): 275–298.

Levinson, Bernard M. *Deuteronomy and the Hermeneutics of Legal Innovation*. Oxford and New York: Oxford University Press, 1997.

_____. *Legal Revision and Religious Renewal in Ancient Israel*. Cambridge and New York: Cambridge University Press, 2008.

Lundon, John. "Lexeis from the Scholia Minora in Homerum." *ZPE* 124 (1999): 25–52.

Luz, Ulrich. *Matthew 21–28: A Commentary*. Translated by James E. Crouch. Hermeneia. Minneapolis: Fortress Press, 2005.

MacDonald, Dennis R. *The Legend and the Apostle: The Battle for Paul in Story and Canon*. Philadelphia: Westminster, 1983.

_____. *The Acts of Andrew and the Acts of Andrew and Matthias in the City of the Cannibals*. Atlanta: Society of Biblical Literature, 1990.

_____. *Christianizing Homer: The* Odyssey, *Plato, and the* Acts of Andrew. New York: Oxford University Press, 1994.

_____. *The Homeric Epics and the Gospel of Mark*. New Haven: Yale University Press, 2000.

_____. *Does the New Testament Imitate Homer? Four Cases from the Acts of the Apostles*. New Haven: Yale University Press, 2003.

_____. *My Turn: A Critique of Critics of "Mimesis Criticism."* Occasional Papers of the Institute for Antiquity and Christianity 53. Claremont, CA: Institute for Antiquity and Christianity, 2009.

_____. *Two Shipwrecked Gospels: The* Logoi of Jesus *and* Papias's Exposition of Logia about the Lord. ECL. Atlanta: Society of Biblical Literature, 2012.

_____. *Mythologizing Jesus: From Jewish Teacher to Epic Hero*. Lanham, MD: Rowman & Littlefield, 2015.

_____. *The Gospels and Homer: Imitations of Greek Epic in Mark and Luke-Acts*. Lanham: Rowman & Littlefield, 2015.

_____. *Luke and Vergil: Imitations of Classical Greek Literature*. NTGL 2. Lanham, MD: Rowman & Littlefield, 2015.

MacDonald, Dennis R., ed. *Mimesis and Intertextuality in Antiquity and Christianity*. Harrisburg, PA.: Trinity Press International, 2001.

Marcus, Joel. "Crucifixion as Parodic Exaltation." *JBL* 125 (2006): 73–87.

_____. *Mark 8–16: A New Translation with Introduction and Commentary*. Anchor Bible 27a. New Haven: Yale University Press, 2009.

Marrou, Henry Irénée. *A History of Education in Antiquity*. Translated by George Lamb. New York: Sheed & Ward, 1956.

Martin, M. W. "Progymnastic Topic Lists: A Compositional Template for Luke and other *Bioi*?" *NTS* 54 (2008): 18–41.

Matera, Frank J. *Galatians*. SP 9. Collegeville, MN: Liturgical Press, 1992.

Mayor, Joseph B. *The Epistle of St. James: The Greek Text with Introduction, Notes and Comments*. Third edition. London: Macmillan & Co., 1910.

McCarthy, Dennis J. *Treaty and Covenant: A Study in Form in the Ancient Oriental Documents and in the Old Testament*. AnBib 21A. Rome: Biblical Institute Press, 1978.

_____. *Old Testament Covenant: A Survey of Current Opinions*. Atlanta: John Knox, 1972.

McKeon, Richard. "Literary Criticism and the Concept of Imitation in Antiquity." *MP* 34 (1936): 1–35.

McNeel, Jennifer Houston. *Paul as Infant and Nursing Mother: Metaphor, Rhetoric, and Identity in 1 Thessalonians 2:5–*

8. ECL 12. Atlanta: Society of Biblical Literature, 2014.

Miles, Gary B. "The *Aeneid* as Foundation Story." *Reading Vergil's* Aeneid: *An Interpretive Guide*. Edited by C. Perkell. Norman: University of Oklahoma Press, 1999.

Miller, John B. F. "Exploring the Function of Symbolic Dream-Visions in the Literature of Antiquity, with Another Look at 1QapGen 19 and Acts 10." *PRS* 37 (2010): 441–56.

Mitchell, Margaret M. "Homer in the New Testament?" *JR* 83 (2003): 244–58.

Montanari, Franco, ed. *The Brill Dictionary of Ancient Greek*. Boston: Brill, 2015.

Moo, Douglas J. *Galatians*. BECNT. Grand Rapids: Baker Academic, 2013.

Morgan, Kathleen. *Ovid's Art of Imitation: Propertius in the Amores*. MnemosSup 47. Leiden: Brill, 1977.

Morgan, Teresa. *Literate Education in the Hellenistic and Roman Worlds*. Cambridge: Cambridge University Press, 1998.

Morgenthaler, Robert. *Lukas und Quintilian: Rhetorik als Erzählkunsti*. Zurich: Gotthelf Verlag, 1993.

Motyer, Stephen. "The Rending of the Veil: A Markan Pentecost?" *NTS* 33 (1987): 155–7.

Moulton, James Hope, Wilbert Francis Howard, and Nigel Turner. *A Grammar of New Testament Greek*. Edinburgh: T&T Clark, 1963–85.

Murley, Clyde. "The Use of Messenger Gods by Vergil and Homer." *Vergilius* 3 (1939): 3–11.

Mursurillo, Herbert. *The Acts of the Christian Martyrs*. Oxford: Clarendon Press, 1972.

Nelis, Damien. *Vergil's* Aeneid *and the* Argonautica *of Apollonius Rhodius*. Leeds: Francis Cairns, 2001.

Norden, Eduard. *Die antike Kunstprosa vom VI Jahrhundert v. Chr. bis in die Zeit der Renaissance.* 2. Aufl. Leipzig: B.G. Teubner, 1909. Reprint. Darmstadt: Wissenschaftliche Buchgesellschaft, 1981.

Orlinsky, Harry M. *Notes on the New Translation of the Torah.* Philadelphia: Jewish Publication Society, 1969.

Pack, Roger A. *The Greek and Latin Literary Texts from Graeco-Roman Egypt.* Second edition. Ann Arbor: University of Michigan Press, 1965.

Padilla, Osvaldo. "Hellenistic *paideia* and Luke's Education: A Critique of Recent Approaches." *NTS* 55 (2009): 416–37.

Page, S. "A Stela of Adad Nirari III and Negal-ereš from Tell al Rimlah." *Iraq* 30 (1968): 139–153.

Patzia, Arthur G. *The Making of the New Testament: Origin, Collection, Text & Canon.* Downers Grove: InterVarsity Press, 1995.

Peerbolte, L. J. Lietaert. *Paul the Missionary.* CBET 34. Leuven: Peeters, 2003.

Penner, Todd C. "Reconfiguring the Rhetorical Study of Acts: Reflections on the Method in and Learning of a Progymnastic Poetics." *PRS* 39 (2003): 425–39.

Penner, Todd C. and Caroline Vander Stichele, eds. *Contextualizing Acts: Lukan Narrative and Greco-Roman Discourse.* SBLSym 20. Atlanta: Society of Biblical Literature, 2003.

Pervo, Richard. *Profit with Delight: The Literary Genre of the Acts of the Apostles.* Philadelphia: Fortress Press, 1987.

_____. *Acts: A Commentary.* Hermeneia. Minneapolis: Fortress Press, 2009.

Phillips, Thomas E. *Acts within Diverse Frames of Reference,* 46–77. Macon, GA: Mercer University Press, 2009.

_____. *Paul, His Letters, and Acts*. Library of Pauline Studies. Peabody, MA: Hendrickson, 2009; Grand Rapids, MI: Baker Academic, 2010.

Plümacher, Eckhard. *Lukas als hellenistischer Schriftsteller: Studien zur Apostelgeschichte*. SUNT 9. Göttingen: Vandenhoeck & Ruprecht, 1972.

Pritchard, James B. *Ancient near Eastern Texts Relating to the Old Testament*. Second Corrected and Enlarged Edition. Princeton: Princeton University Press, 1955.

Preuschen, E., ed. *Der Johanneskommentar. Origens Werke* Bild 4. GCS. Leipzig: J.C. Hinrichs, 1903.

Quasten, Johannes. *Patrology*. Westminster, Maryland: Newman, 1960.

Robbins, Vernon K. "Luke-Acts: A Mixed Population Seeks a Home in the Roman Empire." *Images of Empire*, 202–21. Edited by L. Alexander. Sheffield: JSOT Press, 1991.

_____. "The Reversed Contextualization of Psalm 22 in the Markan Crucifixion." *Sea Voyages and Beyond: Emerging Strategies in Socio-Rhetorical Interpretation*, 258–281. ESEC 14. Dorset: Deo Publishing, 2010.

Romm, James S. *The Edges of the Earth in Ancient Thought*. Princeton: Princeton University Press, 1992.

Rothschild, Clare K. *Luke-Acts and the Rhetoric of History*. WUNT 175. Tübingen: Mohr Siebeck, 2004.

Russell, D. A. "*De Imitatione*." *Creative Imitation and Latin Literature*. Edited by David West and Tony Woodman; Cambridge: Cambridge University Press, 1979.

Russel, D. A. and David Konstan, eds. *Heraclitus: Homeric Problems*. Writings from the Greco-Roman World. Atlanta: Society of Biblical Literature, 2005.

Sandnes, Karl Olav. "*Imitatio Homeri*? An Appraisal of Dennis R. MacDonald's 'Mimesis Criticism.'" *JBL* 124 (2005): 715–32.

Scheller, Paul. *De hellenistica Historiae conscribendae Arte.* Leipzig: Noske, 1911.

Schneemelcher, Wilhelm, ed. *New Testament Apocrypha.* 2 volumes. Revised edition. Translated. and edited by Robert McL. Wilson. Louisville: Westminster John Knox Press, 1991–92.

Scobie, Alexander. *Aspects of the Ancient Romance and Its Heritage: Essays on Apuleius, Petronius, and the Greek Romances.* Hain: Meisenheim am Glan, 1969.

Segal, Alan F. *Paul the Convert: The Apostolate and Apostasy of Saul the Pharisee.* New Haven: Yale University Press, 1990.

Shepherd, Tom. *Markan Sandwich Stories: Narration, Definition, and Function.* AUSDDS 18. Berrien Springs, MI: Andrews University Press, 1993.

Smith, Jonathan Z. *Drudgery Divine: On the Comparison of Early Christianities and the Religions of Late Antiquity.* Jordan Lectures in Comparative Religion 14. School of Oriental and African Studies. Chicago: University of Chicago Press, 1990.

Stackert, Jeffrey. *Rewriting the Torah: Literary Revision in Deuteronomy and the Holiness Legislation.* FAT 52. Tübingen: Mohr Siebeck, 2007.

Steiner, Hans Rudolf. *Der Traum in der* Aeneis. Noctes Romanae 5. Bern: Paul Haupt, 1952.

Stendahl, Krister. "Call Rather than Conversion." *Paul Among the Gentiles.* Philadelphia: Fortress Press, 1976.

Sterling, Gregory E. *Historiography and Self-Definition: Josephos, Luke-Acts, and Apologetic Historiography.* NovTSup 64. Leiden: Brill, 1992.

Steyn, Gert J. "Luke's Use of *ΜΙΜΗΣΙΣ*? Re-Opening the Debate." *The Scriptures in the Gospels*, 551–57. Edited by C. M. Tuckett; Louvain: Louvain University Press, 1997.

Sweeney, Marvin A. "Form Criticism." *To Each Its Own Meaning: Biblical Criticisms and Their Application*, 58–89. Edited by S. L. McKenzie and S. R. Haynes, Louisville: Westminster John Knox Press, 1999.

_____. *King Josiah of Judah: The Lost Messiah of Israel*. Oxford and New York: Oxford University Press, 2001.

_____. *Tanak: A Theological and Critical Introduction to the Jewish Bible*. Minneapolis: Fortress Press, 2012.

_____. *The Twelve Prophets*. Berit Olam. Collegeville, MN: Liturgical Press, 2000.

Taylor, John. *Classics and the Bible: Hospitality and Recognition*. London: Duckworth, 2007.

Taylor, Vincent. *The Gospel According to St. Mark: The Greek Text with Introduction, Notes, and Indexes*. Second edition. Grand Rapids: Baker Book House, 1981.

Thomas, R. F. "Virgil's *Georgics* and the Art of Reference." *HSCP* 90 (1986): 171–98.

Uhlig, G., ed. *Dionysii Thracis Ars grammatica*. Grammatica graeci 1.1. Leibzig: Teubner, 1883.

Van Iersel, Bas M. F. *Mark: A Reader-Response Commentary*. Translated by W. H. Bisscheroux. London: T&T Clark International, 2004.

Van Seters, John. *A Law Book for the Diaspora: Revision in the Study of the Covenant Code*. Oxford and New York: Oxford University Press, 2003.

Von Thaden, Robert H., Jr. *Sex, Christ, and Embodied Cognition: Paul's Wisdom for Corinth*. ESEC 16. Blanford Forum, UK: Deo, 2012.

Walbank, F. W. *Polybius*. Berkeley University of California Press, 1972.

Webb, Ruth. "The *Progymnasmata* as Practice." *Education in Greek and Roman Antiquity*, 289–316. Edited by Yoon Lee Too. Leiden: Brill, 2001.

Whitmarsh, Tim. *Greek Literature and the Roman Empire: The Politics of Imitation*. Oxford: Oxford University Press, 2001.

_____. *Ancient Greek Literature*. Cultural History of Literature. Cambridge: Polity Press, 2004.

Wilson, N. G. *Saint Basil on Greek Literature*. London: Duckworth, 1998.

Winer, Georg Benedikt. *A Treatise on the Grammar of New Testament Greek*. Third edition. Edinburgh: T&T Clark, 1882.

Wiseman, D. J. "The Vassal Treaties of Esarhaddon." *Iraq* 20 (1958): 1–99.

Wright, David P. *Inventing God's Law: How the Covenant Code of the Bible Used and Revised the Laws of Hammurabi*. Oxford and New York: Oxford University Press, 2009.

Youtie, Herbert Chayyim and John Garrett Winter, eds. *Papyri and Ostraca from Karanis*. Michigan Papyri 8; second series. Ann Arbor: University of Michigan Press, 1951.

Contributors and Editors

Michael Kochenash is a doctoral candidate at the Claremont School of Theology. His dissertation, directed by MacDonald, analyzes Luke's construction of the kingdom of God in light of the language and imagery of Roman self-representation; it is titled, "Empire without End: Juxtaposing the Kingdom of God with Rome in Luke-Acts." He has an article, "You Can't Hear 'Aeneas' without Thinking of Rome," forthcoming in the *Journal of Biblical Literature*.

Gregory Riley is Professor of New Testament at Claremont School of Theology, where he has taught for over twenty years. His research spans Gnosticism, Christian origins, and Greco-Roman religion and philosophy. His books *One Jesus, Many Christs* and *The River of God* have been translated into a number of languages.

Marvin A. Sweeney is Professor of Hebrew Bible at the Claremont School of Theology and Professor of Tanak at the Academy for Jewish Religion California. He has written fifteen volumes on Jewish Biblical Theology, Prophetic Literature, Narrative Historical Literature, and Jewish Studies.

Richard I. Pervo taught at Seabury-Western Theological Seminary and the University of Minnesota. His research has focused upon ancient popular literature, especially the various Christian acts, and upon the Pauline legacy.

John S. Kloppenborg is professor at Trinity College, University of Toronto. He has published widely on topics including Q, Christian canonical and non-canonical Gospels, parables, Second-Temple Judaism, and ancient voluntary associations.

Margaret Froelich is a PhD candidate at the Claremont School of Theology, where her research focuses on Christian origins in the context of Hellenistic and early Roman polytheism. Her dissertation examines the Markan miracle tradition as an example of Hellenistic/Roman royal propaganda claiming divine favor.

Matthew Ryan Hauge is Associate Professor of Biblical and Religious Studies at Azusa Pacific University. He is the co-chair of the Society of Biblical Literature seminar on Markan Literary Sources and author of several recent books, including *The Biblical Tour of Hell* and *New Testament and Empire*.

Thomas E. Phillips is Professor of Theological Bibliography and New Testament] and Dean of the Library at Claremont School of Theology. He has published several books and articles on Luke-Acts and its scholarship. In addition, he chaired the section on Acts at the Society of Biblical for 9 years and served as the lead translator for the Gospel of Luke in the *Common English Bible*.

Ilseo Park has earned his MDiv and ThM at the Presbyterian University and Theological Seminary in Korea. He is a PhD candidate writing his dissertation under the supervision of Dr. MacDonald, and adjunct faculty at the Presbyterian Theological Seminary in America.

Made in the USA
Las Vegas, NV
28 September 2022

56163191R00146